# Evaluation and Reform

A Rand Educational Policy Study

# Evaluation and Reform

## The Elementary and Secondary Education Act of 1965, Title I

Milbrey Wallin McLaughlin

Ballinger Publishing Company ● Cambridge, Mass.
*A Subsidiary of J.B. Lippincott Company*

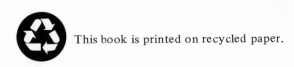 This book is printed on recycled paper.

International Standard Book Number: 0-88410-162-2

Library of Congress Catalog Card Number: 75-11789

Printed in the United States of America

**Library of Congress Cataloging in Publication Data**

McLaughlin, Milbrey Wallin.
   Evaluation and reform.

   (A Rand educational policy study)
   Originally presented as the author's thesis, Harvard.
   Bibliography: p.
   1.  Education, Elementary—United States.  2.  Education, Secondary—United States.  I. Title.  II.  Series: Rand Corporation. Rand educational policy study series.
LA217.M28  1975           379'.151'0973           75-11789
ISBN 0-88410-162-2

# Contents

# Preface

Educational evaluation is not a new phenomenon, but it is only in recent years that it has become institutionalized. The present spate of reporting and the accepted belief in the necessity to evaluate can be traced to the 1965 passage of the massive Elementary and Secondary Education Act (ESEA)—the first major piece of social legislation to mandate project reporting. The unprecedented evaluation requirement was tied to ESEA Title I—a compensatory program targeting more than $1 billion annually to "meet the special educational needs of disadvantaged children." This legislative mandate was initiated with the hope that timely and objective information about the outcomes of Title I projects could reform local governance and practice of education for poor children and that systematic evaluation could make federal management of education programs more efficient.

This case study in policy research examines the congruence between the assumptions and expectations that generated these notions of evaluation and reform and the dominant incentives that shaped the behavior of individuals and institutions in the Title I policy system. The study focuses on the initiation, implementation, outcome and impact of major Title I evaluation efforts undertaken from 1965 through 1972. It is addressed primarily to people who are concerned with formulating evaluation policy or interested in questions about what can be learned from large-scale social action programs and how information about these programs can be used.

Senator Robert Kennedy was the principal architect of the 1965 Title I evaluation requirement. He viewed mandated evaluation as a means of *political* accountability. Kennedy was concerned that the schools would not use Title I funds to develop special and successful programs for the disadvantaged, and hoped that project reports would provide parents with the information (and thus the power) they needed to ensure that Title I dollars were spent in the effective interest of poor children.

Reformers of a different stripe hoped that Title I evaluation could revitalize federal management of education programs. William Gorham, brought to the Department of Health, Education and Welfare to install PPBS *management* principles in the human service areas, expected that data generated by Title I reporting system could be displayed in cost-benefit terms, thereby leading to more effective local practice and more efficient federal decisionmaking.

Although these two types of reformers had different expectations for the role of evaluation, both saw evaluation as central to reform. Both also assumed that federal policy would be self-executing and that the reporting requirements would generate useful information. In addition, they assumed that the new information would be used more or less rationally to inform policy and program decisions.

But not everyone in the Title I policy system was enthusiastic about these notions of reform. State and local schoolmen argued that an evaluation requirement would presage federal control of local education and permit potentially harmful comparisons to be made between schools, districts or states. Schoolmen also contended that evaluation was inconsistent with best practice in that it consumed already limited program resources and employed invidious and inappropriate measures of "success"—achievement scores.

This tension between proponents and opponents of evaluation generated a Title I evaluation history that is a mixture of reform, counterreform, demand, and compromise. And the result, after 7 years, more than $52 million, and a number of alternative evaluation paradigms, has been evaluation that has failed to meet the expectations of reformers, or even to serve the self-interest of federal program managers.

There are numerous reasons why efforts to evaluate Title I failed; the details of these failures constitute the body of this study. The central cause is that school districts had no incentive to collect or report output data, and federal officials lacked the political muscle to enforce evaluation guidelines or to require cooperation with other federal evaluation efforts. The history of Title I evaluation indicates that the success of evaluation—both its conduct and use—is primarily contingent upon the extent to which the evaluation effort is congruent with the dominant incentives at the local and state level. Furthermore, the experience of Title I suggests that the local perception of federal initiatives and commitments as inherently unstable, combined with a basic defensiveness about achievement measures, will most probably continue to frustrate federal attempts to secure objective, reliable program outcome measures. The Title I evaluation history demonstrates both how resistant the educational policy system is to assessment, and that a number of obstacles to objective evaluation are inherent in the system itself.

Reformers who supported evaluation not only underestimated the importance of the balance of power for the conduct of evaluation, but they also failed to take into account the difficulty of evaluating the process of schooling in general and Title I in particular. Consequently, although federal evaluation initiatives represented a reasonable request for a social report, and a rational inquiry from a management point of view, such studies sought answers that could not be given by the Title I program. The more than 30,000 Title I projects across the country reflect multiple goals and treatments. They are not easily transformed into overarching objectives or program models susceptible to precise measurement. Title I evaluation strategies failed chiefly because they ignored this conceptual complexity and underestimated local resistance to or disinterest in evaluation.

Even though these evaluation efforts failed to meet the expectations of reformers, they had uses, often indirect and unexpected, within the policy system. Ironically, the impact and function of the Title I evaluations have been antithetical to the anticipations of reformers. The mandated evaluation scheme has led to local evaluation that is typically seen as little more than an annual ritualistic defense of program activities. And the federal evaluation efforts have not contributed to the formulation of short-run management strategies or long-range planning. Instead they have been used selectively to support policy positions suggested by political or economic constraints, not by new information. On balance, the experience of Title I evaluation indicates that the constituent units of the Title I policy system are more impervious to information and to the intent of federal policies than reformers had expected.

This case study illustrates the importance of viewing evaluation both as a logic of inquiry and as part of a complex social and political system. The experience of Title I highlights the degree to which these two components interact and shape each other and suggests that a realistic and useful evaluation policy should acknowledge the constraints upon evaluation that are inherent to the policy system and the behavior of bureaucracies. The Title I evaluation history suggests that while notions of evaluation and reform may be compatible in theory, they can be expected to conflict in practice when both the interest in reform and the incentive to evaluate originate at the federal level.

**Milbrey Wallin McLaughlin**
Santa Monica, California
December 1974

# Acknowledgments

An undertaking of this sort must rely on the cooperation and candidness of those who are a part of the story. Without exception, the many people contacted in the course of this case study graciously offered their assistance. Bayla White, at present with the Urban Institute, and Susan Smith, now with the Bureau of Social Science Research, were particularly helpful, offering especially generous contributions of time and insight. Both of them have an active sense of history that has led them to retain documents and memoranda that have been indispensable to this study. I also owe a major debt to David Cohen, of the Harvard Graduate School of Education, whose invariably good advice and substantial investment of time are reflected throughout this study.

Others who were especially valuable as historians of the early years, or interpreters of present policy, include: Joan Bissell, Richard Carlson, Emerson Elliott, Joseph Froomkin, Samuel Halperin, Michael Kirst, Larry LaMoure, Walter McCann, Jerome Murphy, Alice Rivlin, and Michael Timpane. Many others made important contributions to this study but cannot be thanked here because of their wish to remain anonymous.

Henry Acland of the Harvard Graduate School of Education and Robert Klitgaard, Robert Levine, John Pincus, and Barbara Williams of The Rand Corporation offered useful comments on an earlier draft.

While this study could have not been done without this assistance, the responsibility for the interpretations and conclusions offered is mine. I am extremely grateful to all these helpful people, and to the Center for Educational Policy Research, Harvard University, and The Rand Corporation for their joint support of this research.

# Glossary of Abbreviations

AERA   American Educational Research Association
AIR    American Institutes for Research
ASPE   Assistant Secretary for Planning and Evaluation
BESE   Bureau of Elementary and Secondary Education
CPIR   Consolidated Program Information Report
CSSO   Chief State School Officers
DCE    Division of Compensatory Education
DHEW   Department of Health, Education, and Welfare
EEOS   Equal Educational Opportunity Survey
ESEA   Elementary and Secondary Education Act
FAP    Family Assistance Plan
GAO    General Accounting Office
LEA    Local Education Agency
NCES   National Center for Educational Statistics
NIE    National Institute of Education
OEO    Office of Economic Opportunity
OMB    Office of Management and Budget
OPPE   Office of Program Planning and Evaluation
PCI    Pupil Centered Instrument
PDI    Project Descriptor Instrument
PPBS   Planning-Programming-Budgeting-System
RFP    Request for Proposal
SAFA   School Assistance in Federally Affected Areas
SEA    State Education Agency
USOE   United States Office of Education

## Chapter One

# Evaluation and Reform: The Climate

Senator Robert Kennedy did not share the general euphoria that pervaded Washington when the 1965 Elementary and Secondary Education Act (ESEA) was ratified.[1] ESEA was enacted with high hopes for benefitting disadvantaged children. Title I of that act, which targets more than $1 billion a year to "meet the special educational needs of educationally deprived children," was the particular cause of excitement and self-congratulation on the Hill. It had broken through the long-standing opposition to federal aid to education and was viewed as an effective way to "break the cycle of poverty."[2] Lawmakers were confident in 1965 that schoolmen knew what to do with the added resources, and that they would thereby establish effective compensatory programs for poor children. Title I was perceived as a central part of President Johnson's War on Poverty.[3]

Reports from some of Senator Kennedy's constituents, however, counselled against such optimism. New York City minority leaders predicted: "Title I will be money down a rathole unless it includes some measure to protect the interests of poor children."[4] This forecast, combined with his own observations of the public schools, made Robert Kennedy skeptical. He concluded that some schoolmen might not use the new Title I dollars in the best interests of poor children unless the act included some way to insure that they would not be cheated of the special attention intended by the legislation.

Civil rights activists argued that the public schools had not been responsive to the particular needs of poor children and that education for disadvantaged pupils was a low priority for most school administrators.[5] In contrast to those educators and legislators who identified the home as a major source of educational failure for the poor and nonwhite, minority leaders contended that the roots of failure lay in the schools, and in the disregard of schoolmen for the views and preferences of the parents.[6] The lack of attention paid low-income parents was compounded, in Kennedy's view, by the fact that they had no recourse. The political power and channels of communication available to parents in Scarsdale were not available to parents in Harlem. Kennedy believed that federal lawmakers therefore had a particular responsibility to act on behalf of the poor:

> [These children] really don't have a lobby speaking for them and do not have parents that can be clamoring down here because they cannot afford to take the bus ride, or cannot afford to fly down here, and they are the ones, I think,

who are of concern. They have been ignored in the past. We are fighting for
them and others have; but the fact is that we are just awakening to the needs
in this part of the country, and what I want to make sure of is not just that
the money is not wasted, because you can find more money, but the fact that
the lives of these children are not wasted.[7]

I think we have a special responsibility to those people who are less
fortunate than we are, to make sure that the money that is being expended
is going to be used so that the next generation will not have to have these
kinds of hearings.[8]

An exchange between Senator Kennedy and Francis Keppel, Commissioner of
Education, shows Kennedy's concern that the schools would not use Title I resources
the way Congress wanted them to:

> *Senator Kennedy:* . . . You describe . . . the family and home background of
> a child and I think that does make for difficulty and creates the kind of
> problems that you have described . . . also would you agree that it is not
> restricted to that, that from your experience of studying the school systems
> around the United States, *that the school itself has created an educationally
> deprived system?*
>
> *Mr. Keppel:* I am sorry to say that is true.
>
> *Senator Kennedy:* And then I come to this other point, that if you are placing
> or putting money into a school system which itself creates this problem or
> helps to create it, or does nothing, very little to alleviate it, *are we not in fact
> wasting the money of the Federal Government and of the taxpayer and put-
> ting money into areas and investing money where it really is going to accom-
> plish very little if any good?*
>
> *Mr. Keppel:* Senator, I think there is an assumption behind your inquiry
> which is that the school systems are not prepared to change their habits.[9]
> [Emphasis added]

As Commissioner Keppel suspected, Senator Kennedy did not believe that the
schools would "change their habits" without new and additional incentives to do so.
Unlike his colleagues who expected that more money to the schools could by itself
promote educational reform, Kennedy thought that merely more money would not
work:

> I think money can make a major difference and can be a big help. But I do
> not think money in and of itself is necessarily the answer. I have seen
> enough school districts where there has been a lack of imagination, lack of
> initiative, and lack of interest in the problems of some of the deprived
> children which causes me concern. My feeling is that even if we put money
> into those school districts, then it will be wasted.[10]
>
> Would not you agree, Commissioner and Secretary, that one of the really
> great problems we have in this country, being blunt about it, is the school
> boards in some of these communities, in some of these States, that they are
> just not going to take the necessary steps to deal with the problem?[11]

Anthony Celebrezze, Secretary of the Department of Health, Education, and
Welfare (DHEW), responded to Kennedy by pointing to national traditions of federalism and pluralism, and their implication for federal policy:

> That is the price of democracy. If you want to keep your education on a local
> level without concentrating it in the Federal Government. But in due time,

Senator, I find that the people of the areas themselves make that adjustment. I think that as I say, it is one of the things that we have to contend with in a democracy unless we want complete conformity throughout the United States.[12]

Kennedy retorted that traditional restrictions were unacceptable in the instance of Title I:

It might be the price of democracy, but we don't have to accept it. We can attempt to do better.
   All I suggest is that we can do something to make sure that we have the highest standards possible and that the money we are going to expend, which is going to be expended, as I understand, in these areas, in my case, is not wasted.[13]

"Obviously," Kennedy remarked, "I am in complete accord with the objectives of this bill. All I wonder is whether we couldn't give further protection to the child by certain requirements?"[14]

The Commissioner and the Secretary were not unprepared for Kennedy's demands. Senator Kennedy's public questioning of Commissioner Keppel and Secretary Celebrezze merely reiterated for the record the major points of the agreement privately negotiated in advance of the formal Senate hearings on ESEA. Adam Walinsky, Kennedy's legislative aide, had telephoned Samuel Halperin, Director of the Office of Legislation of the United States Office of Education (USOE), before the ESEA package was transmitted to the House Subcommittee on Education. Walinsky told Halperin that the Senator was unhappy with the bill as it stood because he believed Title I "wouldn't do enough for the blacks."[15] Halperin was informed that Kennedy would not support ESEA in its present form. In light of President Johnson's demand for swift, clean passage of his landmark education bill, the opposition of the influential junior senator from New York could not be ignored.[16]

Consequently, Halperin arranged a meeting between Robert Kennedy, Adam Walinsky, and the principal drafters of ESEA: Francis Keppel and Wilbur Cohen, who was then Assistant Secretary of DHEW.[17] Kennedy announced in this conference that his support of ESEA would be conditioned upon the addition of a reporting requirement and "good faith administration efforts to hold educators responsive to their constituencies and to make educational achievement the touchstone of success in judging ESEA."[18] According to Samuel Halperin, "Kennedy's notion of evaluation was that poor people should have made available the numbers and figures on how their kids are doing."[19] Kennedy argued for an account of program activities as well as a strong USOE oversight role: ". . . unless there is a meaningful program developed at the local level, which is really tested and checked by you [USOE], I don't think that this program is going to be effective."[20]

From this meeting, there emerged the notions of a reporting and dissemination scheme that was subsequently included in the ESEA legislation, and of the evaluation provision that requires ESEA Title I projects to be regularly assessed for their effectiveness in meeting the "special educational needs of disadvantaged children." Kennedy did not think of this reporting scheme as a way to provide information for teachers or administrators; he saw the evaluation requirement primarily as insurance for those who were previously uninvolved and uninformed, the parents:[21]

I think it is very difficult for a person who lives in a community to know whether, in fact, his educational system is what it should be, whether if you compare his community to a neighboring community they are doing everything they should do, whether the people that are operating the educational system in a State or in a local community are as good as they should be. I think it is very difficult for a citizen to know that.... If I lived in the community where the $2 million [of Title I dollars] was being wasted, I would like to know something about that. *I wonder if we couldn't have some kind of system of reporting, either through some testing system that would be established which the people at the local community would know periodically as to what progress had been made under this program.* [22] [Emphasis added]

## THE EXPECTATIONS OF REFORMERS

If there was a midwife to the emerging notion of accountability, it was Robert Kennedy. Kennedy saw the failure of disadvantaged children in terms of disinterested and inefficient school administration. Kennedy remarked in the Senate Subcommittee hearings on ESEA: "I just question whether they [school administrators] have, No. 1, focused attention on where the real problems are and, secondly, whether they have the ability to really perform the functions."[23] He thought that parents had a right to know what was taking place in the schools, and how Title I dollars were being spent. He expected that the evaluation mandate would provide a new source of political power that parents could use as a "whip" or a "spur."[24] Kennedy hoped a Title I project reporting requirement would force local schools to reform their practices in light of the priorities expressed by parents, and focus on solving the "real problem"—the failure of disadvantaged children.

There was support throughout the federal government for Kennedy's notion of accountability. Commissioner Keppel expected that the evaluation scheme would upgrade local school practices by its appeal to what he called the American sense of pride and competition:

> ... it seems to me [that] the responsibility of the Office of Education [is] to take initiative in bringing to the attention of one State what is going on in another.... I think we really can depend on the competitive instinct, the competition of the American School Systems.

> ... I think we have some instruments here frankly to needle a lot of the schools.[25]

Keppel anticipated that the Title I reporting mechanism would provide information USOE could use to make performance comparisons between districts, states, and regions. The Commissioner suggested that the Office of Education would take an active role in compiling and disseminating such comparative analyses. No state or district, Keppel reasoned, would tolerate unfavorable comments broadcast about its performance:

> *Senator Kennedy:* ... I can see tremendous contrast in what is going on in one community in contrast to another.... Am I wrong, Commissioner, really in my assessment of the fact that there is a tremendous contrast between some of these commissioners of education at the State level and also at the local level as to what imaginative and progressive measures and activities they undertake to deal with this problem?

> *Mr. Keppel:* Of course you are not wrong, Senator. The United States is intensely human and we do have these variations. There is no doubt about it. You are right. I have spent my life at this. I personally think we are going to have to put a lot more energy into it, *and one of the major parts of this*

*bill which I think would not ordinarily be noted is this very reporting provi-*
*sion in which we can get data and demonstrate some of the differences be-*
*tween geographical sections and use the local American pride [to seek the best*
*solutions].*[26] [Emphasis added]

Further, the reporting requirement appeared likely to strengthen the federal government's knowledge of education generally. USOE administrators previously had scant information concerning the nation's school population and its educational needs, or about effective strategies. High-level USOE and DHEW officials welcomed Kennedy's evaluation idea as a way to learn more about education, as well as about the programs under their purview.[27]

Secretary Celebrezze anticipated that the information returned by Kennedy's scheme could serve as a resource for program managers. Celebrezze anticipated that the data could be used to "bootstrap" the nation's education system. The Secretary expressed confidence in the interest and ability of local districts to develop sound performance measures, as well as in the ability of USOE to provide adequate guidelines and assistance for evaluation of Title I program strategies.

Many lawmakers also supported the new concepts of social accounting that Kennedy advanced. As federal spending for education increased dramatically with the passage of ESEA, many in Congress believed that local or state agencies administering and receiving federal monies should render an account of a project's activities and achievements—that program administrators should be held responsible for the effective allocation of federal resources.[28] Furthermore, in 1965 evaluation was becoming fashionable. Although few Congressmen had much sophistication in the areas of data collection, analysis, or evaluation, they believed such activities to be the trademark of a "rational" decisionmaker. More evaluation could only be a good thing.

Also, a number of lawmakers saw Kennedy's evaluation mandate to be compatible with the fundamental workings of democracy. Senator Wayne Morse expressed this view:

I do think that undoubtedly the making available of the money, and the attention that the availability of the money will receive from the State educational authorities and the parents in the community, will have a tremendous effect upon the local school administrators; but that is what I meant when I said that we should make available the facts and . . . just trust that this democracy of ours will put the democratic system to work on the basis of these facts.[29]

The "trust" expressed by Wayne Morse was based on the typically American notion that the public good is better served by adversary proceedings—by public battles of opinions and will, and the resulting compromise—than by a more authoritarian imposition of a centrally (or federally) conceived plan. In this view, as the "facts" about Title I were collected and brought to the marketplace of opinion, they would contribute to devising a strategy for meeting the needs of poor children superior to any that might be designed by Congress or USOE.

Expectations that the new Title I reporting requirements would result in reform were not limited to notions of accountability and competition. Reformers of a different stripe hoped that the Title I evaluation mandate would be instrumental in remodeling educational practices in ways that would lead to more efficient use of resources. This growing concern within the government for the overall efficiency of federal spending and decisionmaking was concomitant with the main ideas about accountability. Whereas Senator Kennedy equated the waste of Title I funds with the waste of a child's educational opportunities, some members of the executive branch saw ineffective expenditure of Title I monies as evidence of inefficient allocation of federal resources and inefficient federal planning and decisionmaking.

Introduction of the Planning-Programming-Budgeting System (PPBS) was symptomatic of this concern.[30] President Johnson announced his intention to install PPBS throughout the executive branch at an August 1965 breakfast meeting of his cabinet. This decision was based on the President's view of the results achieved by the PPBS in the Pentagon and on the forceful arguments of Robert McNamara. PPBS had led to what many viewed as "dramatic" improvements in the efficiency and effectiveness of Department of Defense (DOD) management. It was thought that these systematic planning and budgeting procedures could also be fruitfully applied to the "soft services" of DHEW.

PPBS was introduced to DHEW more or less concurrently with the passage of ESEA. When John Gardner replaced Anthony Celebrezze as Secretary of DHEW in July 1965, one of his first tasks was to reorganize the department to facilitate implementation of PPBS precepts. Positions were created and staffed to introduce and carry out the same systematic management techniques that McNamara's "whiz kids" had brought to the Pentagon. William Gorham was brought to DHEW as Assistant Secretary for Program Coordination (later Assistant Secretary for Program Evaluation—ASPE) principally because of his experience with PPBS at the DOD. He and two new Deputy Assistant Secretaries, economists Alice Rivlin and Robert Grosse, were asked to "develop program goals which might be stated, measured and evaluated in cost benefit terms."[31]

Gorham conceded that "anyone in government knows that most decisions on spending emerge from a political process and are most heavily influenced by value judgments and the pressures brought to bear by a wide range of interested parties,"[32] but he believed that the techniques of systems analysis could increase efficiency even within this context:

> ... the very process of analysis is valuable in itself, for it forces people to think about the objectives of Government programs and how they can be measured. It forces people to think about choices in an explicit way. It is an important tool in the fight against creeping incrementalism—"ten percent to those with the most bureaucratic or political muscle, five percent to all others." A major job of the analyst is to help the decision-maker realize that an extra dollar spent in one way involves greater welfare gain than a dollar spent in another way.[33]

Gorham saw the implementation of a PPBS as a way to sharpen and refocus the decisionmaking process at DHEW and the Bureau of the Budget (BOB). At the outset of his tenure, he spoke of PPBS in terms of "reform":

> An important reform is underway in the United States. It is a reform designed to improve the efficiency with which public resources are used. Its sharpest point of focus at this time is the Executive branch of the Federal Government. . . . It is a framework for planning—a way of organizing information and analysis systematically so that the consequences of particular choices can be seen as clearly as possible.[34]

Gorham thought that the technology of a PPBS had a particular contribution to make in revitalizing and improving local educational practices. Much of his concern focused on Title I, but his perspective of Title I was different from Kennedy's. Whereas Kennedy's view of Title I was "project oriented,"[35] and focused on getting services to the disadvantaged, Gorham thought of Title I as a trial-and-error phenomenon—as a natural experiment, which could be fruitfully investigated by the tools of systems analysis:

> Within any one program the variation in effectiveness among individual projects or localities is tremendous. A surprise to the analysts in HEW was the contribution they could make to upgrading the programs themselves and in identifying successful methods of reaching an objective. Title I of the Elementary and Secondary Education Act, for example, is essentially a vast experiment designed to find effective ways of reaching disadvantaged children. We know that most school systems have not been doing a very good job with these children, but there is no consensus among educators about how to do better.[36]

Because of these different views of the Title I program, Gorham's expectations for the role of evaluation also diverged from Kennedy's. Kennedy thought of evaluation as a means to insure that schools focused on the needs of the poor, to make sure that Title I "worked." Gorham's ASPE staff thought of evaluation as a way to find out "what works," to identify the most effective compensatory strategies:

> Title I allows local educational authorities to spend money in a variety of ways. . . . Among the analyses to which we are giving high priority in the Department at the moment is a major attempt to see what has been learned from this experiment which can help communities spend their money more effectively in the future. Definitive answers . . . may be a long time coming, but even tentative indications may substantively improve the effectiveness with which money is used.[37]

While Kennedy feared Title I monies might be wasted because of disinterested or inefficient local school administrators, ASPE analysts were concerned that the new resources might be used ineffectively because of ignorance about how to do better. Gorham expected that Title I evaluation data would feed into a sophisticated analytical scheme, PPBS, which could increase the efficiency of resource use throughout the Title I policy system, from the local school to the BOB. Kennedy, on the other hand, saw evaluation as an accountability device that could increase the influence of parents in the local school policy arena. And whereas Kennedy's expectation of reform through evaluation was based primarily on a political assessment of the incentives operating at the local school level, Gorham's conception of reform and the role of information was premised on the principles of microeconomic theory.

ASPE's view of the role of analysis assumed specification of a production function—identification of the relative effectiveness of specified inputs, such as money, special services, and the like—in attaining a particular objective, such as gain in academic achievement. It was reasoned that specification of the contributions of particular inputs would lead to an increase of the effectiveness of local compensatory practice and thereby increase the efficiency with which federal funds were spent.

"Efficiency" was a password in 1965, and so ASPE's view of Title I as a "vast experiment" and expectations for the role of evaluation generated important support for the loosely worded ESEA among some members of the executive branch. Budget officials, particularly, viewed a tighter federal rein as necessary to more efficient government:

> The "new guard" [proponents of PPBS] urged a more aggressive federal leadership role and favored detailed statutory provisions designed to produce specific, measurable results. The strongest position was taken by the

staff of the Bureau of the Budget who had long considered the fragmentation of federal school aid an inefficient use of public funds. Bureau staff argued that educational programs, like other federal programs, should be funded and assessed according to their success in achieving explicit goals. Improvements could be expected only when it became possible to finance activities that had demonstrated their productivity and to eliminate those that had not. Those holding this view doubted that educators would voluntarily apply tight standards and favored federal requirements that would force school people to develop and adhere to measures of program efficiency.[38]

Thus the enthusiasm of various participants for Title I's unprecedented evaluation requirement was premised not only on somewhat different views of the role of evaluation but also on dissimilar conceptions of Title I. Nonetheless, both Kennedy and proponents of a PPBS alike were motivated by expectations of *reform* as they advocated a statutory measure to obtain information about the outcomes of Title I projects. Both breeds of reformers saw *evaluation as central to change,* albeit for different reasons.

## THE FEARS OF OPPONENTS

But not everyone in the Title I policy arena[39] was in accord with these notions of reform, evaluation, or the purpose of Title I. Many schoolmen and a number of lawmakers saw Title I as *general aid* that could ease the fiscal pressure generated by rising pupil enrollments, and the escalating cost of professional services. This financial squeeze was greatest in those large, inner city schools that served the largest number of Title I eligible children. Many educators wanted general aid, not categorical aid targeted for the "special educational needs of disadvantaged children." These schoolmen, as well as lawmakers such as Representative Carl Perkins, a long-time advocate of federal assistance to the schools, saw the "reform" of Title I simply in the fact of its passage, and in its successful resolution of the interest-group conflicts that historically had blocked federal aid to the schools.[40] In this view, evaluation of special programs for the disadvantaged was not to the point of Title I.

In addition, the requirement to evaluate was unsettling to many educators. ESEA Title I mandated assessment of an activity with which most schools had little experience. Contrary to Commissioner Keppel's suggestion that models of successful compensatory strategies existed in 1965, special compensatory programs were mostly unknown at that time. Keppel, in the Senate Subcommittee hearings on ESEA, had presented a collection of "promising strategies" that he argued showed "heartening results":

Better than my words, these surveys show what the schools of our nation will do with the resources made available under Title I of the Elementary Act of 1965.[41]

These are descriptions of the kinds of programs that have already been undertaken by imaginative school systems, by school systems under the support of private foundations and others, to show that the type of programs which could be undertaken by Title I could be effective. *I think we have some impressive facts here, sir, some impressive facts that when special attention is paid to a variety of educational problems of children from low-income families, that they can work.* [42] [Emphasis added]

However, in 1965 only three states had compensatory education legislation on the books, and only a handful of school districts had ongoing compensatory education programs. Although many schoolmen may have had ideas they wanted to try, there was little certainty in 1965 about educational strategies that would "work" for disadvantaged pupils. Title I was targeted at the very group of children that the schools had traditionally seemed least able to help.

In addition, few state educational personnel and even fewer local school administrators had any experience with federal programs in 1965. And the requirement to evaluate was unparalleled. Bailey and Mosher observe:

> Perhaps no piece of social legislation in American history has placed a greater premium upon the reporting and evaluating of results than ESEA.
> Most laws, of course, call for or subsume annual reports of periodic financial statements. But these have tended to be pro forma. They have generally been ignored by all except those . . . whose melancholy but necessary function it is to monitor and file government papers.
> In the case of ESEA, however, the legislative mandate for formal reports and evaluation of programs was loud and clear, and unprecedented in scope.[43]

The evaluation required by Title I was simply an unknown to most schoolmen. There was nothing in their experience to tell them how their project reports would be used by local, state, or federal participants. If no operating agency invites critical or public review, it can be expected that such assessment will certainly be unwelcome in an instance where the agencies have no notion of "effective" treatment, no confident prediction of treatment outcome, or no experience in the ways in which the self-reports will be used. Commissioner Keppel suggested that the American sense of pride and competition would motivate the schools to improve practices that led to disappointing evaluations. A more germane question, however, was whether the schools would compile and disseminate unfavorable findings in the first place. Might they not only highlight the positive achievements of the programs, and obscure or minimize the failures or disappointments? In what was essentially an uncharted area, a mandate to evaluate was inimical in important respects to the perceived self-interests of Title I programs or administrators.[44]

It is not surprising, then, that schoolmen raised numerous objections to Kennedy's evaluation plan.[45] A general concern was voiced that a federal requirement to evaluate local programs would be merely a prelude to federal control of the schools. Evaluation or reporting connotes an "authority-subordinate" relationship,[46] and many state and local schoolmen (and some legislators) feared USOE would use the evaluations as the first step in the federal prescription of a national curriculum. Many schoolmen anticipated that federal interest in the *outcomes* of local school activities would justify increasing federal involvement in the *inputs* to schooling, and so contribute to the loss of local control.

Educators also argued that an evaluation requirement violated the tenets of "professionalism." It was maintained that assessment of student progress was the professional responsibility of the teacher. Schoolmen contended that evaluation "is being done every day, by those who should continue to do it, the teachers in the classroom."[47] Opponents of an evaluation requirement contended that educators, like physicians or other professionals, should not be required to document or guarantee their effectiveness, or submit to judgment by standards other than their own.

Nor, from this perspective, did educators welcome the sort of public review Kennedy urged. They argued that the classroom was a province in which teachers were best qualified to function by virtue of their special training and experience; interference by parents and others would only impair teacher effectiveness. A number of educators predicted that dissemination of program outcome data would lead to "coercion" for the classroom teacher, and thereby result in a loss of "ingenuity, flexibility and initiative," and possibly even lead to "teaching to the test."[48]

Educators were also concerned that a mandated reporting scheme would lead to comparisons among teachers, schools, districts, and states. Such comparisons were not only seen as "unprofessional," but were also held to be unfair and potentially destructive, especially to those schools or districts with special student problems or limited resources. Such comparisons, it was contended, would make the schools *less* responsive to special local needs and thus *less* conscientious in devising appropriate local solutions, *especially* for disadvantaged children. As one educator predicted, "the power structure would turn on a lot of heat to get those scores up or else." The result would be less attention to the multiple needs of poor pupils and more attention to the "tested" school performance. The competition that Kennedy and Keppel hoped would promote reform in local education practices was precisely the evaluation outcome the schools most resisted.

Additional objections to evaluation centered on what Commissioner Keppel termed the "evils of testing."[49] Schoolmen considered standardized tests to be a callous instrument, unfair to teachers and students alike. With much empirical support, educators argued that the tests were not an appropriate measure of the achievement of deprived or nonwhite students, and that the validity of these tests was unproven. Further, it was pointed out that the use of achievement scores as an outcome measure ignored other and possibly more important program goals and achievements. Educators were in almost complete agreement that standardized tests were insensitive and inappropriate measures of the effectiveness of a Title I program.

Educators also pointed to instances in which an evaluation requirement conflicts with the intersts of sound project management. They argued that an evaluation requirement cuts into already inadequate program budgets and that the resources used for evaluation would be better spent on more educational services. Furthermore, many program administrators suggested ways in which the requirements of a sound evaluation design are at odds with the effective delivery of services. Program managers argued that Title I is a service program not a demonstration program.[50] Program decisions that may be required by a good evaluation strategy—such as the continuation of an unsuccessful effort for the sake of treatment continuity, or the exclusion of late entrants in the interest of cohort integrity, or the denial of Title I services to eligible children in order that they may serve as controls—are often incompatible with the intent of the law.

In sum, there was little agreement between proponents and opponents of evaluation. Whereas Kennedy and Gorham saw evaluation as promoting reform, educators argued that evaluation would stifle creativity and local flexibility. Whereas Keppel believed that appeal to "local pride and the competitive instinct" would lead to better programs, schoolmen contended that such competition was unprofessional and would result in less attention to specific local needs. Whereas Kennedy contended that parents should have something to say in how the schools serve the needs of their children, schoolmen argued that the professional knew best. Whereas Kennedy insisted that schools should be held to the "highest standards possible," educators replied that assessment was the responsibility of the professional and that it took place daily in the classroom.

And, while Secretary Celebrezze anticipated local interest and initiative in developing and refining an evaluation technology, local schoolmen saw evaluation as a waste of scarce program resources and incompatible with best educational practice. While Kennedy believed that "some sort of testing system could be established [which would let] the people at the local community . . . know periodically . . . what progress has been made under this program,"[51] schoolmen alleged that achievement tests were invidious and inappropriate standards to apply to programs such as Title I.

There was some opposition to the idea of a Title I reporting requirement even within the educational research community. At the 1966 annual meeting of the American Educational Research Association (AERA), members suggested to the executive board that AERA go on record against the Title I evaluation mandate on the grounds that it was "impractical and unrealistic."[52]

Thus, coexisting within the Title I policy arena in 1965 were both strong interest in the collection of reliable, quantitative data on program effectiveness and powerful incentives not to collect and disseminate these data. There also existed a fundamental tension concerning the role of evaluation and the sort of "reform" Title I was to be. Kennedy saw Title I as special programs for the disadvantaged, and evaluation as an accountability measure. Gorham's ASPE staff saw Title I as a "vast experiment," and evaluation as a way to make both federal decisionmaking and local educational practice more efficient. Many schoolmen and a number of lawmakers saw Title I as general aid, and evaluation as inappropriate and irrelevant. Thus, the struggle over Title I evaluation involved not only dissimilar views on the value and function of assessment, but also different ideas about what sort of reform Title I was to be.

## CROSS-PRESSURES AND QUESTIONS

This study is concerned with these crosspressures over Title I evaluation policy and their impact on the resulting evaluations. The Title I reporting mandate was without precedent. So, too, were the expectations of reform that attended the requirement to collect and disseminate information about the activities of a large-scale social action program. The experience of Title I evaluation efforts allows us to explore the assumptions on which Kennedy and Gorham predicted their expectations for reform, as well as the feasibility of the reform notion itself.

Although Kennedy and the analysts who were charged with improving the process of decisionmaking viewed reform somewhat differently, they held two very general and important assumptions in common. First, they presumed that a requirement to evaluate would be "self-executing," and that program information would be available. Both Kennedy and Gorham assumed that a requirement to establish procedures for the "objective" measure of program "effectiveness" would generate reliable, objective, and useful program reports.

Second, both notions of reform assumed a particular ability and inclination of organizations—or Title I policy units—to act on the basis of information. That is, it was presumed that information is, in a sense, "self-winding"—that the input of evaluation data about program activities and outcomes into the Title I policy setting would lead to policy choices or program modifications based on these "facts." Taken together, these assumptions suggest a rational conception of decisionmaking.[53]

However, a DHEW evaluator commented: "If evaluation were a natural disease of bureaucracy, we would have caught it long ago."[54] Some organizational theorists suggest that the actions or decisions of individuals within bureaucracies typically

are not based on "facts" but on vested interest, previous compromise, and perceptions of self-maintenance.[55] Rein, for example, argues that "Organizational goals
and basic policies or strategies for meeting these goals are molded by values and
vested interests of key personnel, and these are typically unchangeable by information."[56]

This literature suggests that both the *generation* and *use* of information will
primarily reflect the perceived self-interest of the policy unit. This means that
information will be collected, disseminated, and used selectively and that the selection will be based on organizational goals of self-maintenance rather than on the
formal organizational or program goals. In this view, information could be expected
to be used to effect "reform" only if "reform" is congruent with agency self-interest
and status quo.[57] Where information is *not* congruent with these perceived self-
interests, organizational theorists predict that it will be suppressed, distorted, ignored, or denied.

The central theme of this study, then, is the conflict between the notions of
reform and evaluation expressed by Robert Kennedy and William Gorham and this
theoretical perspective, which suggests that bureaucracies do not behave in the
manner assumed by reformers and evaluators.

Chapter 2 assesses the outcome of Kennedy's reporting strategy. Chapter 3
examines the cost-benefit evaluation model initiated by William Gorham's staff as
an alternative to the mandated evaluations. The findings and failings of two national surveys of Title I and compensatory education are discussed in Chapter 4.

Chapter 5 concerns yet another approach undertaken to Title I evaluation, case
studies of successful programs. Chapter 6 describes the final chapter in the history
of federal efforts to collect evaluation data on Title I—the massive information-
gathering scheme known as Belmont. Conclusions are presented in Chapter 7.


# Notes to Chapter 1

1. U.S. Congress, House, *Public Law* No. 89-10, 89th Cong., 1st sess., H. R. 2362,
April 11, 1965. For a detailed legislative history of ESEA and an analysis of the
political climate surrounding passage of the act, see, for example, Stephen K. Bailey
and Edith K. Mosher, *ESEA: The Office of Education Administers a Law* (Syracuse:
Syracuse University Press, 1968); Eugene Eidenberg and Roy D. Morey, *An Act of
Congress* (New York: W. W. Norton & Company Inc., 1969); and Philip Meranto, *The
Politics of Federal Aid to Education in 1965: A Study in Political Innovation* (Syra-
cuse: Syracuse University Press, 1967).

2. ESEA Title I was a legislative first in a number of respects. The legislation
embodied the first federal aid to parochial schools, the first federal aid measure to
address deficits attending disadvantaged children, not fiscal or material deficits in
local school systems. ESEA was the first large aid-to-education bill to be passed in
the absence of a national "crisis" (such as the launching of Sputnik). And ESEA Title
I was the first major piece of social legislation to require evaluation.

Elizabeth G. Cohen has commented that "Title I is unique not only in that it was
conceived as a way to solve specific educational problems but it was also seen by
many as a means to meliorate the pervasive social ills in many other parts of
society." *(A New Approach to Applied Research: Race and Education,* Columbus:
Charles E. Merrill Books, Inc., 1970.)

3. See Samuel Halperin, "ESEA: Five Years Later," *Congressional Record,*

House, September 9, 1970, pp. 8492-8494, and Frederick Mosteller and Daniel P. Moynihan, *On Equality of Educational Opportunity* (New York: Random House, Inc., 1972).

4. Interview, Samuel Halperin, February 22, 1972.

5. The HARYOU (Harlem Youth Opportunities Unlimited) report provides perhaps the earliest example of this point of view. See HARYOU, *Youth in the Ghetto: A Study of the Consequences of Powerlessness and a Blueprint for Change,* New York, 1964.

Kennedy's informants presented an argument about the effects of school which has also been central to the position of revisionist historians. Colin Greer argues in *The Great School Legend* (New York: Basic Books, Inc., 1972) that schools have never worked for poor and minority groups and further, that they were *designed* to fail these groups.

6. "Both sides agree that the motivation of slum children to excel in school is low. Both also agree that the lack of motivation stems from economic conditions produced by racial and economic discrimination. On nothing else is there agreement. . . . The major disagreement is that those who blame the home and community conditions claim that the schools are functioning at maximum efficiency; while those who see the problem in terms of deficiencies within the school believe that the schools are functioning at minimum efficiency." (James A. Jones, Research Director of the HARYOU-ACT, "Education in Depressed Areas: A Research-Sociologist's Point of View," in HARYOU, *Youth in the Ghetto: A Study of the Consequences of Powerlessness and a Blueprint for Change,* New York, 1964.)

7. U.S. Congress, Senate Subcommittee on Education, *Hearings on Elementary and Secondary Education Act of 1965,* 89th Cong., 1st sess., p. 529 (hereafter cited as *1965 Hearings*).

8. Ibid., p. 1298.

9. Ibid., p. 511. See also pp. 900-901, p. 1298.

10. Ibid., pp. 1743-1744

11. Ibid., p. 513.

12. Ibid.

13. Ibid.

14. Ibid., p. 512.

15. Interview, Samuel Halperin, February 22, 1972.

16. Ibid.

17. Bailey and Mosher (op. cit., p. 41) explain Wilbur Cohen's part in ESEA in this way: "Keppel continued to consult with HEW Assistant Secretary (later Under Secretary) Wilbur Cohen. This was not only because of the latter's extraordinary experience in the formulation of social legislation over the past three decades; it was also an expression of Keppel's determination to bring the Office of Education into the HEW team in order to get its help and protection."

18. Halperin, "ESEA: Five Years Later," op. cit.

19. Interview, Samuel Halperin, February 22, 1972.

20. *1965 Hearings,* p. 903.

21. Interview, Samuel Halperin, February 22, 1972. See also *1965 Hearings.*

22. *1965 Hearings,* p. 514.

23. Ibid., p. 1746

24. Interview, Samuel Halperin, February 22, 1972.

25. *1965 Hearings,* p. 901.

26. *1965 Hearings,* pp. 513-514.

27. Bailey and Mosher, op. cit., p. 47.

28. For comments concerning changing expectations for evaluation, see Gene V. Glass, "The Growth of Evaluation Methodology," Laboratory of Educational Research, University of Colorado, n.d., mimeo. Also see Stephen M. Barro, *An Approach to Developing Accountability Measures for the Public Schools*(Santa Monica, Calif.: The Rand Corporation, 1970), mono., for a good discussion of the evolution of accountability and the methodological implications.

29. *1965 Hearings*, p. 528.

30. For a brief political history of PPBS, see Charles L. Schultze, *The Politics and Economics of Public Spending* (Washington, D.C.: The Brookings Institution, 1968), and Elizabeth B. Drew, "HEW Grapples with PPBS," *The Public Interest*, Summer 1967, pp. 9-29.

President Johnson attributed the new vigor at DOD to the introduction of "modern" PPBS management principles. However, those who were in and about Washington at that time have suggested that the contribution of PPBS to the Pentagon's management reform is not altogether evident. Robert A. Levine, former director of evaluation at the Office of Economic Opportunity (OEO), has said: "It has never been clear to what extent the initial major and desirable changes in American military policy made by Secretary McNamara and President Kennedy were the result of the new system rather than being the result of eight years of growth in the fallow intellectual fields of the Eisenhower administration." *(Public Planning: Failure and Redirection*, New York: Basic Books, Inc., 1972, p. 143.)

31. Bailey and Mosher, op. cit., p. 181.

32. William Gorham, "Notes of a Practitioner," *The Public Interest*, Summer 1967, pp. 4-8.

33. Ibid. The term "creeping incrementalism" was popularized by Charles E. Lindblom as a characterization of the governmental decisionmaking process. ("The Science of 'Muddling Through,'" *Public Administration Review*, Vol. 19, Spring 1959, pp. 79-88.)

34. William Gorham, "Sharpening the Knife That Cuts the Public Pie," paper presented to the International Political Science Association, Brussels, Belgium, September 1967.

35. Interview, Senate Staff Assistant, October 26, 1972.

36. Gorham, "Notes of a Practitioner," op. cit., p. 8.

37. Ibid.

38. Bailey and Mosher, op. cit., p. 47.

39. Here and throughout this study the term "Title I policy arena" or "Title I policy system" is used. This refers to the multiple policy units, official and unofficial, that effect and are affected by Title I policy decisions. At the federal level, the central Title I policy units, in addition to the Office of Education and its agencies, are Congress, the White House, the Office of Management and Budget, the Secretary's Office of the Department of Health, Education, and Welfare, and the Office of the Assistant Secretary for Planning and Evaluation, DHEW. Outside the federal government, key participants in the Title I policy system include such interest groups as the Council of Chief State School Officers (CSSO), the Council of Great City Schools, Title I parents and their representatives, and those policy units responsible for the implementation of federal Title I policy, the State Educational Agencies (SEAs), and the Local Educational Agencies (LEAs).

40. Interviews, Senate Staff Assistants, October 1972. For a discussion of the degree to which Title I has been used as general aid, see Jerome T. Murphy, "Title I of ESEA: The Politics of Implementing Federal Education Reform," *Harvard*

*Educational Review,* Vol. 41, No. 1, February 1971, pp. 35-63, and Alan Ginsburg et al., "Title I of ESEA—Problems and Prospects," DHEW paper, n.d.

41. *1965 Hearings,* pp. 659 ff.

42. Ibid., p. 881.

43. Bailey and Mosher, op. cit., pp. 162-163.

44. Joseph S. Wholey, a former ASPE analyst has remarked: "Program managers may view evaluation of the impact of their national programs as a process from which they have more to lose than to gain—if not as a threat to their own positions. One possible conclusion of an objective evaluation study, for example, is that the program manager is not performing his job competently, or that the principles underlying a program have proven faulty in whole or in part. In either case, the administrator may prefer to take his chances on ignorance about the growth of the program. There may also be legitimate fears that the evaluation might give misinformation or unbalanced views on the worth of the programs, either because of the undeveloped state of evaluation methodology or because unsuitable output measures might be chosen by evaluators removed from program responsiblities." (Joseph S. Wholey et al., *Federal Evaluation Policy,* Washington, D.C.: The Urban Institute, 1971, p. 67.)

45. See, for example, opinions expressed by state and local schoolmen in "National Educational Assessment: Pro and Con," National Education Association, Washington, D.C., 1966. See also *Phi Delta Kappan,* Vol. 47, No. 1, September 1965, for views on federally sponsored evaluation effects, particularly pp. 8-18.

46. See Anthony Downs, *Inside Bureaucracy* (Boston: Little, Brown & Co., Inc., 1967), for a discussion of implications of this relationship in terms of bureaucratic behavior and decisionmaking.

47. "National Educational Assessment: Pro and Con," op. cit.

48. Ibid.

49. Ibid.

50. Interview, BESE Administrator, February 1972.

51. *1965 Hearings,* p. 514.

52. Kathryn A. Hecht, "Five Years of Title I Federal Evaluation," revised version of a paper presented to the 1972 Annual Meeting of the American Educational Research Association, Chicago, Illinois, April 7, 1972, p. 11.

53. See, for example, characteristics of a rational model of decisionmaking as outlined in Graham T. Allison, *The Essence of Decision Making* (Boston: Little, Brown & Co., Inc., 1971).

54. James G. Abert, "Evaluation at HEW: 1969-1971," April 8, 1971, mimeo., p. 9.

55. See, for example, Allison, op. cit.; Richard M. Cyert and James G. March, *A Behavioral Theory of the Firm* (Englewood Cliffs: Prentice-Hall, Inc., 1963); Daniel Katz and Robert L. Kahn, *The Social Psychology of Organizations* (New York: John Wiley & Sons, Inc., 1966); Herbert A. Simon, *Administrative Behavior,* 2d ed. (New York: The Free Press, 1965).

56. Martin Rein, *Social Policy: Issues of Choice and Change* (New York: Random House, Inc., 1970), p. 469.

57. For a discussion of this point, see James S. Coleman, "Incentives in Education: Existing and Proposed," n.d., mimeo.

# Chapter Two

# The Three-Tiered Reporting Scheme

Senator Kennedy's demand for an evaluation requirement generated considerable stress at all levels of the Title I policy system. Specifically, his "petulance" and insistence on a report of Title I project activities was seen to threaten the delicate consensus that had been established to insure speedy and unanimous passage of President Johnson's landmark education bill.[1] The passage of ESEA was predicated on a fragile coalition of important interest groups, and on a consensus about what the act would mean in such traditionally controversial areas as church-state relations, civil rights, and federal control of education. Because it accounted for five-sixths of the total funds authorized by ESEA, Title I received the primary attention of lawmakers and schoolmen. Accordingly, framers of Title I purposely left ambiguous parts of the bill that might generate conflict and weaken support.[2]

## DIPLOMACY AND AMBIGUITY

Kennedy's support was important to the passage of ESEA, but evaluation was also a traditional bugaboo of schoolmen. Thus, to appease Senator Kennedy and not simultaneously anger educational interest groups, drafters resorted to additional political diplomacy. Kennedy's demand for an accountability measure was met as inconspicuously as possible, with a loosely worded evaluation mandate.[3]

The long hours of debate within USOE and the executive branch that Kennedy's position precipitated focused chiefly on the political viability of an evaluation requirement as federal policy, not on the substance of Kennedy's concern. Keppel's chief legislative aide, Samuel Halperin, remembers that the Commissioner's "immediate reaction" to Kennedy's demand for evaluation was to "recite the problems and hostilities he had encountered over the Carnegie National Assessment program."[4] In addition to the battle over National Assessment, in his function as "broker" for the Gardner Task Force on Education,[5] Commissioner Keppel had been exposed to the sentiment of various educational interest groups concerning evaluation. Keppel was conversant with the views of educators and the staunch opposition to evaluation by groups such as the American Federation of Teachers (AFT) and the Council of Chief State School Officers (CSSO). He feared that the insurance device Kennedy insisted upon could destroy the consensus necessary to smooth passage of

ESEA. Halperin recalls: "Keppel felt that an evaluation requirement would be a red flag to the Chief State School Officers and that it could greatly damage if not kill the bill."[6] The Commissioner supported Kennedy's notion of evaluation, but insisted in the interest of the Act as a whole that any requirement to evaluate be very open-ended and nonspecific.[7] Consequently, as Kennedy's proposal was translated into legislative language, "the guiding concern was that the amendment be broad and general, and open to multiple interpretations at the local level."[8]

Commissioner Keppel instructed Samuel Halperin to "slip" the evaluation amendments into the legislation as inconspicuously as possible, so that attention would not be called to the Kennedy additions as the bill was sent to the House. Accordingly, Halperin transmitted the "Kennedy Amendments"[9] to John Brademas, a member of Carl Perkins' Executive Subcommittee, without "explaining to Brademas what they were"—substantive additions to the legislation that should have House debate and vote before being included in the legislation.[10] Representative Brademas was "allowed to believe" that the evaluation provisions were "perfecting amendments" that did not substantively change the nature of the bill and thus would require no vote.[11] As Keppel and others had hoped, the evaluation requirements did not receive notice from professional-interest groups, and ESEA was enacted with the Kennedy Amendments undebated and intact.[12]

The broad language of the Title I evaluation requirement allowed considerable state and local discretion in meeting the new federal mandate. A local project was required to ensure that ". . . effective procedures, including provisions for appropriate objective measurements of education, will be adopted for evaluation at least annually of the effectiveness of the programs in meeting the special educational needs of educationally deprived children."[13] The law did not specify what "appropriate objective measurements" might be, or indeed even what might be identified as the "special educational needs of educationally deprived children." The overall evaluation plan defines a three-tiered (or pyramid) reporting scheme for Title I. The Local Educational Agency (LEA) is required to report annually to the State Educational Agency (SEA). SEAs, in turn, are required

> . . . [to] make to the Commissioner (A) periodic reports including the results of objective measurements . . . evaluating the effectiveness of payments under this Title and of particular programs assisted under it in improving the educational attainment of educational deprived children and (B) such other reports as may be reasonably necessary to enable the Commissioner to perform his duties under this Title. . . .[14]

The reporting responsibilities of USOE were left ambiguous in the 1965 legislation, but it was understood that an annual report on Title I would be made to Congress and that the information required by law would be included in this report.[15]

## IMPLEMENTING THE MANDATE

In order to placate both Kennedy and the important educational interest groups, the language and intent of the evaluation requirement was purposely vague. Consequently, the legislative mandate transmitted to the Office of Education was ill-defined, and interpretation of the Title I evaluation requirement was left until the implementation stage.[16] It was USOE's responsibility to give administrative substance to Kennedy's ideas by formulating specific evaluation guidelines. This task was accomplished under severe time and staff constraints. The Division of Program

Operations (DPO)[17] in the Bureau of Elementary and Secondary Education (BESE) had the major administrative responsibility for Title I evaluation guidelines. Since no planning time had been allocated, DPO officials faced a 30-day deadline in which to write guidelines for school-year Title I programs that had already begun.

Another problem was that the job of writing the evaluation guidelines was delegated to an unprepared and inexperienced Policy and Procedures Unit[18] within DPO. But this office's lack of experience was not exceptional. USOE had little experience in administering programs of the size of ESEA, and USOE had no experience with evaluation.[19] Neither was there any office within the whole of DHEW involved in 1965 with evaluation of the type proposed by Title I. DPO, essentially a grants-management unit, had no full-time evaluator on its staff for the first 6 months of Title I operation, and recruitment of qualified staff was difficult.[20] The number of available professionals was limited anyway, and few experienced evaluators were willing to take the risks involved in an USOE career.[21]

But lack of time and expertise were not the most important factors in determining the parameters and tone of Title I evaluation guidelines: the guidelines were written and implemented with an eye to USOE's traditional role in educational policy system. For while passage of ESEA had precipitated extensive reorganization of USOE, those primarily responsible for administration of Title I were not reformers like Keppel.[22] Arthur L. Harris, a long-time USOE executive, was selected to manage BESE. DPO (DCE) was headed up by John F. Hughes, a former USOE chief administrative officer. And, "the traditional professional cadre of the Division of Program Operations consisted almost entirely of a scattering of experienced middle-level staff transferred from a variety of posts in the old USOE organization."[23]

Thus the bulk of the BESE/DPO staff had been educated in the school of grants management and weaned on the traditions of a weak USOE. There were few if any spokesmen for the new, aggressive leadership role envisioned by Robert Kennedy, Francis Keppel, and William Gorham. Instead, those responsible for framing Title I evaluation guidelines had been part of USOE when "it had few friends apart from the National Educational Association, the American Association of School Administrators, and the Council of Chief State School Officers (and was) the 'kept' Federal agent of these major private educational associations."[24]

Further, the law itself contained provisions that muddied the question of evaluation and USOE's new role. While ESEA required that USOE Title I staff review the effectiveness of Title I, at the same time USOE officials were prohibited by Section 604 from exercising "discretion, supervision or control" over state and local administration of ESEA.

It is not entirely surprising, then, that for any or all of these reasons USOE's formulation of the Title I evaluation guidelines reflected greater concern for old, valued friendships and familiar patterns of state-federal relationships than for the ideas of reform that motivated Kennedy. In constructing the evaluation guidelines, the DPO staff tried to strike a course for Title I evaluation that would not disrupt the policy system. At the outset, explicit decisions were made within DPO to avoid evaluation issues that might frighten local or state administrators, or cloud the new "partner-client" relationship. For example, as discussions concerning the evaluation guidelines got underway, an implicit decision was made not to set uniform reporting standards, not to require measurement by standardized tests, and not to suggest what the preferred components of "effectiveness" might be.[25] More sophisticated methodological notions, such as the provision of control groups, were rejected as running against the grain of legislative intent.[26]

Throughout the drafting process, USOE officials took extraordinary care to obtain the concurrence and support of SEA and LEA officials.[27] And much of this concern focused on the issue of evaluation as a federal requirement:

> ... the statutory emphasis on measuring the educational achievement of the beneficiaries of Title I projects appeared to lead in the direction of a national assessment of a school's effectiveness—a development long feared and resisted by school administrators throughout the country.[28]

As many of the CSSO pointed to the shadow of federal control in the evaluation measures of the first draft guidelines, USOE responded by revising the ESEA guidelines.[29] The final version of the Title I guidelines was sent to the SEAs on December 3, 1965, halfway into the school year. The evaluation issue was treated cautiously:

> ... the document was considerably condensed and revised editorially, especially the sections on project design and evaluation, which were placed after, instead of before, the section on fiscal administration— *presumably in order to reduce their prominence.*[30] [Emphasis added]

As a result of USOE's caution and concern, the guidelines were little more concrete than the legislative language itself. This enabled LEAs to exercise complete discretion in determining the content and format of their reports.

The pusillanimity of USOE about evaluation persisted beyond the drafting of guidelines into the implementation stage. USOE personnel anxiously sought to reassure SEA and LEA officials that their evaluations would not be used in a punitive fashion, and that continuation of their local projects would not be premised on their program reports. USOE's initial position toward Title I reporting deemphasized the difficult job of evaluation, as well as the purpose of the enterprise itself. Contrary to Senator Kennedy's expectation that evaluation would permit USOE to check the effectiveness of LEA program administration, the posture of USOE suggested that the outcome of the evaluations would have little substantive effect on the future of local and state Title I projects. Certainly Commissioner Harold Howe (who replaced Francis Keppel shortly after the passage of ESEA) carried this message to schoolmen:

> Maybe too much fuss is being made about evaluation. Evaluation procedures are already built into Title I projects, now you simply carry them out. . . . I don't think it is unreasonable to expect schoolmen to do a careful job on evaluation. We're really not asking them to do any more than they normally would do on their own. . . . *No one is going to be penalized as a result of the evaluation.*[31] [Emphasis added]

Few of the central participants in the implementation stage of Title I addressed Kennedy's expectations concerning the function of project reporting, nor did they appear eager to assume the oversight role that reformers anticipated. In fact, in the early years of Title I few of the major officials showed much interest in evaluation at all. Commissioner Howe, for example, saw little immediate value in Title I evaluation. Dr. Joseph Froomkin, who headed the Office of Program Planning and Evaluation (OPPE) from 1967 to 1969, recalls that Howe was primarily interested in desegregation and that his interest in evaluation was marginal. Further, according to Froomkin, Howe was skeptical about the value of Title I evaluation. The Commissioner believed that the result of Title I could not be measured at current levels of spending and that too little time had passed to assess the effort of the program.[32]

Lee Wickline, formerly Assistant Director, Division of Plans and Supplementary Centers, USOE, remembers Senator Kennedy pressing Commissioner Howe on the question of Title I evaluation in the 1966 Senate hearings on ESEA:

> Senator Kennedy asked Commissioner Howe, "What have you accomplished with the billion dollars that you got for elementary and secondary education last year?" In reply, Commissioner Howe began listing the number of books that had been purchased, the amount of money that had been expended for teachers, the amount of money that had been used for the purchase of equipment and materials, and so on. When finished, Senator Kennedy was quite impatient, and asked, "What happened to the children? Do you mean that you spent a billion dollars and you don't know whether they can read or not?" Commissioner Howe countered by saying, "You know this program has been operating for less than a year and it is just like planting a tree; you don't plant it one day and then pull it up every week and look at the roots to see if it's growing." Needless to say, Senator Kennedy was not very happy with this answer.[33]

And Director of DCE, Jack Hughes, appeared to have little interest in evaluation. Hughes defined the role of USOE as "checkwriter" and was concerned mainly with getting the money out, not checking up on its impact.[34] Joseph Froomkin has said:

> There was a lot of confusion when Title I was passed. It was seen as a funding program. There was no pressure to find out what was happening. Jack Hughes ran Title I like an accounting operation. Hughes wanted to see money go to the right places.[35]

A member of the Title I staff said:

> Jack Hughes saw Title I not as a program to be enforced, but as a program to be administered. He saw the intent of a significant part of Congress to be "a little bit to everybody." Therefore there was a small Title I staff and so on. He saw his job just to get the checks out, not evaluate.[36]

As ESEA Title I got underway, then, there was little explicit interest within USOE in making school administrators responsible to their constituencies, or in making educational achievement the "touchstone of success in judging ESEA,"[37] as Robert Kennedy had been promised in return for his support. Kennedy's expectations were eclipsed by more powerful policy system incentives, and by USOE's perceived need to maintain harmonious relations with the states. Evaluation was an issue only as it affected these intergovernmental relations.


## THE RESULTS

The results of this approach to evaluation were evident in the first round of Title I reporting. Commissioner Howe noted that although the first annual report on Title I

> . . . lacked some of the specifics of a technical evaluation report, . . . nevertheless, a great amount of useful and illuminating information has been accumulated by the states and territories. From that information emerges a picture of how American schools met the mandate of Congress to provide for educationally deprived children.[38]

This report painted the success of Title I in glowing terms, and suggested that the local school administrators were moving quickly to devise effective compensatory strategies. Title I seemed to be working beyond anyone's highest expectations.

One state reported that Title I was "bringing about an educational revolution." USOE editorialized that a similar impact was "echoed in the reports of our states one after the other." The enthusiastic LEA reports synthesized by the states were largely promotional and impressionistic. For example:

> In a short period of time we have passed through the embryonic state of a revolutionary venture. . . .

> . . . these [Title I] experiences have provided for many children a new outlook on life.

> . . . the impact of Title I is summed up by words such as vibrant, exploratory, reflective, child-centered and challenging. . . .

> . . . early, informal observation and evaluation by educators indicate that this impact will be unquestionable and dramatic. Most teachers were stimulated to restate old and new objectives with the feeling that they might now reach fruition. . . . The image of the "poverty school culture" is changing from one of inferiority to one of progressing professionalism.

And, the USOE report concludes:

> Hundreds of diverse and innovative projects sponsored in communities across the nation testify to the creative energies released by Title I. New ideas were sought, not for change's sake, but because new approaches were needed to break through the apathy and intellectual inertia which often surround the child from poverty areas.

The anecdotal nature of the first annual report was generally excused as a result of "start up confusion."[39] However, the second annual report, *Title I/Year II*, turned out to be similar in format and substance, emphasizing impressionistic local reports, testimonial data, and photojournalism.

The failure of the second annual report to meet the expectations of reformers, or even to meet the precepts of sound evaluation practice, was roundly criticized, both within the Title I policy system and without. Robert Dentler, of the Center for Urban Education (CUE) in New York, characterized the report and its conclusions as "elegantly incontestable." The variance between the Title I program outcomes reported in the second annual report and his own research prompted Dentler to write an article, "Urban Eyewash," which pointed out many substantive problems of analysis and interpretation evident in the report:

> In the summer of 1968, the U.S. Government Printing Office published a handsome document entitled *Title I/Year II*. I became fascinated with that part of the report that evaluates the effects of Title I in big cities, because of the great difference between its conclusions and the conclusions one might reach from reading the more than 60 Title I evaluations prepared by CUE since 1966. *The federal report is, with cautions, a success story. The Center reports document a series of earnest attempts and invite impression of cumulative failure.* [40] [Emphasis added]

The very positive and inoffensive national summaries of the first 2 years of Title I activities can be viewed as an effort by USOE officials to meet two potentially contradictory objectives. On the one hand, these reports side-stepped the issue of "federal control" with an uncritical synthesis and interpretation of the project reports submitted by 18,000 local school districts and 50 State Departments of Education. On the other hand, these evaluations formally fulfilled the demands of reformers such as Robert Kennedy, who insisted on an account of Title I project effectiveness.

This approach to evaluation may have been the best solution to the dilemma presented to USOE, but it did not give Kennedy or other proponents of project evaluation what they wanted. Few would contest the idea that the local reports, and the state and federal reports based on them, are essentially public relations documents. In other words, Kennedy's evaluation requirement created Title I evaluation at the local level only in form, not in substance. LEAs comply with the letter of the law in the annual submission of an evaluation document, but their evaluation effort does not reflect the spirit that motivated the requirement or concern for objective self-assessment. A number of studies demonstrate that LEAs make little use of the data they are producing.[41] Former ASPE analyst Bayla White has said: "The content of [LEA] evaluation reports is designed to provide information that state and federal officials want—not necessarily what local school officials need to know."[42]

A BESE document acknowledges the ritualism that characterizes local evaluations: ". . . evaluation is rarely used by LEAs as a tool for reasoned management decisionmaking, but instead as a mandated exercise necessary to prolong receipt of federal funds."[43] An Urban Institute report of Title I evaluation efforts concludes:

> Unfortunately, millions of federal dollars are being spent each year on noncomparable, unrelated evaluations of individual local projects. Under present plans, additional millions of federal dollars will be spent in the future on such evaluations. These noncomparable, unrelated evaluations of individual local projects, often done simply to satisfy Federal evaluation requirements, are generally useful neither for national program planning nor local program planning.[44]

Even though this three-tiered reporting scheme continues, and consumes the lion's share of available evaluation funds—approximately $10 million annually— federal interest in the results of the mandated reporting scheme ended with the publication of *Title I/Year II*. There is no evidence that local reporting practices have improved with time. Reviews undertaken by the American Institutes for Research (AIR) and the Center for Educational Policy Research, Harvard University, found that these evaluations were as unsatisfactory in 1972 as they were in 1966. In fact, OPPE personnel can identify only five state reports that contain data potentially useful to the planning areas within USOE.[45] Most Title I project reports continue to resemble educational travel brochures, with extensive anecdotes and little objective data to support claims of "success." The evidence presented is often unrepresentative, impressionistic, and incomplete, if not false.[46] Indeed, if one were to rely solely on these required reports in judging the impact of Title I, one would have to conclude that it has been an astonishing success—a conclusion that, as we shall see, finds little support in other efforts to evaluate Title I. The local evaluations have not provided the "facts" and "figures" Kennedy hoped for. These anecdotal and promotional reports could hardly serve as a "whip" or a "spur" for the "embittered parents of ghetto children, most of whom have seen precious little change in the quality of their children's education."[47]

The worth of these evaluations can be inferred from their reception at USOE. After their arrival has been duly noted on all the proper forms, the state reports remain in their packing boxes or in files in a remote corner of USOE, until they must be moved to make room for next year's shipment.[48] With few exceptions, the SEA evaluations are not used or even read by the USOE staff.[49] Even the area desk men, whose job it is to know what is happening in Title I programs in their assigned states, ignore the annual reports.[50] One area desk man said:

> State reports? The whole thing is done for appearances.... [Do we use them?]... Just look at the number of outstanding audits and narratives on state procedures. We know that state reports are done just to make the states look good.[51]

And another said:

> [They're] not read because we feel before we would start that they are garbage. [The fact that they are not read] also reflects our experience with the states.... You talk with the states about evaluation and planning and then you go visit local districts and find out that Title I is still general aid and supplanting. So what are you evaluating?[52]

## SOURCES OF FAILURE

/ This area desk man points to an important reason for the failure of Kennedy's evaluation plan: an inconsistency between the way reformers saw Title I and local perceptions of the purpose of the program. LEAs wanted general aid, not categorical aid targeted for disadvantaged children. In practice, many LEAs have used Title I funds as general aid, some quite blatantly and others simply by stretching the operational definition of "category" to its broadest interpretation. But the net effect has been the same, and "So what are you evaluating?"[53] Evaluation of a "program" that exists only on paper could only be pro forma.[54] But LEAs did not act on these preferences for evaluation in a vacuum; the laissez-faire administrative climate of the Title I policy system permitted it. ASPE evaluator Alan Ginsburg comments:

> LEAs, particularly those under considerable financial pressure, would prefer to use these funds as general aid. The popularity of SAFA [School Assistance in Federally Affected Areas] money indicates this. It is reasonable to expect the LEAs to spend funds according to their own priorities, when there is little fear of enforcement.[55]

The predisposition of LEAs to see the Title I program and the role of evaluation differently from Kennedy was compounded and reinforced by the posture of other parts of the Title I system. For one, temporary settlements, whether in the area of foreign affairs, labor relations, or public policy have a tendency to become permanent. Organizations, particularly bureaucracies, typically act so as to minimize their uncertainty. Thus, once a temporary measure has become known and has been incorporated by the operating system, its replacement will be resisted. The initial posture of USOE may have undermined Kennedy's evaluation scheme. The temporary measures that were designed to take the sting out of an evaluation requirement perhaps cost USOE an important opportunity to establish a strong evaluation policy. In the absence of precedent on this issue, the way these controversial questions were resolved at the outset may have afforded federal officials their best chance to exercise initiative and leadership. Having elected, for a multiplicity of reasons, to begin by underplaying the issue of evaluation, it is not surprising that USOE was unable to strengthen its position on evaluation or accounting later. In addition, the organizational literature observes that subordinate agencies tend to model their priorities and actions on those of their superiors. In the early years of Title I, there was little in the behavior of USOE to demonstrate much federal interest in the exercise of local project evaluation.

Thus the initial USOE response to the evaluation mandate established patterns that were difficult to modify later.[56] By late 1967, the balance of power in the Title I policy arena had become established. The weak posture of USOE simply served to strengthen the hand of SEAs and LEAs and permitted them to follow their own predispositions concerning evaluation and the use of Title I funds. By the time *Title I/Year II* was published, whatever initial fears schoolmen may have had about "federal control," or whatever opportunity USOE may have had to exercise, superordinate sanction had vanished.[57]

Neither did the states have much interest in assuming responsibility for the intent of Kennedy's evaluation requirement.[58] Title I represents but a small portion of a SEA's budget, and target children a small percentage of state school children. SEAs must deal with the local districts on numerous more important issues, such as accreditation, licensing, and school finance. SEAs, like USOE, have been unwilling to destroy good working relationships with the local districts over the relatively trivial matter of Title I data collection and evaluation.

Further, state education personnel have little practical interest in the sort of evaluation Kennedy had in mind. SEA officials did not want to publicize the disappointments or shortcomings of Title I programs in their state; nor did they see evaluation as relevant or appropriate in the instance of Title I. Many SEA personnel saw the focus of the Title I evaluation as too narrow to be useful to them. Commenting on the state role in Title I evaluation, Bayla White remarks:

> The state is responsible for monitoring local operations to see that they conform to the letter and spirit of the law. State evaluation activities should have at least two objectives: (a) to yield information to state program officials which can be used to improve the operations of local Title I programs; (b) to yield information about Title I activities within the state which can be used in federal program planning. How well do state Title I evaluation activities accomplish these activities? Not well at all.[59]

The states' pro forma approach to evaluation is evident in Bayla White's analysis of SEA evaluation activities:

> States send out evaluation guidelines or requests for information to the LEAs long after the school year has begun. Since the local projects are already underway, the state is in a very poor position to influence either the evaluation design or the kind of information maintained on the Title I projects. States are required by the Office of Education to supply data on the effect of Title I on student achievement. But most states merely collect whatever test data exist, as opposed to requiring uniform testing or the use of selected tests. The evaluation reports filed by the LEAs reach the state officials long after decisions on project approval for the next year are made.
>
> The consequences of the state efforts to meet federal requirements are twofold: (1) the extent to which the state shapes the local evaluation efforts is minimized and (2) the utility to state decisionmaking of the information collected is greatly reduced. As presently constructed, the annual state reports provide little information on the extent to which individual local projects are meeting stated objectives. ... These problems, coupled with the timing of the evaluation cycle, mean that the local evaluation reports play almost no part in the Title I project approval process.[60]

The states, then, generally do not concern themselves with local Title I evaluation even as a basis for review of local Title I project applications. Thus the responsibility for overseeing the evaluation guideline (like other program guidelines) has slipped between the cracks of the policy system. Phyllis McClure remarks that ". . . Title I was caught in the 'political thicket' of education politics in which no level of government assumed responsibility for enforcing the law."[61] A state administrator has been quoted as saying that since USOE didn't seem too interested in evaluation, he didn't see any reason why he should be.[62]

The outcome of the weak USOE position on evaluation and the concomitant lack of state interest in program reporting, ironically, has been precisely the sort of implementation of an accountability measure that Kennedy did *not* want and sought to prevent. Kennedy intended that the evaluation provisions of ESEA would preclude local school domination of the collection, assessment, and dissemination of information about project activities and effectiveness. He hoped that a requirement to report would force the schools to focus their attention on the needs of disadvantaged children, and enable their parents to negotiate from a position of strength. But the effective withdrawal of SEAs and USOE from evaluation policy left the determination of Title I project evaluation in the hands of those who had opposed it from the outset. Thus, in practice, the Title I evaluation policy reflects *local* interests and priorities for evaluation, not the concerns of federal reformers such as Kennedy, who pushed for evaluation. And, incentives at the local level to do the sort of evaluation that Kennedy wanted are slim or nonexistent.

Local administrators confronted several policy options as they made decisions about the character and form of Title I programs and Title I evaluation. The passive role of the federal and state Title I administrators regarding evaluation effectively removed any sanction or incentive—most specifically continuation of funding—to conduct evaluation in a manner that conflicted with local interests. The critical and public self-assessment expected by Kennedy is inimical in some important respects to local perception of self-interest. Any rewards or incentives that may be tied to required reporting from the perspective of local administrators tend to solicit precisely the sort of public relations document produced by most LEAs. An evaluation engineered to spotlight program success and obscure failures would be expected to reduce interference from the Title I parents, minimize checking up and poking about by state and federal officials, and promote a positive image for the school and school personnel in the education community. Since continued funding of local projects is contingent only on submission of an "evaluation," and does not depend on the quality or reliability of the report, there is little reason for LEAs to view evaluations as other than an irritating annual ritual.

Any movement toward "accountability" or evaluation as a result of the Title I evaluation requirement, then, was generally pro forma. The institutionalization of Title I evaluation requirements represented little substantive change in school accountability or in the relationships between schools and the community. The local incentives that weighed against accountability of the type Kennedy envisioned were more powerful than the pressures to provide this sort of social report.[63]

This resistance gives lie to an assumption underlying Kennedy's expectation that a statutory reporting scheme would help to generate the data requisite to reform of local school administrative practice and priorities. Kennedy expected that the evaluation requirement would be its own brief—that ipso jure, a reporting mandate would result in objective reports on Title I program activities and accomplishments.

But experience has shown that this is not always true. Operating units within a bureaucratic structure exhibit a tendency to interpret policy directives in light of their own priorities and interests. A consequent paradox for social planners is the typical perversion of intent that occurs as federal policy directives move through the multilevel operating units of a bureaucracy.[64] Furthermore, federal officials have limited authority to oversee or enforce the implementation of federal intent at the local level. The degree to which local implementation of federal policy conforms to federal intent appears to depend on the degree to which the federal policy agrees with local preference. Wirt and Kirst have remarked:

> A legal requirement in the statute or an administrative structure in the federal regulations is conceived of as a policy output. But if state and local education officials are antagonistic to these legal mandates, they can prevent them from becoming outcomes merely by not enforcing them. Or by their own means and in response to their own values, they may transform outputs into outcomes unanticipated—even undesired—by the authorities originally producing them. It is not enough to provide information about the output to have it be received, accepted and acted on. ... it would take an army of federal auditors and program analysis to check on compliance in 19,300 local school districts.[65]

Kennedy's notion of reform, then, was not borne out by the Title I evaluation mandate. The legislation in the largest measure did *not* make information available that could be used either by parents to change the priorities of local school administrators or by USOE to oversee the effective targeting of Title I funds. And USOE did not try to force local program managers to comply with the intent of the evaluation requirement.[66]

Parents and their spokesmen feel that in theory the Title I reporting scheme is adequate, and that if properly implemented at the local level, it could serve the parent community as Kennedy hoped.[67] However, in reality, local values play an important part in determining how a federal initiative (or policy) is implemented locally. The outcome of the three-tiered reporting scheme suggests that local schoolmen don't want to collect and disseminate objective information about the activities and achievements of a national program. Additional incentives beyond those contained in a federal policy guideline may be required to motivate local schoolmen to act in ways that are contrary to their fundamental preferences. However, because Kennedy's scheme failed, there is no way to know whether his second assumption— that evaluation would be used by parents and USOE to hold programs accountable and to check up on Title I program effectiveness—was correct. The reporting scheme didn't generate useful program data, so we cannot judge how such information would have been used within the Title I policy system—whether to effect reform as Robert Kennedy hoped or for some other purpose. But the posture of USOE toward evaluation suggests that, at least for Title I, there was as little federal demand for rigorous and comprehensive evaluation data as there was interest at the local level in supplying them.

## IMPACT ON THE TITLE I POLICY SYSTEM

Although the evaluation mandate failed to lead to reform of local school practice, the reporting measure did have an impact in the Title I policy system. By late 1967, as the first annual Title I report had been reviewed and the shape and content of the second report was apparent, both Kennedy and Gorham's ASPE staff abandoned the three-tiered reporting scheme.

The glowing evaluations submitted by LEAs were in stark contrast to the disheartening reports Kennedy was receiving from parents and community leaders in New York City who claimed that Title I had not bought better educational services for poor children,[68] and that Title I monies were being misused by local schools. In Kennedy's view, the Title I evaluation plan had failed. This judgment diminished his confidence in the ability of USOE personnel to monitor the targeting and impact of Title I funds, and reinforced his initial fears that local school administrators would waste Title I resources.[69] He therefore turned from evaluation to legislation as a way to reform local school administration and educational practices for disadvantaged children. Kennedy interpreted the outcome of the mandated evaluation plan as a warrant for substantive federal intervention in local school affairs. Samuel Halperin has said that "Kennedy told Howe that he wanted to see evaluations of working programs. By 1966 and 1967, Kennedy wanted to identify five or ten working programs and *make* the local schools adopt them."[70] As a lawmaker, Senator Kennedy wanted to make Title I work using the means with which he was most familiar and over which he had some degree of influence. Since statutory requirements had failed to achieve the reform he felt was necessary, Kennedy wanted to go one step farther and require the adoption of program strategies thought to be successful.

Kennedy's conclusions about the outcome of the three-tiered reporting scheme were shared by Gorham's ASPE staff, but ASPE analysts had another response. Whereas Kennedy responded with a recommendation for stronger legislation, ASPE analysts responded with a plan for additional evaluation. ASPE was created primarily to implement PPBS. Up-to-date and reliable information is central to these responsibilities. Michael Timpane, former ASPE Director of Educational Planning, has described the function of this policy unit:

> ASPE is concerned with planning studies, program development, cost benefit and projective analysis. We are concerned with the evaluation and management of federal programs in the context of all other things going on. ASPE ends up counterpunching OE; we serve as a critical review for OE.[71]

Kennedy demanded evaluation to make sure the new Title I resources reached poor children; he did not want to "learn" from evaluations in the way that ASPE did. Initially, ASPE analysts anticipated that Kennedy's reporting scheme could also serve their data needs. The "facts and figures" Kennedy thought could be an accountability device were compatible with the input and output data required by a PPBS. At the beginning, it was expected that the required Title I reporting scheme would serve a dual purpose—that the local project reports could promote the sort of reform Kennedy had in mind, as well as provide the data necessary to ASPE-inspired programmatic and managerial reforms.

However, the impressionistic and anecdotal Title I evaluations created in response to Kennedy's demands were antithetical to ASPE's information needs. These evaluations were hardly scientific, reported no cost or other input data, and furnished no goal statements or output data that could be reduced to quantitative terms. In short, no data were generated through the Kennedy evaluation scheme that would allow ASPE analysts to identify successful strategies or that would permit application of cost-benefit techniques. Publication of the first annual Title I report, then, precipitated ASPE's immediate intervention in the area of Title I evaluation.

# Notes to Chapter 2

1. Interview, Samuel Halperin, February 22, 1972.

2. See Stephen K. Bailey and Edith K. Mosher, *ESEA: The Office of Education Administers a Law* (Syracuse: Syracuse University Press, 1968).

3. U.S. Congress, House, *Public Law* No. 89-10, 89th Cong., 1st sess., H.R. 2362, April 11, 1965, Sec. 205.

4. Interview, Samuel Halperin, February 22, 1972. The Exploratory Committee on Assessing the Progress of Education was appointed by the Carnegie Corporation in July 1964. The Council of Chief State School Officers (CSSO) expressed strong objections to the suggestions of this Committee, which they feared might lead to federal involvement in the evaluation of local school outcomes, or to the drawing of comparisons between states, districts, or schools. Schoolmen also worried about who would have access to the National Assessment data.

5. The Gardner Task Force was a blue ribbon pannel commissioned by President Johnson to study the nation's education needs and to offer suggestions for new federal education policies. Francis Keppel served as "broker" between USOE and the Gardner Task Force, "consulting with various professional and interest groups in an attempt to resolve the issue dividing them—especially the issues of church-state relations and the degree of Federal control. In short, Keppel performed a key role as an intermediary broker of ideas, moving among various arenas: the task force; HEW and USOE planning staffs; the White House; the Congress, the press; professional associations, and interest groups." (Bailey and Mosher, op. cit., p. 41.)

See Charles Philip Kearney, "The 1964 Presidential Task Force on Education and the Elementary and Secondary Education Act of 1965," Ph.D. diss., University of Chicago, 1967, for an analysis of the role the Gardner Task Force recommendations played in the drafting and passage of ESEA. Kearney suggests that the report of the Task Force (which still has not been made public) was used by the Administration primarily to provide allusion to "expert judgment" and thus to legitimate President Johnson's education initiatives, contained in ESEA, especially Title I.

6. Interview, Samuel Halperin, February 22, 1972.

7. One federal participant in the 1965 sessions has suggested that Commissioner Keppel made a mistake in treating the issue of evaluation with such deference. This former Office of Management and Budget (OMB) official believes, in retrospect, that "we could have asked for anything we wanted (regarding an evaluation requirement) in 1965 and gotten away with it. Commissioner Keppel overestimated the clout of the states and the Chiefs." (Interview, February 25, 1972.) Most other participants, however, do not share this view.

8. Interview, Samuel Halperin, February 22, 1972.

9. The "Kennedy Amendments" include not only the evaluation requirement contained in Sec. 205 of Title I, but also the dissemination requirements contained in Titles III, IV, and V of ESEA.

10. Interview, Samuel Halperin, February 22, 1972. President Johnson had expressed a strong wish that ESEA be passed with no debate. For this reason, the Act has been dubbed the "Railroad Act of 1965."

11. Ibid.

12. See Bailey and Mosher, op. cit.

13. U.S. Congress, House, *Public Law* No. 89-10, 89th Cong., 1st sess., H.R. 2362, April 11, 1965, Sec. 205.

14. Ibid., Sec. 206.

15. Kathryn A. Hecht, "Five Years of Title I Federal Evaluation," revised

version of a paper presented to the 1972 Annual Meeting of the American Educational Research Association, Chicago, Illinois, April 7, 1972, p. 2.

16. See Bailey and Mosher, op. cit.

17. DPO was renamed the Division of Compensatory Education (DCE) in August 1966.

18. This office was later renamed the Office of Program Planning and Evaluation (OPPE) and removed from DCE.

19. USOE's experience with administering the programs of the magnitude of ESEA was limited to the National Defense Education Act, a formula grant which made no attempt to evaluate outcome. See Michael W. Kirst, "Administrative Problems in Evaluation of Title I of the Elementary and Secondary Education Act," a paper included in an Urban Institute report on federal evaluation practices, December 1969, mimeo.

20. Hecht, op. cit., p. 3.

21. See Elizabeth B. Drew, "Education's Billion Dollar Baby," *The Atlantic Monthly,* Vol. 218, July 1966, pp. 37-43.

22. ESEA was responsible for precipitating an extensive reorganization 'of USOE. For discussions of the important changes in USOE staffing, attitudes, and priorities brought about by the passage of ESEA, see Robert Bendiner, *Obstacle Course on Capital Hill* (New York: McGraw-Hill Book Company, 1965); Bailey and Mosher, op. cit.; and William G. Land, "The Shakeout in USOE," *Phi Delta Kappan,* Vol. 47, No. 1, September 1965, pp. 31-33.

23. Bailey and Mosher, op. cit., p. 93.

24. Ibid., pp. 17-18.

25. See Kirst, op. cit.

26. Ibid.

27. Bailey and Mosher, op. cit., p. 113.

28. Ibid., p. 101.

29. See Jerome T. Murphy, "Title I of ESEA: The Politics of Implementing Federal Education Reform," *Harvard Educational Review,* Vol. 41, No. 1, February 1971, pp. 35-63, for interpretive comments on the compromises made as the original ESEA guidelines were constructed by USOE.

30. Bailey and Mosher, op. cit., p. 112.

31. Quoted in Hecht, op. cit., pp. 3-4.

32. Interview, Joseph Froomkin, February 25, 1972; letter from Joseph Froomkin, June 19, 1974.

33. Lee E. Wickline, "Educational Accountability," in E. Wayne Roberson (ed.), *Educational Accountability through Evaluation* (Englewood Cliffs: Education Technology Publications, 1971), pp. 7-8.

34. Interviews: Richard Carlson, February 25, 1972; Alice M. Rivlin, February 9, 1972; Bayla F. White, February 7, 1972.

35. Interview, Joseph Froomkin, February 25, 1972.

36. Interview, Title I Staff Member, February 24, 1972.

37. Samuel Halperin, "ESEA: Five Years Later," *Congressional Record,* House, September 9, 1970, pp. 8492-8494.

38. U.S. Office of Education, *The States Report: The First Year of Title I, Elementary and Secondary Education Act of 1965* (Washington, D.C.: U.S. Government Printing Office, 1967).

39. Hecht, op. cit.

40. Robert A. Dentler, "Urban Eyewash: A Review of Title I/Year II," *The Urban Review,* Vol. 3, No. 4, February 1969, pp. 32-33.

41. See Daniel C. Jordan and Kathryn A. Hecht (Spiess), *Compensatory Education in Massachusetts: An Evaluation with Recommendations* (Amherst: The University of Massachusetts Press, 1970).

42. Bayla F. White, "The Role of Evaluation in Title I Program Management," paper presented at the National Academy of Public Administration Conference on Evaluation in Education Programs, Rockville, Maryland, May 26, 1972, p. 6 (hereafter cited as "The Role of Evaluation").

43. U.S. Office of Education, Bureau of Elementary and Secondary Education, "A Plan for Program Evaluation: FY 1969," n.d., mimeo.

44. Joseph S. Wholey et al., *Title I: Evaluation and Technical Assistance,* Appendix B (Washington, D.C.: The Urban Institute, February 1971), p. 1.

45. Interview, OPPE Evaluator, February 23, 1972.

46. See, for example, the conclusions presented by AIR's recent Title I evaluation: Michael J. Wargo, "Needs, Resources, Management and Impact: A Comprehensive Evaluation of ESEA Title I Since 1965," American Institutes for Research in the Behavioral Science, Palo Alto, California, February 1972. (This report was rewritten, toned down, and officially released in March 1972 under a different title: "ESEA Title I: A Reanalysis and Synthesis of Evaluation Data from Fiscal Year 1965 Through 1970.") See also *Title I of ESEA: Is It Helping Poor Children?* a report prepared by the Washington Research Project of the Southern Center for Studies in Public Policy and the NAACP Legal Defense and Educational Fund, Inc., Washington, D.C., 1970. (This report is also popularly known as the "Martin-McClure Report," after principal authors Ruby Martin and Phyllis McClure.)

47. Samuel Halperin, "ESEA: Five Years Later," op. cit.

48. Interviews: OPPE Staff Member, February 23, 1972; Area Desk Man, February 24, 1972.

49. Joseph Froomkin, former USOE Assistant Commissioner for Planning and Evaluation, believes he was probably the only person at USOE who ever looked at the reports. Shortly after he arrived at USOE to head OPPE, Froomkin explored the documents as a possible source of program data. Froomkin has said: ". . . no one read state evaluations until I came and no one has read them after I left."

50. An "area desk man" is the member of the Title I/DCE staff who functions as the USOE liaison for SEA personnel in states in specific areas of the country. The area desk man is responsible for overseeing the implementation of Title I in his region and for providing technical assistance to the states.

51. Interview, Area Desk Man, February 24, 1972.

52. Interview, Area Desk Man, February 23, 1972.

53. See, for example, Washington Research Project Report, op. cit., for a discussion of "nonprograms."

54. Whether or not a slide project purchased with Title I funds is used for all children in a school or just for Title I eligible children is, of course, difficult for a federal auditor to determine. Thus, the number of borderline instances in which Title I funds have been used as general aid may never be known. However, the number of "gross" misuses of Title I funds identified by federal auditors indicated that the practice of using ESEA Title I as general aid is fairly widespread. ASPE analyst Alan Ginsburg has written: "Misuse of Title I funds is considered 'severe' and when asked if this meant that it was 10-15 percent, [DHEW] auditors thought it was substantially greater." (Ginsburg et al., "Title I of ESEA—Problems and Prospects," DHEW paper, ca. 1970.)

55. Ginsburg, ibid., p. 2.

56. James Abert, an ASPE analyst, has suggested: "Evaluation fell victim to a

sort of Gresham's Law. The immediate crisis drove out consideration of the long run." ("Evaluation at HEW: 1969-1971," April 8, 1971, mimeo., p. 2.)

57. Michael W. Kirst, a former BESE official, commented: "Two years into the program, there was no more fear of the 'Commissar' of Education. The state and local people know they won't be bugged by the feds." (Interview, July 31, 1972.)

58. See, for example, Hecht, op. cit.

59. White, "The Role of Evaluation," p. 4.

60. Ibid., p. 405.

61. Phyllis McClure, statement before the Congressional Black Caucus Hearings on Government Lawlessness, June 29, 1972.

62. From Frederick M. Wirt and Michael W. Kirst, *The Political Web of American Schools* (Boston: Little, Brown & Co., Inc., 1972), quoted in Hecht, op. cit., p. 10.

63. ASPE analyst Joseph Lipson, discussing another evaluation venture, made a comment much to this point: "The [educational policy] system was [found to be] resistant to change and restoring forces returned to an equilibrium state much like the one which generated the movement for change." ("An Overview of Educational Problems," Commissioner's Planning Unit for NIE, August 30, 1971, mimeo., p. 19.)

64. Robert A. Levine, *Public Planning: Failure and Redirection* (New York: Basic Books, Inc., 1972).

65. Wirt and Kirst, op. cit., p. 171. See also Murphy, op. cit., and Philip Meranto, *The Politics of Federal Aid to Education in 1965: A Study in Political Innovation* (Syracuse: Syracuse University Press, 1967).

66. See Levine, op. cit., and Wirt and Kirst, op. cit.

67. Interviews with Title I parents in Hartford, Connecticut, and in Los Angeles, California, Spring 1971. See also Phyllis McClure, op. cit.

68. Reports on Title I prepared by the Center for Urban Education, New York City, substantiate the claims made by Kennedy's constituents.

69. In the 1967 Senate hearings on ESEA, Kennedy chided Commissioner Howe about what he viewed as USOE's inertia in the area of evaluation, and about its loose management of Title I. Consequently, Howe asked the states to nominate "successful" Title I programs for inclusion in an additional USOE review of Title I activities. The result of this inquiry, *A Chance for Change,* was the first USOE publication to talk about specific projects. Samuel Halperin recalls Kennedy's response to the document: "I ordered forty copies of the report. The Senate hearings were still on and I wanted to show Kennedy that we [USOE] had been working on the problem. I found Kennedy in the hall and handed him a copy. He thumbed through it and threw it back at me. He said it had 'too many pictures.'"

*A Chance for Change* was little different from the Title I evaluations that had prompted it. It was a public relations document. Samuel Halperin relayed Kennedy's comments in an interview (February 22, 1972).

70. Ibid.

71. Interview, Michael Timpane, February 24, 1972.

# Chapter Three

# TEMPO: A Cost-Effectiveness Study

The ASPE staff moved in two directions to remedy the failure of the three-tiered reporting scheme. First, they attempted to make the mandated Title I evaluation system more effective. USOE administrators were urged to tighten up on the Title I evaluation and to communicate federal concerns about the quality of Title I reporting to SEAs. The ESEA evaluation requirement was also expanded. DHEW Secretary John Gardner carried ASPE's concern for a stronger reporting measure to Congress, and Congress amended ESEA to give the force of law to much broader evaluations of Title I. The 1967 amendments required that the Secretary of DHEW annually submit to Congress "... a report evaluating the results and effectiveness of programs and projects assisted thereunder," including Title I.[1] Material for the Secretary's report was to be supplied by the Commissioner of Education, who was instructed to "study and report annually" on the effectiveness of USOE programs.

Second, whereas Senator Kennedy interpreted the disappointing results of the required evaluation scheme as evidence of disinterest (if not malfeasance) on the part of local school administrators, ASPE attributed the failure of the evaluation requirement to the inexperience of local evaluators. The ASPE staff thought that the Title I reporting requirement should be continued as a "good thing" and as "character building" for LEAs and SEAs,[2] but that the difficult job of gathering and evaluating the data required by PPBS should be left to those with suitable background and training.

## ASPE INTERVENES: A SYSTEMS ANALYSIS APPROACH

Consequently, ASPE also stimulated and directed another study of Title I through USOE's Bureau of Research. ASPE analyst Alice Rivlin, Deputy Assistant Secretary for Program Analysis, and her assistant, Joseph Wholey, were especially interested in the use of cost-benefit analysis as a means of judging the effectiveness of Title I, and as a technique for identifying successful compensatory strategies.[3] Consequently, early in 1967 the TEMPO Division of the General Electric Company was commissioned by the Bureau of Research to undertake a preliminary cost-benefit analysis of compensatory education and Title I subsequently known as the TEMPO study.

TEMPO was conceived as a pilot study designed to relate academic achievement to compensatory education program components and costs. The study plan called for examination of exemplary Title I projects and identification of the features of successful compensatory programs. This evaluation strategy was expected to lead to more efficient purchase of Title I educational services and thereby more effective educational programs for disadvantaged children. Specification of successful compensatory strategies, it was reasoned, would eliminate wasteful trial and error, as well as treatments shown to be unsuccessful.

ASPE's expectations for the use of evaluation were different from Senator Kennedy's. The TEMPO design was not supposed to foster LEA responsiveness to Title I parents, but to provide information that federal decisionmakers could use to formulate policy and to give concrete direction to the Title I program. ASPE analyst Bayla White comments: "The [ASPE] philosophy was that planning and evaluation should have a central function. The model was McNamara. Planning and evaluation was seen as a tool, in an active sense, for running a program."[4]

ASPE's interest in Title I program data and the identification of successful strategies became more urgent with the release of two important reports on the effects of schools. The 1966 Equal Educational Opportunity Survey (EEOS),[5] also known as the Coleman report, raised doubts among some policymakers about the value of compensatory education (and Title I) as a social strategy. Many interpreted the Coleman findings to mean that schools "don't make a difference" in overcoming the unequal educational attainment that accompanies low socioeconomic status. And shortly after the Coleman report was released, the 1967 report of the U.S. Commission on Civil Rights generated more questions about the wisdom of investment in compensatory education as a federal antipoverty strategy.[6] While the EEOS addressed the effectiveness of schools generally, the Commission study specifically examined the success of compensatory programs that attempted to remedy achievement differences between poor children and more affluent ones. The Commission report offered guarded but gloomy conclusions about the impact of compensatory education:

> The Commission's analysis does not suggest that compensatory education is incapable of remedying the effects of poverty on the academic achievement of individual children. There is little question that school programs involving expenditures for cultural enrichment, better teaching, and other needed educational services can be helpful to disadvantaged children. The fact remains, however, that none of the programs appear to have raised significantly the achievement of participating pupils, as a group, within the period evaluated by the Commission.[7]

These two reports created doubts about beliefs that had been part of the American credo since the days of Thomas Jefferson. The Coleman results, together with the Commission findings, challenged the very underpinnings of ESEA Title I.[8] As Rivlin and Wholey note, the results of the Coleman analysis (as well as the Commission report) could suggest two policy alternatives: "1. Give up on schools. 2. Use schools to overcome socioeconomic-status deficits."[9] Title I represented explicit legislative confidence in the second alternative. The idea of improving the life chances of poor children through education is valued by most Americans:

> No one knew whether investment in education was the most effective way of alleviating poverty, but it seemed like a possible way. Alleviating poverty by education is a more attractive idea to most Americans than simply handing out money to the poor under welfare programs.[10]

ASPE's response to the challenge of the Coleman report was optimistic. Much of the euphoria that had accompanied the passage of ESEA still remained in Washington, and the reports submitted by LEAs were highly positive. But above all, ASPE analysts hoped that the science of systems analysis could provide information to justify federal expenditure on education as well as a management strategy to improve local practice and federal decisionmaking.[11] Economists, after all, are trained to deal with maximization and optimization, the two analytical techniques that are central components of "efficiency." These tools had served effectively in other areas —defense and transportation, for example—so why not in education? Alice Rivlin recalls ASPE's rationale:

> . . . analysis of this natural experiment [Title I] appeared likely to uncover something about what worked and what did not. Couldn't we measure success in some way—changes in test scores, drop out rates, attitudes, and so forth—and see whether success thus measured was associated in some regular way with level of resources per child, age of child, or type of program?[12]

Certainly, to ask how much of a given resource leads to what increment in a specified outcome was a rational way to approach an activity in which failure was frequent and in which there was no consensus about how to do better. In addition, it was a question that had not been systematically asked by the federal government of education programs. In fact, the professional tools and vocabulary of ASPE economists startled many educators. Alice Rivlin relates:

> The first step [in deciding upon a way to measure success] was to gather together some distinguished educators and systems analysts to talk over the problem. The first meeting established only that they do not speak the same language. The educators were frightened by words like "input" and "output" and "production functions," and the systems analyst did not understand their fear. But the effort persisted and funds were finally provided for several studies of the relationship between inputs and outputs in compensatory education projects. One of these [was] . . . TEMPO.[13]

The managerial model promoted and refined by Robert McNamara at DOD and brought to DHEW by William Gorham was drawn from the world of microeconomic theory. ASPE analysts attempted to apply similar theoretical perspectives to human service areas.[14] Implicit in the TEMPO design were several assumptions that form an economist's view of how the world works. The basic presupposition is that individuals and organizations behave so as to maximize some identifiable outcome or set of outcomes. An analyst, then, should be able to model organizational choices and deduce desired objectives and the relative effectiveness of different strategies for attaining them. This analytical framework presumes the existence of a stable production function, a regular and quantifiable relationship between the inputs to an activity and the outputs.

Translating these precepts into educational evaluation and the process of schooling, it was expected that (1) increasing academic achievement was a dominant objective for schools and so for Title I programs; (2) an increment in an educational input (in this instance dollars) should, if the Title I program were successful, result in a positive change in the outcome of schooling (that is, academic achievement); (3) alternative educational policy choices have quantitatively different and identifiable benefits; (4) ASPE's scientific procedures could assist in making educational policy choices more efficient and effective by objectively displaying program data in terms of costs and benefits.

Within this theoretical framework, the TEMPO analysis plan outlined three general questions: (1) What is the impact of Title I or compensatory education upon pupil achievement? (2) What school, pupil, and background variables are regularly associated with gains in academic achievement? (3) What are the distinguishing features of successful compensatory strategies?[15]

The TEMPO design expresses ASPE's persistence in the face of fears expressed by educators, their confidence in their assumptions and analytical tools, and their hope that they could learn something in a systematic way from the natural variation that exists in Title I. The study sample was deliberately unrepresentative in that the school districts selected for inclusion in the study were those thought to contain "successful" Title I projects. TEMPO analysts solicited school district nominations from USOE and SEA Title I staffs, from OPPE evaluators, and from members of the National Advisory Council, who had made site visits to Title I projects throughout the country. TEMPO authors explain:

> The effects of compensatory education programs on pupil performance were assessed by comparing results on achievement tests and attendance rates prior to and after exposure to compensatory programs. Data for this study were obtained from 11 school districts chosen for analysis because there was reason to believe that successful compensatory programs were in operation in at least some of the schools.[16]

After a preliminary analysis of the data collected from the 11 school districts suggested that there could be a problem in specifying the components of "success," and even in identifying a Title I impact, the original study design was expanded to include case studies that examined the experiences of 5 selected school districts in much greater depth and detail.[17] The case study analysis was little more successful than the preliminary analysis at retrieving the information ASPE analysts wanted.

## THE DISAPPOINTMENT OF TEMPO

The TEMPO effort culminated in a two-volume report: "Survey and Analysis of Results from Title I Funding for Compensatory Education," and the companion case studies, "Analysis of Compensatory Education in Five School Districts." Joseph Wholey wrote the following summary of the TEMPO findings:

1. There appears to have been a very slight decline in average pupil achievement in the Title I schools studied. One school district showed a significant improvement and two districts showed significant declines between 1965-66 and 1966-67. Observed changes in other districts were not significantly different from zero.

2. On the other hand, there appears to have been a slight *improvement* in achievement of the lowest 10% of the pupils in the schools studied.

3. Schools with 40-60% Negro pupils showed the poorest response to compensatory education programs.

4. There was a slight negative correlation between changes in achievement (between 1965-66 and 1966-67) and grade.

In examinations of school programs in two school districts extremely wide variations were found in expenditures for regular school programs and in expenditures for compensatory education programs. In the first district, a positive correlation was observed between changes in achievement scores and level of per pupil education expenditures.[18]

These TEMPO findings were received at ASPE with great disappointment and "something approaching disbelief."[19] Both Alice Rivlin and Bayla White commented: "We didn't know what we didn't know."[20] Even within a universe of supposedly "successful" programs, TEMPO analysts were able to identify neither a Title I population, nor a Title I program, nor significant achievement gains that could be attributed to Title I funds. The incomplete, confusing, or nonexistent records at the local level made it difficult for TEMPO analysts to determine which services were being purchased with Title I dollars, or to specify the group receiving special attention through Title I. In practice there seemed to be no real Title I program to evaluate.

ASPE and TEMPO analysts were unprepared for these findings and for the fragility of the data base. Only 11 of the 14 sampled districts had sufficient data to be included in the first aggregate analysis; only 5 of the 11 districts had adequate data to permit a case study. Even these case study reports are prefaced and qualified throughout, cautioning the reader that conclusions are at best tentative and based on incomplete and possibly erroneous data.

The report explains: "fragments of information on the regular school programs and compensatory activities had to be assembled from many sources." Data on programs, school/pupil characteristics, attendance records, financial records, and evaluation reports were all inadequate.[21]

From ASPE's point of view, TEMPO was a complete washout—not because it demonstrated that Title I programs failed to produce significant gains in the achievement of poor children, but because TEMPO analysts were unable to gather data on the dependent and independent variables specified by the study design. Bayla White has commented that "at best, all you could conclude from TEMPO was that Title I was a non-program."[22] And Alice Rivlin has said:

> The results of this effort were not spectacular. . . . In fact, the TEMPO study did not show anything at all, one way or another, about Title I. It showed only how hard it is to find out anything about input-output relations in education, especially from a quick, low budget project using existing data.[23]

Although other readers of the study might have concluded that Coleman was right, ASPE's interpretation of TEMPO was consistent with its assumptions. The TEMPO study had been undertaken with the expectation that PPBS could be fruitfully applied to schooling in general and to Title I specifically, and "that some techniques or forms of organization or combinations of resources now in use are probably more effective than others—if only we could find out what they are."[24] ASPE assumed that an increase in the resources spent for education programs through Title I would lead to an observable increase in outcome—that different amounts of money spent in different ways would be significantly and differentially successful in effecting academic achievement. As Alice Rivlin said: "We thought we could classify programs by types and make gross conclusions and classifications about effective strategies."[25]

The failure of TEMPO to furnish these data was interpreted primarily as a particular methodological failure. The primary conclusions ASPE analysts drew from the TEMPO study had little to do with the TEMPO paradigm, with school effects, with educational process, or with Title I as a social strategy, but rather with issues of methodology and data. For example, one of the major "lessons" ASPE drew from the TEMPO study was about the reliability of LEA data. Bayla White has said: "One of the most important things we learned from TEMPO was that we couldn't rely on the pyramid reports."[26]

ASPE's interpretation of TEMPO and scant reappraisal of the theoretical premises underlying the study are especially noteworthy in that the model selected for the TEMPO study was without precedent as a federal education study and was only one of a number of possible evaluation strategies. In fact, by specifying TEMPO as a "pilot study," ASPE analysts themselves made no claims that the TEMPO design was the best way to evaluate Title I.[27] For example, ASPE could have looked at the efficiency of the delivery of Title I services, or examined the effects of Title I on the redistribution of educational services between socioeconomic groups. Certainly, such study designs are more typical of evaluations conducted in other areas of DHEW.[28]

In some respects, the TEMPO design can be seen as a reflection of the assumptions held by some backers of Title I—especially in Congress. Title I was sold as a way to "compensate" for the effects of poverty on educational achievement and lifetime opportunities. Even though the Title I legislation never specified academic achievement as an objective for the program (and, in fact, assiduously avoided such specification), many believed that effective "compensation" would result in enhanced performance on standardized achievement tests. TEMPO, then, sought to evaluate these assumptions. But TEMPO was primarily a response to factors that were not purely methodological. The TEMPO design was prompted by the 1966 coincidence of (1) the challenges and questions raised by the Coleman report and the preliminary work of the Civil Rights Commission and (2) the pervasiveness of "McNamarism." Had either of these factors been absent in 1966, it is possible that TEMPO might never have been carried out.

The Coleman report and the Commission analysis framed their discouraging conclusions about the effects of schooling in terms of achievement scores. These reports established thereby a frame or a standard for evaluating the effectiveness of educational intervention efforts such as Title I. Although TEMPO represented an unprecedented approach to evaluation of federal social programs, if TEMPO was to furnish evidence that would amend the implications of Coleman, a similar reference point was needed. (A distributional analysis of Title I, for example, could not answer the questions raised by the Coleman and the Commission reports.)

Further, "McNamarism" was almost a religion within certain circles of the federal government in 1966, and administrative posts at DHEW and ASPE had been staffed with disciples. PPBS was riding high as a nostrum of universal utility and application; throughout the federal agencies, economists were taking what has been characterized as a "blunderbuss" approach to public policymaking.[29] The analytical tools of PPBS were applied uncritically and confidently to Title I. Questions about the compatibility of the Title I program—the process of education—to the substance of the TEMPO design were not explored.

Given the almost missionary zeal with which Gorham's ASPE staff worked to implement PPBS, and the practical constraints under which ASPE analysts worked, it is understandable that these basic questions were not explored at the outset. ASPE had a job to do. Within the context of budget cycles and Congressional calendars, there was scarcely time to undertake the searching analysis that ideally should precede development of an evaluation model. The scope of ASPE's "search" was confined by pressure of time to established routines, time-honored variables, and standard operating procedures.

But had any of the substantive assumptions underlying TEMPO been explored, there was much evidence available that might have eroded ASPE's confidence in this particular analytical model. For example, ASPE viewed Title I as a "vast experiment ... primarily as an invitation to random innovation."[30] The literature on research in teaching suggests that identification of an unusually effective strategy within such a setting, and by means of the particular TEMPO paradigm, would have been an astonishing accomplishment, and altogether incongruent with past experience.

The Gage *Handbook on Research in Teaching,* for instance, presents considerable evidence indicating that efforts designed to enhance student achievement seldom produce startling or impressive results. Further, Stephens' book, *The Process of Schooling,* takes a historical view of innovation and experimentation and demonstrates that academic achievement has seldom been found to be affected by introduction of new strategies. Stephens documents the lack of variation to be found in the effects of schooling:

> The constancy of the schools' accomplishment is one of those things that everybody knows. It is part of the folklore that, in educational investigations, one method turns out to be as good as another and that promising innovations produce about as much growth as the procedures they supplant, but no more.[31]

In addition, the immutability of the outcomes of educational strategies is not exactly news:

> Nachman and Opochinsky (1958) ... feel safe in stating, as a matter of common knowledge, that "Reveiws of teaching research have consistently concluded that different teaching procedures produce little or no difference in the amount of knowledge gained by the students." In truth this has been a refrain ever since Rice (1897) discovered the surprising constancy of spelling attainment in the face of marked variations in the time devoted to study and since Merriam (1915) reported regular growth in school subjects in the absence of formal instruction in those subjects.[32]

The evidence marshaled by Gage and Stephens implies that assumptions about the impact of "more" or "different" resources on academic growth are at the very least moot, or are hard to detect by input-output relations such as those specified by TEMPO. This literature speaks to the difficult task of determining the relevant inputs to educational effectiveness and, further, evidences scant agreement even on what the most important variables might be.

## WHY DID TEMPO FAIL?

There are numerous reasons why TEMPO failed to meet ASPE's expectations. The most obvious is that the data ASPE hoped to analyze—information on Title I programs, student participation, and program accomplishments—simply did not exist. Despite Title I application and evaluation requirements, most LEAs had not in fact collected the necessary information.

But another view of the failure of TEMPO relates to the conceptual model of the study and suggests that TEMPO would have failed to meet its goals even if the desired information had been available. The TEMPO study posed questions that the

Title I program, by its nature, was unable to answer. Within Title I there are no controls, little agreement on objectives, and little comparability of treatment, target groups, or outcome measures. Alice Rivlin has said:

> The main problem [with TEMPO] was not the study; it was the design of the Title I program. Even from a better study with uniform testing of the same children in different years, and more adequate descriptions of compensatory programs and of the resources devoted to them, we still might not have learned much because the program simply was not designed to yield information on effectiveness. There was no experimental design. There were no control groups. There was no attempt to define promising methodologies or approaches and try them out on enough places to test their operation under different conditions.[33]

In one sense, this is a non sequitur; the main problem of TEMPO was its design. This is not to argue that questions about the input-output model and the program's overall value were not important for federal planners to ask. The questions posed by TEMPO embodied legitimate expectations for a social report. The problem of TEMPO was the slippage between the particular definition given this input-output model and the reality of the Title I program. TEMPO applied demonstration or experimental methodology to a large-scale service program.

A central requirement of an impact, cost-benefit study—the ability to tie inputs to outputs—does not coincide with the operational reality of Title I. An attempt to trace the flow of Title I dollars to specific programs and outcomes is beset with problems. In what Michael Kirst calls the "Byzantine world of school accounting," it is difficult if not impossible to trace the course of Title I dollars through the school system.[34] Some cities, especially larger cities, have over 100 sources of income. As the number of revenue sources increases, the ability of evaluators to identify the impact of any single source diminishes.

Complicating these "Byzantine accounting practices" is the fact that most Title I project directors view Title I resources as "soft" money and subject to withdrawal on short notice. A significant number of local school people hesitate to commit Title I funds to primary instructional efforts (which of course are the very activities assessed by an impact study). Local personnel more typically invest Title I funds in ancillary or supplementary services (such as movie projectors, cultural enrichment, additional health and guidance personnel) that enhance but do not define the central instructional efforts.

Further, application of this evaluation design to Title I ignores the experience of other social programs, particularly in health care, which suggests that social programs have either high impact or high coverage, but not both.[35] This experience implies that measurable benefits from large-scale social action programs such as Title I can be expected to be marginal. Both the nature of the target population and of the program militates against finding "significant Title I impact." Emerson Elliott, former Office of Management and Budget (OMB) examiner for human resources, has said: "We're putting very little money into a very large pot. Therefore it is naive to think Title I is having any large impact on schools."[36]

An impact evaluation such as TEMPO also assumes some degree of agreement on treatment. means and ends. That is, an analysis of impact on achievement assumes increased achievement to be a program goal and that the treatment activities could conceivably have some effect on academic achievement.[37] Title I, however, evidences no such agreement among local programs on either means or ends. Thus, evaluations that measure the impact of programs on achievement describe the goals

and objectives of Title I with seductive simplicity. Title I has been variously interpreted and implemented by different groups. It is little more meaningful to assume
that better academic achievement is the single most important goal of Title I than
it is to insist that its most important objective could be measured by counting the
number of hot lunches served, the number of eyeglass prescriptions filled, or the
number of private school children served. As the legislative history of ESEA demonstrates, enhancing academic achievement is but one of many objectives announced
for Title I. To conclude on the basis of standardized test scores that Title I is not (or
is) "working" is not justified.

⤪ Thus the failure of TEMPO can be traced both to the unavailability of data and
to the conceptualization of the study itself. And, from ASPE's point of view, the
result was no useful information at all.

## THE IMPACT OF TEMPO

But TEMPO did not lead ASPE to ask questions about the nature and character
of Title I, or to reassess its assumptions about the process of schooling. Instead, the
outcome of TEMPO prompted ASPE to support new ways to ask the same questions.
For one, ASPE supported an OEO funded experimental program: Follow Through/
Planned Variation.[38] ASPE viewed the Follow Through/Planned Variation experiment as an opportunity to assess systematically the effects of planned educational
strategies for different target groups over a period of time. It was hoped that the
Follow Through/Planned Variation idea could remedy the methodological deficiencies of TEMPO and result in the specification of models of compensatory programs.
These models, then, could be used to make the educational system work better.

ASPE also responded to the disappointment of TEMPO by supporting another
federal effort to find out what was happening within the Title I program and to
measure the effect of its funds. In conjunction with USOE, the "lessons" of TEMPO
were incorporated as the basis for a national survey of Title I programs and the
impact of compensatory education. It was reasoned that better instruments and the
direct involvement of federal personnel in the data collection could succeed where
TEMPO had failed.[39]

But elsewhere in the Title I policy system, TEMPO was not dismissed as inconclusive. Despite the disclaimers of both ASPE and TEMPO staff that the TEMPO
results did not warrant conclusions about the effectiveness of Title I, the study had
a profound and wide-ranging impact on the climate of opinion surrounding Title I
and education.[40] TEMPO also played a part in the formation of educational policy,
but not in the way ASPE had expected. TEMPO did not contribute to the formulation of short-run management strategies, or to longer-range planning. Instead it was
used in a post hoc fashion to defend policy positions reached quite independently of
the study itself.

Organizational theorists argue that information typically is used in this
"bureaucratic" or "nonrational" fashion. Martin Rein, for example, suggests that
the use of evaluation or information is not determined simply by the character of
the evaluation itself or by its prima facie implications.[41] That is, evaluation does not
arrive in an organizational unit as a full-blown policy directive. The use of information is determined primarily by its perceived consequence for a policy unit: "Much
research and experience support the view that individuals select information to
support their basic commitments, and that where they cannot select, they distort

or deny."[42] The TEMPO study was used in this way—to support preconceived notions about the direction of federal policy as well as to advocate the basic commitments of policy units or individuals within the Title I system.

USOE, of course, was distressed by the TEMPO findings. It also perceived in TEMPO, however, an opportunity to issue a program guideline which its officials had urged from the outset of the program but which had met stiff resistance in Congress: concentration of funds.[43] The tone of the relationship between USOE and Congress in the area of guidelines and relations with LEAs and SEAs had been set by the Congressional response to the Keppel/Daley dispute. Commissioner Keppel, early in the history of Title I, requested that Chicago return Title I funds that USOE judged had been misused. Mayor Daley responded to Keppel's request with angry phone calls to the White House and to members of Congress. Worried Congressmen requested that Keppel withdraw his request in the interest of peace, harmony, and local control. USOE retreated. The TEMPO finding of a positive correlation (in one district) between per pupil expenditures and academic achievement gave USOE an opportunity to issue a concentration guideline based on "fact" not "opinion" about best practice. Thus, Congress could not charge undue federal control of local programs; sanctified by "science," USOE's move became unassailable.[44]

Although USOE selectively used the TEMPO findings to push a concentration guideline, other USOE public documents sought to de-emphasize the existence of TEMPO and soften its findings. The only public acknowledgment TEMPO received from USOE was a fleeting reference in its second annual report, *Title I/Year II*. The TEMPO findings presented by the USOE report were drawn from the Wholey summary but were sanitized and understated.[45] For example, Wholey wrote: "There appears to have been a very slight decline in average pupil achievement." But *Title I/Year II* reports: "The data did not indicate any change in average pupil achievement [and] the measures were not sufficiently reliable to suggest general findings." Again, Wholey noted: "There was a slight negative correlation between changes in achievement and grade." But, according to the USOE report: "There was little correlation between changes in achievement and grade level." Further interpretations offered in the report have little meaning. For example: "The study measured the effects of compensatory education by comparing achievement test data in a specific grade and school for one year with those for children in the same grade and school the following year. Hence a finding of no change from one year to the next may or may not have represented an improvement over previous years."

Bureaucratic organizations tend to distort or deny information they cannot select. The omission of TEMPO, a widely publicized report, from an annual report on the evaluation of Title I would have been indefensible. Thus USOE chose the next best alternative—to bury an innocuous reference to the TEMPO study in the appendix of its report to Congress.

The major consumers of the TEMPO study were in the executive branch—OMB and the Office of the President. The TEMPO study figured centrally in the advocacy politics that accompany the transmission and approval of the President's budget.[46] Despite President Johnson's assurances that Title I's $1 billion allocation for the education of the disadvantaged was "just the beginning," the political and economic climate of the years following the passage of ESEA forced the President to shift his priorities from butter to guns. The fiscal years 1967-1968 and 1968-1969 saw a marked escalation in the war in Southeast Asia, and a concomitant realignment of executive budget policy and priorities. The eclipse of education and the Great Society as a chief Presidential concern was commonly acknowledged in Washington. For example, a *New York Times* article reporting Secretary Gardner's departure from DHEW said:

> Some sources have said that Mr. Gardner quit his job after two and one-half years of effective leadership because President Johnson shifted his highest priorities from the Great Society and the healing of its ills to the war in Vietnam.[47]

And Alice Rivlin has commented:

> In the later Johnson years, decisions about Title I were made at the White House. DHEW still asked for major increases, but our requests were not congruent with Presidential priorities.[48]

The USOE administrators, too, were aware of the budget constraints imposed upon education by a growing commitment of national resources to defense. So certain, in fact, was the USOE budget staff that famine would follow the feast of 1965 that the budget plans were drawn with an eye to this fiscal "fact."[49]

Emerson Elliott, former OMB examiner for human resources, has identified three possible "uses" to which budget officials could put impact information such as that furnished by TEMPO:

> If it indicates that the program is in real trouble—
>
> 1. one outcome could be to reduce funds or to terminate the program.
>
> 2. or hold the program level and try to remedy the problems pointed up by impact.
>
> 3. or put more money into it and try to alter it.
>
> Which strategy is chosen depends upon the current administration stance. If it is a program proposed by the current administration, it becomes a "pet" and is protected and bolstered.[50]

Elliott's comments, however, imply an ideal fiscal and political flexibility that did not appear to exist as TEMPO was released. The executive decision to "hold" on Title I funding did not represent serious consideration and rejection of these three policy options. The Title I funding decision was the only viable alternative given other policy system considerations. The program funds could not be substantially reduced; it was an LBJ program and an executive "pet."[51] To cut the program would have been interpreted as an admission of political failure for Johnson. Nor could the program be increased by any amount that could have resulted in an increase in the level of spending for Title I projects at the local level. As Elliott said: "The increases which would have been necessary to significantly change the level of spending at the local level just could not have been made in a tight budget year."[52] Politically and economically, then, the suggested course for Title I funding, quite apart from the evidence, was to hold the line.[53]

Although the decision to hold Title I funding was seen by most USOE and OMB staff members as "inevitable,"[54] there were influential members of Congress who could be expected to be unhappy about this executive policy. Title I had become an extremely popular program in Congress. Furthermore, members of the Senate Sub-committee on Education had indicated that they were anxious to see an increase in funds for Title I, even if the Vietnam war necessitated cutbacks in other areas.

These views concerning Title I funding were expressed in the Senate hearings on the USOE budget requests in the previous year. OMB's reduction of the USOE Title I request from $1.3 billion to $1.07 billion drew sharp criticism. In these hearings, members of the Senate Subcommittee on Education pushed hard to find out exactly how USOE administrators felt about the budget cuts. The Subcommittee members appeared to be searching for evidence they could use to argue that executive decisions were crippling a program vital to national interest.

USOE officials, as they appear before this Subcommittee, are placed in a curious position: agency officials must change hats, and become witness for the Administration. As such, they are often obliged to support executive decisions that may conflict with their own opinions of agency or program best interest. Both witnesses and examiners alike are aware of the political constraints that shape these hearings. These "rules of the game" often generate a strained dialogue.

For example, Senator Clark engaged in protracted conversation with Commissioner Howe, trying to determine what the 1966 budget figures really meant: "What bothers me is whether this is a public relations figure or is this some really basic information into which the Committee can get its teeth."[55] Clark hoped that the Committee could consider USOE estimates of funds *necessary* for education. As Howe continued to dodge the question, Clark put his request more bluntly: "Well that is all very interesting, but I don't think it really answers my question. How much did you ask for and how much did you get out of the Budget Bureau?"[56]

The members of the Subcommittee did not see their interests reflected in the fiscal priorities articulated by OMB. Subcommittee members, especially Senator Robert Kennedy, felt that the executive solution to the spending dilemma was wrong. Kennedy argued that the government should not try to balance its budget by reducing its commitment to education. Consequently, he put the Commissioner through the hoop Clark had raised regarding the correlation between USOE's budget need and the OMB administration budget. Kennedy's questions posed a politically delicate quandary for Howe:

> Senator Kennedy attempted to test the sincerity of Howe's testimony by asking him how he could support the lower request figure when, just a few months before, his office had submitted a request substantially larger. This line of questioning was an attempt to place Howe on the horns of dilemma. Either the commissioner would have to admit that his original request was inflated, or he would have to challenge the President.[57]

Howe responded to Kennedy's questions in the vague manner he had answered Clark. Kennedy finally stopped Howe and said: "Let me just ask you a question: Are you, in fact, saying that the Bureau was right and you were wrong in this request?"[58] Commissioner Howe's response was perhaps the only one available to him. Howe replied: "I am saying that I really don't know."[59] In response, Kennedy pushed Howe even harder:

> But I can't believe, with the experience that all of you have had, the commitment you have had to education, the studies that you have made that you didn't feel when you made that application that this money was needed.
>
> It is difficult for me to reach the conclusion that you did not know what you were talking about.[60]

Howe weakly suggested that Title I funds would be used more "efficiently" in the future than in the past, "so that there is at least the possibility that these funds will do the job." "I'm sure there is a possibility," snapped Kennedy, "there is a possibility of anything." Kennedy set forth his priorities for education in unequivocal terms:

If we are going to cut down on our spending because of the struggle that is taking place in Vietnam, in my judgment we are making a very, very, very bad mistake in doing that in the field of education. I don't think there is any area where the money is needed more.... If we are going to deal with ghettoes, if we are going to deal with the crime rate, and if we are going to deal with all these basic kinds of problems affecting our society over the next decade we have to do what is necessary in education.[61]

In light of such opposition to curtailed executive support for Title I, then, the TEMPO study served much the same "legitimizing function" for OMB as it had for Commissioner Howe and USOE. OMB was able to use TEMPO to defend its actions on the grounds of "rationality" and as congruent with the precepts of efficient program management. Members of Congress cherish and cultivate an image of thrift and wisdom; the waging of active battle in support of Title I would not have made political sense in view of the TEMPO findings. A former OMB staff member remarked, "there were some of us who would have liked to increase Title I; we just couldn't find the evidence to balance off the implication of TEMPO."[62]

The way in which OMB used the TEMPO study illustrates the role evaluation often plays in fiscal decisionmaking. Many participants in the Title I policy system believe that the OMB staff usually does not rely on evaluative evidence in formulating the budget. Michael Timpane, former Director of Educational Planning, ASPE, said: "OMB does not have a clear role in education evaluation at this time. They are very rah-rah about it, but they really don't care about it."[63] Genevieve Dane, who is responsible for preparing DCE budget justification and estimates, said:

> There are overriding considerations in making budget decisions (beyond a program's effectiveness). The President's budget places number one priority on defense. A program is never funded in a vacuum. It is all appropriations politics, it isn't based on evidence.[64]

In contrast to the assumptions concerning the role of information that underlay Gorham's and ASPE's notion of reform, and that prompted TEMPO, the adversary process of appropriation politics appears to use new information in just the manner that analysts hoped PPBS could modify—if only at the margins. TEMPO was not used to fight "creeping incrementalism"; ironically, the study was used to sanction and support it. The use of TEMPO was primarily an after-the-fact application of "evidence" as warrant for decisions generated by broader policy system considerations and commitments. Evaluation or information is just one input into the complex process of policymaking. It would appear, in the instance of Title I, that the policy alternatives open to decisionmakers precluded the "rational" utilization of information ASPE hoped to promote.

The input of TEMPO to the budget progress may have been more symbolic than real, but TEMPO did have a substantial impact in the area of opinion. Critics of federal investment in compensatory efforts quickly seized upon the TEMPO study as "proof" that schools could not "work" to overcome the effects of childhood poverty. And TEMPO sowed seeds of doubt among those not quite so willing to give up entirely on education as a social strategy. With TEMPO, the high hopes surrounding the passage of ESEA were dissipated. Further, the repercussions of this "modest pilot study" were felt beyond Capitol Hill and the federal agencies; TEMPO contributed to a wholesale erosion in public faith in education across the country. Alice Rivlin observed: "TEMPO added to the layman's impression that compensatory education doesn't work and led some to believe that 'there is nothing we can do through education that will help poor children.'"[65]

Social strategists such as Daniel Patrick Moynihan viewed TEMPO as confirmation of the Coleman findings and as closing evidence in the debate on the wisdom of federal investment in education as an antipoverty strategy.[66] TEMPO added fuel to a climate of opinion in which the burden of proof was shifting from "radical" social planners such as Moynihan, who were proposing alternative federal intervention policies such as the Family Assistance Plan (FAP), to educators. Upon assuming the position of Commissioner of Education, James Allen warned the CSSO that federal investment in education no longer enjoyed unchallenged support:

> One of the attitudes I have encountered with increasing frequency from many quarters since coming to Washington is a growing sense of reservation over whether current funds are being effectively used and, or even greater concern, whether more money for our public school system as presently constituted is the best educational investment for the 1970's. Clearly indicated is the fact that future support for education rests on our ability to make a hard, tight case to back up our requests.[67]

In sum, both the outcome and the impact of TEMPO were unanticipated by ASPE analysts. ASPE's "modest pilot study" not only failed to uncover information that could help reform local educational practice and inform federal decisionmakers, but, perversely, it served to undercut support for the social enterprise that ASPE hoped to strengthen through scientific analysis.

# Notes to Chapter 3

1. U.S. Congress, *Public Law* No. 90-247, 90th Cong., 1st sess., 1967, Sec. 404(a).
2. Interview, Bayla F. White, February 7, 1972.
3. Ibid. See also Alice M. Rivlin, *Systematic Thinking for Social Action* (Washington, D.C.: The Brookings Institution, 1971); Michael W. Kirst, "Administrative Problems in the Evaluation of Title I of the Elementary and Secondary Education Act," a paper included in an Urban Institute report on federal practices, December 1969, mimeo.

More or less concurrently with the initiation of the TEMPO study, ASPE also funded two feasibility studies to explore the problems and contributions of a cost-benefit approach to Title I evaluation. Kirst notes: ". . . two contractors (Abt and Technomics) were selected in March 1966. These contractors submitted elaborate models which have never been empirically tested. The National Center for Educational Statistics thought the Abt model was of high quality and deserved a fair test. OE contracted with Abt for a computer program to carry out the model. As of February 1969, this program was 9/10th completed. (OE does not expect to fund an implementation of the Abt model but says the computer program 'may be used in-house.')" (Kirst, op. cit., p. 6.)

The Technomics contract resulted in a report, "A Study of Cost/Effectiveness in Title I Schools," February 1968. The report concluded that cost/effectiveness analysis could be fruitfully applied to education and offered a revised cost/effectiveness model suitable for "immediate implementation" at the local level.

4. Interview, Bayla F. White, February 7, 1972.
5. James S. Coleman et al., *Equality of Educational Opportunity* (Washington, D.C.: U.S. Government Printing Office, 1966).
6. U.S. Commission on Civil Rights, *Racial Isolation in the Public Schools* (Washington, D.C.: U.S. Government Printing Office, 1967).

7. Ibid., p. 138.

8. Secretary John Gardner describes the faith that promoted ESEA Title I: "The Elementary and Secondary Education Act is a great piece of legislation because, perhaps more than any other, it expresses the profound faith of the American people in the equality of opportunity. We know in fact that people may be born into widely different circumstances. But we believe that whatever their starting point, the path ahead must be open for them to achieve the best that is in them. And throughout our history, we have used education as an instrument of equality of opportunity.

"In the enactment of this law, Congress faced the cruel paradox that when schools attended by the poor are inferior to schools attended by the well-to-do, education itself becomes a potential tool for the reinforcement of inequality." (U.S. Congress, Senate, *Hearings on S. 3046*, pp. 299-300.)

9. Alice M. Rivlin and Joseph S. Wholey, "Education of Disadvantaged Children," *Socio-Economic Planning Sciences*, Vol. 2, 1969, pp. 373-380.

10. Ibid.

11. See William Gorham, "Notes of a Practitioner," *The Public Interest*, Summer 1967, pp. 4-8; Rivlin, op. cit.

12. Rivlin, *Systematic Thinking for Social Action*, pp. 80-81.

13. Ibid.

14. At this time, William Gorham had undertaken a number of similar studies focusing on other DHEW activities. These studies resulted in a series of DHEW reports, such as "Maternal and Infant Health Care," which detailed successful strategies. The TEMPO analysis was presumably to be included in this "how to do it" series.

15. E. J. Mosbaek et al., "Analysis of Compensatory Education in Five School Districts: Summary," TEMPO, The General Electric Company, Washington, D.C., n.d., p. 1 and p. 30 (hereafter cited as TEMPO "Summary").

16. TEMPO "Summary," p. 31.

17. Ibid., p. 32.

18. Joseph S. Wholey to James Mauch, Memo, "TEMPO Contract," January 15, 1968.

19. Interview, Bayla F. White, February 7, 1972. Michael W. Kirst expressed a similar view in an interview, July 31, 1972.

20. Interviews: Bayla F. White, February 7, 1972, and Alice M. Rivlin, February 9, 1972.

21. ASPE certainly had not anticipated this absence of data. In fact Commissioner Howe had assured the Senate Subcommittee in 1966 that almost all local Title I projects had gathered the baseline data that were necessary to measure progress.

22. Interview, Bayla F. White, February 7, 1972.

23. Rivlin, *Systematic Thinking for Social Action*, pp. 82-83.

24. Ibid., p. 86.

25. Interview, Alice M. Rivlin, February 9, 1972.

26. Interview, Bayla F. White, February 7, 1972.

27. Michael Timpane, "Hard Lessons in the Assessment of Social Action Programs: The Case of ESEA Title I," n.d., mimeo.

28. Interview, Richard Carlson, February 25, 1972. Most health programs, for example, are not assessed in terms of "impact"—that is, has the death rate gone down—but rather in terms of delivery—how many people are receiving what sorts of new health services as a result of the program.

29. See "Economics and Public Policy," *The Public Interest*, Summer 1968, pp. 67-129.

30.   Rivlin, *Systematic Thinking for Social Action,* p. 88.

31.   J. M. Stephens, *The Process of Schooling* (New York: Holt, Rinehart & Winston, Inc., 1967), p. 10.

32.   Ibid.

33.   Rivlin, *Systematic Thinking for Social Action,* pp. 83-84.

34.   See, for example, Michael W. Kirst, "Delivery System for Federal Aid to Disadvantaged Children: Problems and Prospects," in U.S. Congress, Senate, *Hearings Before the Select Committee on Equal Educational Opportunity of the U.S. Senate,* 92nd Cong., 1st sess., pt. 17 (Washington, D.C.: U.S. Government Printing Office, October 7, 1971); and David O. Porter et al., "The Mobilization of Federal Aid by Local Schools: A Political and Economic Analysis," report submitted to the Syracuse University Research Corporation.

35.   See Peter H. Rossi, "Boobytraps and Pitfalls in the Evaluation of Social Action Programs," in Carol H. Weiss (ed.), *Evaluating Action Programs: Readings in Social Action and Education* (Boston: Allyn & Bacon, Inc., 1972), pp. 224-235.

36.   Interview, Emerson Elliott, February 24, 1972.

37.   See David K. Cohen, "Politics and Research: Evaluation of Social Action Programs in Education," *Review of Educational Research,* Vol. 40, No. 2, April 1970, pp. 213-238.

38.   Timpane, op. cit.

39.   Interview, Bayla F. White, February 7, 1972.

40.   Alice M. Rivlin comments: "When [TEMPO] was completed and its results released, newsmen jumped on the fact that the average test scores between the two years had not increased and the headlines read, 'U.S. Priming of School "Pumps" Fails To Raise Learning Level.' Many of those involved spent days on the phone explaining to Congressmen, their aides, and others that the study did not show that at all; that it was a limited sample; that it was only for one year; that the test scores were not for the same children; that many of the children tested had not had any special services, and so on. But few were interested in the explanations." *(Systematic Thinking for Social Action,* p. 83.)

41.   Martin Rein, *Social Policy: Issues of Choice and Change* (New York: Random House, Inc., 1970).

42.   Ibid., p. 469.

43.   Jerome T. Murphy notes: "One of the critical issues addressed in the original draft guidelines was the concentration of limited resources for a limited number of students. USOE officials believed that if Title I was to have any impact, the money could not be spread thin. The original provision on the draft guidelines (Fall 1965) stated that the number of children served could be no greater than the number of children in the district counted under the poverty formula. This effort to concentrate funds met with strong disapproval from both the Congress and professional interest groups who argued that the standard was not consistent with Congressional intent. In November 1965, the word came down from Commissioner Keppel to 'slenderize' the documents. The concentration provision was removed from the guidelines." ("Title I of ESEA: The Politics of Implementing Federal Education Reform," *Harvard Educational Review,* Vol. 41, No. 1, February 1971, p. 48.)

44.   While Congressmen had to accept the USOE guideline—based as it was on "evidence"—they were not constrained to support it. The concentration guidelines, like other USOE Title I guidelines that conflicted with constituent interests, emerged in a watered-down, emasculated version.

45.   Joseph S. Wholey to James Mauch, Memo, "TEMPO Contract," January 15, 1968.

46. For a full discussion of "appropriation politics," see Richard F. Fenno, Jr., *The Power of the Purse: Appropriations Politics in Congress* (Boston: Little, Brown & Co., Inc., 1966); Aaron Wildavsky, *The Politics of the Budgetary Process* (Boston: Little, Brown & Co., Inc. 1964).

47. *The New York Times,* March 2, 1968.

48. Interview, Alice M. Rivlin, February 9, 1972.

49. The BESE budget that was being prepared concurrently with the release of TEMPO, for example, notes that the analysis of Bureau planning and budget needs "Lays the base and vehicle in FY 1970 for marked increase in federal support when 'peace breaks out.'" (U.S. Office of Education, Bureau of Elementary and Secondary Education, "Bureau Strategy Plan: ESE, FY 70-74," n.d., mimeo., p. 13.)

50. Interview, Emerson Elliott, February 24, 1972.

51. Ibid.

52. Ibid.

53. Robert A. Levine, *Public Planning: Failure and Redirection* (New York: Basic Books, Inc. 1972), offers a similar analysis of the fiscal fate of OEO programs.

54. Many USOE staff members believe that the funding decision for Title I would have been the same even if TEMPO had found a significant impact on student achievement as a result of participation in compensatory programs. The only difference, many felt, is that it would have been necessary to give Title I a "cost of living" increase.

55. U.S. Congress, Senate, *Hearings on S. 3046,* p. 317.

56. Ibid.

57. Eugene Eidenberg and Roy D. Morey, *An Act of Congress* (New York: W. W. Norton & Company, Inc., 1969), p. 189.

58. U.S. Congress, Senate, *Hearings on S. 3046,* pp. 345 ff.

59. Ibid.

60. Ibid.

61. Ibid.

62. Interview, Former OMB Staff Member, February 1972.

63. Interview, Michael Timpane, June 9, 1972.

64. Interview, Genevieve Dane, June 12, 1972.

65. Rivlin, *Systematic Thinking for Social Action,* p. 83.

66. Daniel P. Moynihan, testifying before the House Subcommittee on Education, summed up this interpretation of TEMPO: "We had thought [as legislation such as Title I was passed] we knew all that really needed to be known about education in terms of public support, or at the very least that we knew enough to legislate and appropriate with a high order of confidence.... We knew what we wanted to do in education and we were enormously confident that what we wanted to do could work. That confidence... has eroded.... We have learned that things are far more complicated than we thought. The rather simple input-output relations which naively no doubt, but honestly, we had assumed to obtain in education simply, on examination, did not hold up. They are not there." (U.S. Congress, House, *Hearings on H.R. 33, H.R. 3606, and Other Related Bills,* pp. 7-8.)

67. James E. Allen, Jr., "Strengthening the Office of Education for Service to the States," address before the Annual Meeting of the Council of Chief State School Officers, Phoenix, Arizona, November 17, 1969, p. 5.

## Chapter Four

# A National Survey of Compensatory Education

The TEMPO study revealed serious deficiencies in the information system and in the knowledge base presumed to support decisionmaking throughout the Title I policy system—from the local school district to the OMB. TEMPO indicated that even within a universe of reputedly exemplary programs, no one knew what worked, or who was receiving what. The study pointed to a dearth of knowledge about effective educational strategies, generally, and about local implementation of a federal initiative, specifically. Even though the Title I formula specified a population, and program applications outlined a program, and despite the successes portrayed by local project evaluations, neither the population nor the program, or outcome, could be identified by the TEMPO staff. Over 1 billion federal dollars seemed to be disappearing into the nation's educational system with scarcely a trace.

Where were the effective programs Keppel had suggested would result from additional resources for disadvantaged children? Who were the recipients of the Title I services listed on application forms? How were the pupil participation and expenditure figures reported in the Title I evaluations determined if local school districts had no reliable way to trace the allocation of funds or to identify participants?

This lack of information about the use and impact of Title I funds created problems both for ASPE and for USOE. It frustrated ASPE's attempt to assess the efficiency of Title I as a social strategy and to identify the most effective program choices for its projects. As a result of TEMPO, ASPE viewed SEA and LEA reports as "virtually useless."[1] USOE, consequently, could not justify reliance on the three-tiered reporting scheme as a source of data for fulfilling its expanded reporting responsibilities. Thus, both ASPE and USOE, albeit for somewhat different reasons, interpreted the failure of TEMPO as warrant for creation of a new Title I information system that did not rely on the reporting machinery set up by the Kennedy Amendments.

The outcome of the TEMPO study not only prompted a new data collection plan, but it also suggested its instrumentation and methodology. Dr. James Mauch of the Division of Compensatory Education (DCE), who was responsible for Title I evaluation, responded to the deficit in program information by proposing a survey plan that in many ways was essentially a bigger and better TEMPO. Based on the TEMPO experience, Mauch suggested a new survey instrument to gather national baseline and impact data on the Title I program and other compensatory activities. Instead

of the project model used by LEA evaluators or the school district model employed
by TEMPO, Mauch proposed that the new survey employ a pupil-centered design to
assess the impact of compensatory education on disadvantaged students, as well as
describe the multiple factors that might influence achievement. Mauch's reasoning
was based in large part on the TEMPO recommendation that a pupil-centered model
would maximize the possibility of uncovering an impact of participation in compensatory programs.[2] Further, Dr. Mauch, like ASPE analysts, believed that a short-
term, 6-month study such as TEMPO was inadequate to assess accurately the impact
of Title I funds or to identify successful strategies.[3] The new 1968 survey was
proposed as the first step in a long-range research plan whose eventual payoff would
be in the provision of cumulative evidence about the impact of compensatory education.

The new survey design did not rely on data collected by local projects but
proposed to gather new information. The TEMPO report was laced with caveats
about the reliability of an analysis based on the data collected by LEAs. E. J.
Mosbaek and his colleagues suggested that just as data indicating positive impact
may have been due to sampling error, the positive effect of Title I might have been
missed for lack of data.[4] It was thought that new instruments and new data would
solve many of the problems resulting from the inadequate local data.

## THE 1968 SURVEY OF COMPENSATORY EDUCATION

The 1968 survey began as a collaborative effort by James Mauch at DCE, BESE
evaluators, and Alice Rivlin's ASPE staff. The survey idea met many of ASPE's own
needs, and ASPE readily agreed to support Mauch's proposal. It was frustrating for
ASPE staff to admit to ignorance about the content and outcome of a program under
their purview, especially a program as large as ESEA Title I. And, as a DHEW
planning document indicates, ASPE felt itself completely in the dark concerning
Title I:

> At the present time, we know very little about the kinds of projects being
> ·funded in the Title I program and almost nothing about the results of Title
> I projects in improving the performance of educationally deprived children.[5]

ASPE's motives in supporting a new national survey of compensatory education
were more aggressive than USOE's. Whereas Mauch and Joseph Froomkin at OPPE
(see Chapter 5 for a discussion of Froomkin's response to TEMPO) needed data
primarily for Commissioner Harold Howe's new reporting requirements, ASPE
wanted to use evaluation to make the schools work better and to make federal
decisionmaking more efficient.[6] Dr. Mauch's idea of a Pupil Centered Instrument
(PCI) was appealing to ASPE because it gathered data on the *multiple* educational
influences that might contribute to a child's success or failure in school. The PCI
seemed more promising as a way to identify effective compensatory strategies than
a purely program-focused device:

> ... [while] project evaluation may be an extremely valuable means of exam-
> ining the process of teaching a particular skill, verbal or vocational, project
> evaluations do not ... provide any clear picture of all the programs and
> activities which may affect the performance of an individual pupil, since an
> individual pupil in a Title I eligible school might be a participant in several
> compensatory projects simultaneously. By way of contrast, the pupil-cen-

tered model permits an examination of the relationship between inputs to an individual pupil—in terms of the intensity and extensiveness of his participation in compensatory education programs—and any changes in his own academic performance.[7]

As a result of the lack of knowledge about educational practices revealed by TEMPO, and because TEMPO indicated that Title I projects were so different from other compensatory projects operating at the local level, ASPE was no longer concerned just with the impact of Title I. Alice Rivlin and her staff were curious about the effects of schooling, and of compensatory education in general; the statutory provisions of Title I served to legitimate their active involvement in this politically delicate area:

> ... Title I provides the opening wedge for federal concern over the outcomes of elementary and secondary education. Title I provides the bucks and the requirements to evaluate performance that give OE the opportunity to become involved in this critical area.[8]

Mauch's plan represented an opportunity to institutionalize a data collection effort congruent with ASPE's information needs and to justify, under the banner of the Commissioner's new reporting requirement, more direct and extensive federal involvement in assessing the outcomes of local educational practices. Bayla White predicted that "This first year's effort should be viewed primarily as baseline data. If this kind of evaluation is repeated for several years in the same schools, we will have some very interesting information of the kind TEMPO wanted to get on what changes are occurring over time."[9]

Thus, both the ASPE analysts and the USOE program staff saw the new national survey as a promising way to remedy the failure of Kennedy's reporting scheme, as well as to meet deficits in information relevant to educational policymaking. ASPE anticipated that the 1968 survey would generate useful input-output data; USOE hoped that the evaluation would furnish positive evidence about the impact of pupil participation in compensatory programs.

Since the PCI was congruent with a new information strategy being developed by BESE, BESE took the lead in designing the survey with assistance from ASPE analysts. Both BESE and ASPE expected that better sampling procedures and more sensitive instruments could generate useful data not only about the overall impact of Title I but also about the particular combinations of resources that systematically enhance the academic achievement of disadvantaged children. The substantive assumptions about particular input-output relationships underlying the 1968 survey were similar to TEMPO's. Like TEMPO, the 1968 survey plan tried to identify an impact of educational treatment on student achievement.

Concerns beyond methodology also played a part in the survey design. While the overall logic of inquiry was shaped by the findings and failings of the TEMPO study, the 1968 survey was also influenced by the political climate. As Bayla White comments:

> There were two powerful lobby groups which influenced Title I evaluation policy:
>
> 1. The Chief State School Officers. Some very key people in this group were rabid state's righters. They didn't want a national evaluation.
>
> 2. The Council of Great City Schools. This group was important because Title I was primarily an urban program. Their membership included the 21

largest school systems. Title I made them a lobby group; their power in 1967 was relatively untested.

To design and conduct evaluation, you have to have the cooperation of both groups.[10]

Since the 1968 survey was a new evaluation effort that required the cooperation of state and local education personnel, planning for the survey required renegotiation of federal-state policies on federal evaluation of local educational programs. The issues that played a part in the formulation of the 1965 evaluation guidelines continued to be important, since the CSSO continued to resist any evaluation plan that might lead to comparisons among states, districts, and schools.

George Mayeske, an OPPE evaluator, recalls unequivocal expression of this sentiment at federal-state planning meetings. One of the more powerful Chief State School Officers stated flatly: "I'll never let you into my state to draw comparisons between schools."[11] According to Mayeske, those not preoccupied with the potentially damaging conclusions that could be drawn were opposed to evaluation "because it was really an unknown."[12] The Chiefs knew that a new evaluation initiative would mean an unknown increase in data collection responsibilities for SEAs and LEAs, who already resented the burden imposed by the existing reporting requirements. But they did not know what conclusions would be drawn from the study, or who would use the information, or how.

At the time that the 1968 survey was being designed, plans for the National Assessment of Educational Progress were on the drawing board. ASPE had considerable interest in seeing the successful initiation of this data collection effort and so did not want to raise issues over the 1968 survey that might kill national assessment.[13] Accordingly, an operational agreement concerning the survey was reached with the Chiefs, which constrained USOE (1) to make no state-by-state comparisons; (2) not to aggregate pupil data by school or state; (3) to clear for release all federal reporting forms through the Chiefs.[14]

Joseph Froomkin, Assistant Commissioner for Planning and Evaluation (OPPE), observed the process of consensus building that preceded the survey with distaste: "ASPE, Gorham and Rivlin reflected the educational establishment at the time. They were trying to get along with everyone and their research reflected it."[15] However, the compromises ASPE made were required by the larger policy system, if the survey was to take place at all. (Indeed, as the following chapter will discuss, Froomkin's alternative evaluation plan ignored these political constraints and met with disaster.) These negotiations suggest how far removed the realities of federal policymaking often are from the ideal of the rational paradigm of decisionmaking. In designing the 1968 survey, ASPE sought to construct a survey that could meet its information needs on the one hand, but would keep peace in the larger Title I policy system on the other.

Consequently, the survey design was constrained in a number of respects before planning even began. The position of schoolmen on the issue of evaluation precluded a host of questions about the differential effectiveness of particular sorts of schools or teachers. Furthermore, the failure of LEAs to keep financial data on a school-by-school basis precluded the cost-benefit questions posed by TEMPO. ASPE's notions of reform generated clear-cut information requirements, but paradoxically the implementation of an evaluation to answer these questions was not similarly straightforward. ASPE could not go to the local schools, for example, and ask what services at what cost led to how much gain in achievement. The 1968 survey design, then, was a product of the disappointment of TEMPO, the politics of the Title I policy system, and the logic of PPBS.

Within these constraints, a survey design emerged. The survey's gross categories and classifications differed only incrementally from those of the TEMPO study. The Request for Proposal (RFP) outlined three general objectives:

1. To describe the characteristics of pupils, teachers, school facilities, and compensatory education services in Title I eligible schools.

2. To examine the relationship between economic and educational deprivation of pupils in Title I eligible schools, the extensiveness of compensatory services and resources provided those pupils, and their participation in compensatory education activities.

3. To examine the relationship between pupil participation in compensatory education programs, the quality of their environment, and pupil development as measured by standardized achievement tests and teacher perceptions of changes in the classroom behaviors of pupils.[16]

The 1968 survey employed a multistage sample design consisting of (1) school districts; (2) schools within the sample school districts; (3) all teachers in grades 2, 4, and 6 in the sampled schools; and (4) a sample of students within each teacher's classroom. The universe of school districts consisted of 90 percent of the 13,000 districts in the 50 states and the District of Columbia, which enrolled more than 300 students and received ESEA Title I funds. A sample of 465 of these schools was selected by systematic random sampling for inclusion in the analysis.

Since the 1968 survey was initiated under the authority of the Commissioner's reporting requirement, responsibility for implementation of the new survey rested with the Office of Education. Although USOE had proposed the survey idea as a way to remedy the failure of the three-tiered reporting scheme and gather useful new data on Title I, USOE's approach to implementation of the study did not suggest a new interest in evaluation.

The 1968 survey was launched with the old apologetic USOE posture toward evaluation, and overriding concern for the maintenance of good relations with the states and interest groups. The timidity with which USOE announced the new survey was reminiscent of the cautious drafting and distribution of the original evaluation guidelines in 1965. Communications with the states implied that USOE was simply "carrying out" a new requirement imposed by Congress.[17] Perceptive and knowledgeable Chief State School Officers probably relished the tortured diplomacy with which USOE introduced the new survey. For example, although LEA and SEA reports were widely regarded as worthless,[18] Program Information Letter No. 126 praised the states for their good evaluation efforts in the past:

> This approach [the new 465 survey] has been based on the fine Title I project information provided to us by the states during the past two years. Your information has helped us to revise our measurement instruments in a manner that now allows us to focus on our most important concern—the disadvantaged child. . . . Although this document [the SEA reporting form] provided good information on the impact of Title I in individual states, it was quite general. . . .[19]

The Program Information Letter reassured the states that the final survey report would result only in national estimates, and extended a pro forma invitation to the SEAs to contribute their further thoughts and suggestions to the survey design.[20]

USOE was reluctant to state its preferences or to make a requirement regarding the survey mechanics. It was unwilling to require even the most expedient means of distributing the survey forms: "we would prefer to mail directly to the school. However, we will complete distribution in any way the SEA wishes. Please keep in mind that it will be faster, easier, and less open to loss if you select the third alternative. In any case, you will see the copies first."[21]

ASPE intervened in the spring of 1968 to bolster USOE's timorous efforts. Shortly after the survey forms were mailed, a team of "flying feds" was dispatched to four regional meetings, set up to explain the mechanics of the survey. Since LEA and SEA participation in the survey was voluntary, federal personnel also used these meetings to urge cooperation, to allay any concerns school people might have about the new survey, and to attain visibility for the federal evaluation effort.[22]

The pampering and cajoling of SEA and LEA personnel paid off to some extent. The survey's net response rate was high, much higher than had been expected.[23] For example, 93 percent of the school district survey forms were returned and 87.9 percent of the individual school forms. However, most of the completed forms lacked achievement data. Out of 180,000 questionnaires mailed, only about 8,000 to 10,000 were returned with usable achievement data,[24] and the data that were reported were not representative of the national sample, either in terms of pupil performance or in terms of type of compensatory participation.

Many state personnel contended that the achievement data requested by the survey were not available. However, a USOE in-house study that examined the frequency of standardized achievement testing throughout the country estimated that *at least twice as much achievement data were available than were reported by LEA officials.*[25]

✦Successful implementation of an evaluation effort such as the 1968 survey is contingent upon the cooperation of SEA administrators and local practitioners. The survey presented new incentives to cooperate with a federal evaluation effort: federal interest was clear, the study design was constructed to remove anxiety about comparisons among specific schools, districts, and states, and the value of the survey to its sponsors and nonfederal partners was iterated in numerous communications. ASPE and USOE claimed that the survey would be useful as more than a national policy document—that the states and local agencies would receive helpful information as well. But despite the energy and effort invested in the striking of consensus and alleviating concern, many local schoolmen still hesitated to furnish the achievement data USOE requested, and others did not collect any standardized information at all.

The survey return, therefore, implies that if any reordering of local priorities and incentives concerning evaluation did occur, it was not sufficient to overcome the opposition of many schoolmen to impact evaluation. Schoolmen responded to requests for descriptive information, but the achievement measures that would have permitted specification of a relation between program inputs and outcomes either were not submitted or not collected despite USOE and ASPE guarantee of respondent anonymity and promise of aggregate analysis. But, as anyone who has asked others to complete a questionnaire of a sensitive nature can testify, paper guarantees do little to diminish an unwillingness to record potentially damaging information.

• Theorists suggest that an important factor in organizational behavior is a tendency to avoid uncertainty, to deal with known and predictable consequences. The 1968 survey was a significant unknown. Some SEA and LEA personnel had no background in evaluation or data analysis, and simply did not know what evaluation per se was all about. Others, a bit more sophisticated in the ways of evaluation, understood the perverse applications to which statistics could be put. Few within the larger Title I policy arena were quite sure what to expect from the 1968 survey. There had never been a national evaluation of Title I (nor of any other such program, for that matter), and there was no precedent as to how the findings of the survey would be used. It is not surprising, then, that many schoolmen were not eager to collect or to furnish outcome data that would permit assessment of the effectiveness of compensatory programs.

Nor did explicit federal involvement in evaluation enhance the importance of evaluation or achievement testing in the eyes of state and local schoolmen. And the classroom teacher had even less reason to believe USOE claims that an analysis aggregated at the national level would be valuable. As a comment of one Chief State School Officer suggests, classroom teachers showed little interest in the reliability or validity of the 1968 survey data. "In our districts a number of teachers mixed up the pre and post data. In fact, they often put down anything as long as they could turn in their records and get their $30 for filling out the forms."[26]

The general absence of outcome data made it difficult to interpret the 1968 survey data. Dr. Karl Hereford, head of BESE evaluation, spent fully a year writing and rewriting the survey report.[27] The data were put in one frame and then another, requiring further data analysis and numerous cuts to present the data in a way that would place compensatory education and the Title I program in a positive light. The 1968 survey report went through at least three drafts.[28] It was not released to the Title I policy community until April of 1970, when it was submitted to Congress as "the first annual report prepared and presented in response to the 1967 ESEA amendments that require a national evaluation [of Title I] and a report on the results."[29]

The text of the report is guarded, ambiguous, and more nearly resembles a census than an evaluation report. Most of its content is concerned with the characteristics of Title I districts, schools, and the target population. The preface states:

> ... this is the first report that endeavors to examine the nature and extent of Title I activities overall, and to examine Title I performance as an instrument of national policy.... It provides ... an overview of the massive problems that confront the schools, as well as encouraging evidence that the schools are beginning to grapple with these problems on other than an *ad hoc* basis.[30]

Dr. Hereford's preface indicates more nearly what he hoped the report would be, rather than what it actually was. There was scant evidence on the "nature and extent of Title I activities overall," and "encouraging evidence" was slim to nonexistent. The first 122 pages of the report present an "Overview"; "Title I and District Characteristics"; "Characteristics of Title I Elementary Schools"; "Characteristics and Needs of Disadvantaged Children"; and "School Programs Provided with Title I Funds." Chapter VI, "Benefits from Title I Supported Programs," deals in 5 pages with the "performance" of Title I "as an instrument of national policy."

The report begins with the following "significant findings and conclusions":

1. *It is now possible to define the dimensions of the problem of reaching educationally deprived children in the Nation's public schools.*

> There may be as many as 16.8 million school-age children who must be regarded as "educationally disadvantaged...." These 16.8 million youngsters suffer from economic deprivation and/or educational disabilities which require special treatment or attention in school....

2. *All available evidence seems to support the selection by Congress of the public school district as the main vehicle for reaching disadvantaged youngsters.*

All disadvantaged children live in a public school district somewhere in the Nation. . . .

3. *The problems that public school districts face in providing special programs for the disadvantaged seem far more complex than many of these districts are able to treat effectively.*

Public school districts vary greatly in their ability to mount and maintain appropriate compensatory programs for disadvantaged pupils; indeed, they vary greatly in their ability to support the good general education curriculum upon which special compensatory programs must be built.

Schools vary in their ability to use Title I funds in ways that really match and meet the special needs of their disadvantaged pupils. Public schools with very heavy concentrations of disadvantaged pupils, for example, confront a different and far more difficult problem than schools which enroll relatively smaller proportions of disadvantaged pupils.

4. *Under the legislatively prescribed formula, Title I funds in 1968 did not flow to school districts and their disadvantaged students proportionately to their needs. Place of residence remains a primary determinant of the quality of services available to the Nation's disadvantaged pupils.*

Forty-six percent of low-income children receive their education in low-expenditure school districts. These low-expenditure districts receive fewer Title I funds for each child than do high-expenditure districts and both tend to spread their Title I money among more pupils than they have poor children.[31]

This presentation seems to dress up the meager data in the mantle of "policy significant results" as well as to congratulate Congress on its wisdom in legislating Title I as a vehicle of social reform. The first three conclusions, for example, are neither "significant" nor "suggestive." Evidence that economic deprivation and educational disadvantage go hand in hand, or that all disadvantaged children (like all advantaged children) live in a school district somewhere in the nation, or that the problems of poverty are multiple and complex, or that schools enrolling large numbers of poor children have different and more difficult problems than other schools, was not surprising in 1968 and certainly was not news in mid-1970. The 1965 hearings on Title I had produced volumes of data in support of these same conclusions.

The fourth conclusion is of some import. It suggests that the Title I formula was not working as intended. The 1968 survey found, as did TEMPO, that the addition of Title I funds did not lead to comparability in the services available to poor children and advantaged children. But further, the 1968 survey findings suggest that schools, especially those with "different and more difficult problems," tended to use Title I as general aid, not as categorical aid for poor children. The 1968 survey evidence on misuse of Title I funds was, however, so obscured and underplayed as to be lost to all but the most concerned and persistent reader. The use of Title I as general aid was fairly common knowledge within USOE, and many Congressmen knew about it also. But because of its implications for questions or "federal control," it was also an issue few chose to raise.[32]

The report has little concrete to say about the impact of Title I. Although there are abundant statistical tables, the activities and impact of Title I programs are discussed in two short narrative chapters. Because of the poor return rate on achievement items, there was little Karl Hereford could find to report about the "performance of Title I as an instrument of national policy." The following general conclusions are presented concerning the impact of participation in Title I on reading achievement:

While these data do not constitute a statistically valid sample of . . . districts or pupils, they do offer some indications of the impact of compensatory reading programs upon the pupils—a close analysis of the data reveals the following:

1. Schools did, in fact, select as participants in compensatory reading programs those pupils with low scores on reading achievement tests.

2. For participating and non-participating pupils, the rate of progress in reading skills kept pace with their historical rate of progress.

3. Pupils taking part in compensatory reading programs were not progressing fast enough to allow them to catch up to non-participating pupils.

4. A number of pupils among both participants and non-participants had reading achievement levels below national norms. For both participants and non-participants that "deficit" grew progressively greater in each succeeding grade level sampled (grades 2, 4, and 6).

The survey also found that:

Those pupils who had large gains in reading achievement were, in every sense, less socially disadvantaged than those who did not gain. "High-gain" pupils came from families of higher income, their parents had more education, the occupations of the parents required greater skills, and they were predominately white.[33]

The language and format of the report obscures the implications of the achievement data that were returned. Title I was not found to help remedy the academic problems of poor children; further, gains, where they were found, were positively correlated to socioeconomic status. In plainer language, compensatory education programs were not "closing the gap"; in fact, participation in compensatory programs seemed to be having no effect at all. Student achievement continued to be correlated most closely with family background, and to be unaffected by educational intervention.

## THE 1969 SURVEY OF COMPENSATORY EDUCATION

In this story of disappointment and failure, however, the 1968 survey is only the penultimate chapter. Before the 1968 survey data had been fully analyzed and interpreted, an updated version of the instrument was on its way to the schools. The 1969 survey of compensatory education was launched in the spring of 1969.[34]

The 1969 survey was intended essentially to replicate the 1968 effort. SEAs and LEAs had been told that the 1969 survey would not be radically different. Further, it was hoped that a repeat of the 1968 survey would gather comparable data. Thus, the 1969 survey was sent out with only a few cosmetic changes.

The 1969 survey did not receive much more than haphazard monitoring from the BESE staff once it was underway. A former staff member remarked that "no one even asked Gene Glass what he was doing until he was almost through with the data analysis. At that point, Hereford made some suggestions for a different sort of analysis which Glass refused to carry out."[35]

This lack of direction is ironic in view of USOE's increased explicit concern for "informed decisionmaking." The communications surrounding the 1969 survey point up the purely symbolic function that the *activity* of evaluation had come to play within the Title I policy system, particularly for USOE.

As we have seen, by late 1968, federal objectives had changed markedly as the government shifted its priorities from a War on Poverty to a war in Southeast Asia. Thus, TEMPO raised questions about the efficiency of USOE's Title I management at a time when the executive directive had been issued to get "more bang for the buck," in both domestic and foreign policies. And the pressure on Title I to look good, if only from the management point of view, was further increased as Richard Nixon took office. President Nixon did not share LBJ's priority for education as a social investment, and categorical programs such as Title I were viewed as "Democrats' programs."[36] Consequently, USOE scrambled to satisfy the premises and precepts on which Title I was administered. The USOE communications surrounding implementation of the 1969 survey echoed tenets revered by ASPE and OMB. For example, Richard Jaeger of BESE's evaluation staff informed ASPE that:

> Data [from the 1969 survey] to be analyzed during 1970 will provide federal policy makers and program managers with definitive information on efficiency of implementation of Title I ESEA programs and the effectiveness of that program in meeting the needs of disadvantaged children.[37]

Even the RFP attempted to convey an image of vigorous efficiency:

> ... providing an annual report for Congress was the main purpose which caused the initiation of the 1968 national survey. ... the other and more important goal of the 1969 survey is that of promoting sound management decisionmaking at the state and federal levels, by providing good data on which decisions can be based.[38]

In light of the indifferent attention given the 1969 study, it is difficult to view these declarations as other than shibboleths offered to appease the gods of fiscal and programmatic authority.

Since the 1969 survey was little different from its predecessor, its conclusions were not unexpected. The discouraging results of the 1968 survey had prepared USOE for the equally discouraging outcome of Gene Glass's report, *Data Analysis of the 1968-1969 Survey of Compensatory Education (Title I).*[39] The 1969 survey had no more success than the 1968 effort in obtaining usable achievement data. In fact, the return on achievement data was even poorer than that for the preceding year.[40] In the absence of these output data, the body of the Glass report presents narrative statistics about Title I schools, districts, and so on. And, in the tradition of Coleman, the Civil Rights Commission, TEMPO, and the 1968 survey, Glass—on the basis of the available output data—was unable to identify significant achievement gains that could be attributed to participation in compensatory programs. Glass, too, found family background to be the strongest predictor of student achievement, and concluded that the influence of poverty was not mitigated by educational intervention. Glass offers the following conclusions concerning the impact of Title I programs:

1. Participants in reading programs for the disadvantaged had lower pretest and posttest scores than non-participants. It would appear that compensatory programs were indeed reaching those who needed special help in reading.

2. Negative gain scores for most "participating" groups in all grades seem to indicate that even when a lower "starting point" is considered, participants progressed at a slower rate than non-participants.

3. For non-participating pupils, progress in reading achievement generally kept pace with their academic [record] in years of schooling; i.e., at the end of one year's school experience they had gained one or more grade equivalents in reaching achievement on the average. This was not true for most participants in compensatory reading programs. Perhaps evaluation of the progress of those who have environmental and other types of disadvantagement should not be compared with those who are not characterized by these handicaps, who are not receiving compensatory programs. . . . (Such comparisons were not possible within the survey data.) Rate of learning, motivation, etc., would in this case be largely equitable, and program impact more validly discerned.

4. Increasing the number of hours spent by pupils in remedial reading, at least within the limits represented by on-going programs reported in the 1969 survey, did not reverse the losses suffered by participants.

In general and for whatever reasons, compensatory reading programs did not yield evidence in terms of performance on standardized reading tests that the reading deficiencies of participants had been overcome.[41]

The Glass report was completed at a time when the press, civil rights groups (such as the Washington Research Project), ASPE, and members of the executive branch were all complaining about the administration and impact of the Title I program, and hounding USOE for "action." So while the 1968 survey was written and rewritten, and its publication delayed for more than a year, the Glass report was not released at all. Although compiled and printed, it was not "available" in the summer of 1970 even to qualified researchers under contract to DHEW's Title I Task Force. Gene Glass himself was not, at that time, able to distribute copies of the report.[42] It was still difficult in the spring of 1972 to obtain a copy of the document, and the report now remains buried somewhere in USOE. Thus, the report that was to provide "definitive information on the efficiency of implementation of Title I ESEA and the effectiveness of that program" has never seen the light of administrative day, nor has it (officially) informed a single decisionmaker. Since it failed to serve its main purpose for USOE—to provide positive data for a report to Congress—the report has been, for all practical purposes, suppressed.[43]

## SLIPPAGE BETWEEN EVALUATION DESIGN AND PROGRAM REALITY

While USOE officials can be criticized for repressing the 1969 survey report, their defensiveness is understandable. The national surveys undermined the credibility of education programs and the morale of the Title I staff, but on balance they were not evaluations of Title I. As Richard Fairley, Director of DCE, has argued, compensatory education as assumed by TEMPO and the national surveys has never really existed.[44] The TEMPO evaluation was initiated with specific questions in search of particular answers, and Title I was viewed from the perspective of information needs. The Title I program (and its evaluation requirement) was simply a "wedge" for the technology of systems analysis. As progeny of TEMPO, the national surveys also sought to answer the impact questions prescribed by PPBS, as well as to gather descriptive information about compensatory education practices. But, as the preceding chapter argued, the impact design of the surveys, which seemed appropriate to ASPE's notions of reform, did not square with the fact of the Title I program. Thus the persistent failure of these federal evaluation efforts to accomplish the management and information objectives of ASPE reformers lies in large part in the inconsistency between this particular analytical paradigm and the operational reality of the Title I program.

Robert Hartman, former ASPE economist, argued this position in a series of memos to the ASPE staff:

> Ideally, Title I's benefits would be measured by the degree to which it redressed some of the migratory and equity imbalances in our federal system. In the present state of the art, the best we can do is look at intermediate measures: Title I's fiscal impact in different states and cities. Period. . . . It is illegitimate and misleading to measure Title I by the success or lack thereof of compensatory programs. . . . the greatest study of test scores or attitudes before and after, designed by the greatest statisticians in the world, done 15 years after Title I, *will not be measuring Title I's benefits*. It *will* be answering Brandl's production function questions. But it will not answer questions about the role of the federal government in a federal-state-local system and how that system can break down when public services levels and tax burdens get out of whack.[45] [Emphasis in original]

Hartman's memos arguing against impact evaluation of Title I, and urging ASPE's attention to other questions about the Title I program, resulted only in a flurry of rebuttals from Alice Rivlin and other ASPE staff members. His arguments concerning the illegitimacy of an impact design for Title I were, on balance, correct. His arguments are somewhat off point, however, in assuming that the central purpose of these evaluations, from ASPE's view, was an assessment of the Title I program. Alice Rivlin and others responded in unequivocal defense of this design because in their view the primary importance of the evaluation effort lay in the questions it asked, not in the judgment it suggested about Title I. Hartman was correct in arguing that questions of distribution are more appropriate to an evaluation of Title I. However, these questions are not relevant to ASPE's notions of reform.

Hartman's arguments assume that ASPE's expectations for the function of evaluation are akin to Kennedy's. Kennedy wanted to use evaluation to check up on the local programs, to hold them accountable. Hartman, like Kennedy, saw Title I evaluation undertaken primarily to announce the "success or lack thereof of compensatory programs." But ASPE did not have a "report card" view of evaluation. ASPE saw evaluation both as a management tool, and as a purely scientific tool to satisfy its thirst for knowledge—apart from evaluating Title I. Thus, the tension that existed in this phase of Title I impact evaluation was caused not so much by the failure of a national program, but rather by the incompatibility resulting from the information needs of a federal policy unit, the methodology appropriate to these needs, and the social program to which these tools were applied. These impact evaluation efforts failed to meet the expectations of their sponsors essentially because analysts did not pause to square their theoretical assumptions about behavior and relationships within the policy system with the practical reality of a new social initiative.

## IMPACT ON THE TITLE I POLICY SYSTEM

The consequence of this incompatibility between the analytical model and the Title I program has been reflected in many different ways. One important way has been the impact that the national surveys of compensatory education have had within the Title I policy system. The most pervasive and significant impact of the 1968 survey (like TEMPO) was in the area of opinion. Coming on the heels of TEMPO, the report stoked the fires of "Colemanism" within DHEW, OMB, and Congress, and corroded USOE morale. With the publication of the 1968 survey report, the golden days of Title I, and widespread confidence in education as a social strategy, ended. Secretary Robert Finch's comments in the Senate Subcommittee hearings on the 1969 ESEA amendments, for example, contrast starkly with the optimism expressed previously by Commissioners Keppel and Howe and Secretaries Celebrezze and Gardner:

> Well, before we try our moon shot on education, we have to at least get somebody out there that can defy the laws of gravity. I must say that I am convinced that, given the state of the art right now, I am not sure that we have the capabilities for an educational moon shot in the 70's. We need to be more precise about the state of the art than we are and that is what we are trying to dig into.[46]

The outcome of the 1968 survey led the executive branch and ASPE analysts to turn their attention from Title I, specifically, to the state of the art of education generally. But evaluation retained its status as the principal vehicle of reform. Although Secretary Finch's expectations for educational outcomes were very different from the sentiment expressed in 1965, his views on the role of evaluation were almost identical with those expressed by William Gorham. Finch said:

> Evaluation is a necessary foundation for effective implementation and judicious modification of our existing programs. *At this point, evaluation is probably more important than the addition of new laws to an already extensive list of educational statutes.* . . . Evaluation will provide the information we require to strengthen weak programs, and drop those which simply are not fulfilling the objectives intended by Congress.[47] [Emphasis added]

ASPE's notions of the questions appropriate for education evaluation also persisted. The response of ASPE analysts to the failure of the 1968 survey was to abandon Title I as a way to find out about more successful compensatory strategies. The failure of the national survey was seen as symptomatic of the more general "failure thus far to organize social service systems to facilitate investigation of their effectiveness."[48]

One obvious way to remedy this shortcoming was to acquire more control over program inputs and design, which meant either moving away from service programs to controlled experiments or turning service programs into experiments.[49] Thus, as Title I failed to provide the data ASPE wanted, ASPE analysts turned from the natural experiment setting of Title I to focused, controlled, and systematic experiments. Since a major problem of TEMPO and the national surveys had been the specification of costs and other inputs, an approach was adopted in which the inputs, at least, were established. With ASPE's support, programs such as Right To Read and Experimental Schools were initiated to test "best bets."

The unstable character of the information generated by this mismatch between evaluation design and social program is also reflected in the multiple interpretation and use given the findings. The weakness of the data returned enabled advocates to cite them as "facts" or "best available evidence," and allowed opponents to find methodological flaws, poke conceptual holes, or turn up an equal number of exceptions.

Ironically, the same body of evidence, the TEMPO study and the national surveys, has been used to support *antithetical* executive policies on funding for compensatory education. First, the 1968 survey findings made possible an executive move that was congruent with President Nixon's priorities for federal involvement in the area of education, but was politically controversial. The 1968 survey, in combination with the TEMPO report, lent empirical support to the President's 1970 education message proposing a National Institute of Education (NIE) and announcing the abeyance of funding for categorical compensatory programs.

The 1970 proposal for an NIE was not new. Its precursor had been suggested as long ago as 1958 by the National Academy of Science and the National Research Council. But, as we have seen, the form and extent of federal involvement in education and evaluation became a highly charged and partisan issue in Washington. Many Republicans and a number of Democrats traditionally had opposed federal involvement in the area of education research. "They feared federal control of the schools, establishment of a national curriculum and so on."[50] Further, powerful educational lobby groups, principally the CSSO, had been adamant in opposing federal evaluation initiatives. Past recommendations for an NIE had met with stiff resistance from schoolmen, who justified their opposition in terms of the drain such an organization would impose on the limited funds available for education. TEMPO and the 1968 survey, however, could meet this opposition by providing evidence that more research was needed, because local schools did not seem to be devising effective solutions to their problems. President Nixon cast the evaluation findings in just this frame:

> We must stop letting wishes color our judgments about the educational effectiveness of many special compensatory programs when—despite some dramatic and encouraging exceptions—there is growing evidence that most of them are not yet measurably improving the success of poor children in school.
>
> We must stop pretending that we understand the mystery of the learning process, or that we are significantly applying sciences and technology to the techniques of learning....
>
> When educators, school boards and government officials alike admit that we have a good deal to learn about the way we teach, we will begin to climb up the staircase toward genuine reform.... Therefore, I propose that the Congress create a National Institute of Education as a focus for educational research and experimentation in the United States.
>
> ... The purpose of the National Institute of Education would be to begin the serious, systematic search for new knowledge needed to make educational opportunity truly equal.[51]

Further, the President anticipated objections of "federal control" by suggesting that NIE would *prevent* the increased federal involvement in local practices that might appear to be warranted in light of the evidence:

For years the fear of "national standards" has been one of the bugaboos of education. . . . The problem is that in opposing some mythical threat of "national standards" what we have too often been doing is avoiding account-ability for our own local performance. We have as a nation too long avoided thinking about the *productivity* of schools.

This is a mistake because it undermines the principle of local control of education. Ironic though it is, the avoidance of accountability is the single most serious threat to a continued and even more pluralistic educational system. Unless the local community can obtain dependable measures on just how well its school system is performing for its children, the demand for national standards will become even greater and in the end almost certainly will prevail. When local officials do not respond to a real local need, the search begins for a level of officialdom that will do so, and all too often in the past this search has ended in Washington.[52]

Similarly, the President was able to present the 1968 survey evidence as justifi-cation for executive decisions about Title I funding. Categorical aid to education was contrary to Richard Nixon's views of the most effective ways to treat either the problem of inequality or to allocate resources to education. Genevieve Dane has said: "These programs are all LBJ programs. If you work in them, you're branded a Democrat and in favor of categorical aid."[53] But, as Emerson Elliott has commented, "to be against Title I was to be against the disadvantaged."[54] President Nixon believed in general aid to the schools, not targeted, categorical assistance. The President also subscribed to ASPE's views concerning controlled, scientifically rigor-ous experimentation.[55] A USOE staff member observed, "the current administration didn't want to support any more categorical programs" and wanted to conduct national policy in the area of education in its own style.[56]

Thus the President used the 1968 survey data and other material to justify lack of increase in Title I. President Nixon said:

The most glaring shortcoming in American education today continues to be the lag in essential learning skills in large numbers of children of poor families. . . . *the best available evidence indicates that most of the compensa-tory education programs have not measurably helped poor children catch up.*

Thoughtful men recognize the limitations of such measurements and would not conclude that the programs thus assessed are without value. It may be necessary to wait many years before the full impact of such programs on the lives of poor youngsters can be ascertained. But as we continue to conduct special compensatory education for the disadvantaged, we must recognize that our present knowledge about how to overcome poor back-grounds is so limited *that major expansion of such programs could not be confidently based on their results.* [57] [Emphasis added]

The President was able, using these evaluations as rationale for his priorities, to neutralize opposition from lawmakers such as Representative Perkins and Senator Morse who advocated substantial increase for Title I and from schoolmen who were against the idea of NIE.

Hardly 2 years later, however, the political climate forced the President to alter his position on funding for education. In response to the bitter national controversy over the issue of busing, President Nixon proposed repackaging of $1 billion in funds for education in his March 1972 message to Congress.[58] The President's initiative purported to equalize educational opportunity *within* existing structures and facili-ties and so to obviate the need for busing. This meant that while the President required evidence in 1970 to justify holding the line on spending for compensatory programs, and for establishing an NIE to investigate the causes of the failure of schools to devise successful strategies, the 1972 policy message required just the opposite documentation. Michael Timpane commented: "The broad base decision to move against busing had been made at the White House. The question was how best to present the position as a legislative package."[59] "Facts" were needed to justify spending $1 billion on schools, just as they were needed to support a redirection of these resources. Accordingly, in late winter of 1972, Secretary Richardson was instructed by the White House to prepare a document that would give rationale to the President's new policy initiative in education.[60]

This executive request fell upon ASPE at a difficult time. The report of an AIR study of Title I effectiveness, the only large evaluation of Title I to be undertaken after the 1969 survey, had just been received.[61] The AIR conclusions were discouraging in terms of Title I effectiveness and also highly critical of USOE administration of Title I.[62] The AIR report suggested that the Title I programs conformed no more closely to Congressional intent in 1972 than they did in 1965. The AIR report concluded that compensatory education still wasn't "working," and that USOE was not effectively administering the program. This report hardly furnished the evidence to justify $1 billion for compensatory education. Consequently, Richard Fairley, head of DCE, sat on the AIR report [63] and Constantine Menges, Assistant Director of the Office of Civil Rights (who, ironically, had been the one to push for the AIR study to begin with), was dispatched on a "flying trip to California in search of successful programs."[64]

The resulting DHEW document described its purpose as providing affirmative evidence to the major questions inherent in the President's proposal:

> The President's proposal involves . . . an affirmative answer to the following two questions:
>
> Can compensatory education be made to work?
>
> Does the application of concentrated compensatory resources (usually at higher dollar cost) in basic learning programs enhance the probability of success in compensatory education.[65]

The document set about to ". . . amplify in additional detail our affirmative replies to these questions and set forth some honest and prudent qualifications which should be attached to these 'yes' answers."[66] It framed its answer to the first question with a redefinition of "success." Whereas federal officials had previously viewed "success" as "closing the gap" between the achievement of disadvantaged and advantaged students,[67] the DHEW document adopted a less-demanding standard of "success":

> Our assumption is that if schools can produce improvements in learning for disadvantaged of even a relatively modest order, this both constitutes success when weighed against the formidable challenge to the schools which these other (SES) conditions present and warrants further support and exploration.[68]

Drawing on evidence reported by local and state Title I agencies, the document concluded that ". . . the drift of the evidence seems to be unmistakable; that compensatory education often enhances the achievement of poor children."[69]

Ironically, in framing an "affirmative answer" to the question of effectiveness, DHEW was forced to rely heavily on the very data that had been judged to be "useless" in 1967 and that ASPE had disclaimed in a report to Congress earlier that same year. The DHEW report to Congress for FY 1971-72 stated that "The evaluations which have been carried out by states and localities . . . have been disappointing and have not provided a sound or useful basis for assessing the effectiveness of (Title I)." [70] But, while the DHEW analysis undertaken in response to the White House request acknowledges the implications of TEMPO and the 1968 and 1969 surveys that compensatory education "has not worked and probably cannot be successful with disadvantaged children," the DHEW authors argue that the evaluations upon which such pessimistic conclusions are based are rife with methodological problems:

> . . . we would note that the first study (TEMPO) reviewed a strikingly unrepresentative sample of projects in the initial stages of Title I's implementation, and that the two USOE ('68 and '69) evaluations were severely limited.
> . . . they are derived from an information system rather than an on-site review. . . . they are severely limited in representativeness on this issue because they were marked by very high (over 90 percent) non-response rates for useable achievement data. Furthermore, we know that the funds under this national Title I program were, on the average, spread very thinly among many students and that the average child received no more than one or two hours per month assistance in reading. [71]

TEMPO, it will be recalled, was in fact based on a "strikingly unrepresentative sample of projects." They were thought to be "exemplary." And, while ASPE presents the methodology of the national surveys as less desirable than a methodology of on-site review, the surveys were designed specifically to avoid the data-collection problems involved in on-site review. Dismissing TEMPO and the national surveys on methodological grounds, the analysis concludes that "the evidence indicating that compensatory education has not worked is, we judge, sobering but not overwhelming, a counsel of caution but not of despair." [72] Thus, while TEMPO and kin had been raised in 1970 to justify President Nixon's priorities for education, they were in this moment brushed aside as methodologically inadequate, inconclusive, and unsuitable for policy purposes.

Following this review of major evidence, the DHEW document takes on the other major contributor to the climate of disenchantment with education—the Coleman report. Although, as we saw earlier, the Coleman findings, as interpreted by Moynihan, provided the rationale for the President's proposal to hold down Title I funds and to initiate the Family Assistance Plan, DHEW's analysis takes exception to the relevance of the Coleman findings for compensatory education strategies:

> There is no direct evidence in the Coleman Report for the conclusion . . . that compensatory education does not work. The Coleman Report analyzed the existing range of school conditions in 1965-1966 and had nothing to say about situations in which very substantial additional resources above normal school expenditures were provided for basic learning programs. The Coleman Report did not analyze any such intensive program. [73]

(The Civil Rights Commission report, released concurrently with the Coleman report, did however analyze intensive programs, and reached discouraging conclusions about education as an antipoverty strategy.)

And, in line with the President's antibusing stand, the DHEW document contends that Coleman didn't intend to imply that "physical desegregation is the only educational treatment that can have any positive achievement effects":

> We have not presented compensatory education as an alternative to desegregation but rather as a complementary policy. It is our view that both before,

during and after transfer from racially and/or economically isolated environments to more favorable learning centers, educationally disadvantaged children can benefit from compensatory education services.[74]

In providing an affirmative answer to the second question "Does the application of concentrated compensatory resources . . . in basic learning programs enhance the probability of success in compensatory education?" DHEW analysts relied heavily on a paper by Dr. Herbert Kiesling, "Input and Output in California Compensatory Education Projects." The DHEW document states:

> Dr. Herbert Kiesling's analysis of successful compensatory education programs in California concluded that there is a consistent and strong relationship between educational resources in the range of $200-$300 and achievement gains for disadvantaged children.[75]

The "consistent and strong relationship" identified by Dr. Kiesling, however, concerned process not cost variables. In Dr. Kiesling's view, DHEW had purposely and significantly distorted the findings presented in his paper.[76] As Kiesling pointed out, there are probably almost as many unsuccessful programs within that expenditure range as there are successful ones. "The point is that it's *how* you spend the money *not necessarily how much* money you spend that makes the difference."[77]

On balance, it is difficult to view the DHEW document as much more than a political brief. It uses the very data to support the President's initiative that had earlier been judged useless, and discounts those evaluations previously used to defend executive policy positions. Michael Timpane has commented that "on the basis of research [concerning the effectiveness of compensatory education], no sweeping claims could have been made for either policy."[78] But the inconclusiveness of the evaluations initiated by technologists served well the purposes of the politician. No "facts" were available about schools, learning, or the most efficient social strategies that were unassailable and so compelling as to sweep away perforce other political and organizational considerations.

## THE FEDERAL APPETITE FOR INFORMATION

The way in which the national surveys were used reflected more than just the instability of the knowledge base. The use of the surveys also pointed up the information requirements of various participants in the Title I policy system. Despite the rubric of rationality that adorns communications and memoranda issued by federal policy units, the actual federal appetite for information within decision settings is somewhat different from that assumed by ASPE's evaluation model or PPBS.

Congress, for example, has wanted a different kind of information about the Title I program from that sought by ASPE. With a few notable exceptions, such as Robert Kennedy and John Brademas, Congress has demonstrated greatest concern with the *distribution,* not the overall impact, of Title I funds. According to a Staff Assistant to the Senate Subcommittee on Education,

> The Hill needs district by district information [on Title I], so they know how much is going to the folks back home. Give them something TEMPO-like, and it just upsets people. All Congress wants to know from [Title I] evaluation is "are the bastards misusing the money." That's why the House turned down the 1 percent evaluation authorization.[79]

ASPE analyst Alan Ginsburg has said:

> The fact that Congress doesn't want impact information on Title I can be seen from the amount of time they spent on the formula issues. It's neat and the kind of thing Congress wants; you can talk about the number of kids involved, the amount of money for them and so on. Plus, Congress has leverage over the formula, and who gets what. They don't have any control over the programs.[80]

A BESE administrator concurred:

> Congress doesn't want to hear that Title I doesn't work. They mouth that, but they really want to know where the money's going.[81]

And a former budget examiner commented:

> There is an analogy in the health field to the kind of information Congress wants about Title I. Congress is happy with purely descriptive-type statistics. For example, they don't want to know about a drop in death rate or other "impact" information about health programs, they just want to know how many people received services and where. Congress would be happy with the same kind of information for education. They aren't concerned about impact but about delivery.[82]

Thus, while TEMPO and the national impact surveys found an interested ear in ASPE and in the executive branch, members of Congress were primarily interested in other sorts of reports from their states and districts. As Kirst explains, the focus on impact analysis is discordant with Congressionally defined objectives for Title I:

> Congress has displayed particular concern with [one of] Title I objectives— interstate equalization through channeling federal funds to low income states and cities. Indeed, the recent political support of Title I has rested more on its success as an equalizing financial vehicle among states than as a proven instrument of educational improvement. While the systems analysts and behavioral engineers found a receptive and interested Executive branch audience for studies of pupil achievement data, Congress was listening to state and local officials who complained about not receiving a fair share of the federal financial pie.[83]

The overarching Congressional concern about the flow of federal funds to the districts, and the general lack of appetite for information concerning the impact of these funds, seemingly are not particular to the Title I program but part of a general pattern of information use. Unclouded as it is with highly charged issues such as race, church-state relations, and poverty, the response of Congress to impact evidence about SAFA (School Assistance in Federally Affected Areas) shows more clearly the extent of Congressional interest in where the money goes, as well as the reception of lawmakers to impact information about programs such as Title I.

SAFA, which provides supplementary funds to those districts responsible for the education of the children of federal employees, has been an extremely popular program in Congress.[84] The legislative intent of SAFA was to compensate school districts for the fiscal burden added by federal personnel. However, a comprehensive study by the Battelle Memorial Institute demonstrated that SAFA was having an effect quite unanticipated by the lawmakers. Federal employees tend to live in middle- and upper-middle-class neighborhoods. Consequently, the effect of SAFA has been to help the rich suburban districts get richer, while the central city areas struggle to balance their budgets.

Presidents Johnson and Nixon have both tried unsuccessfully to cut SAFA. Gorham describes Johnson's failure:

> In 1967 the budget proposals of the present administration called for reduction [in SAFA] on the grounds that a more generous program of aid to elementary and secondary education has just been passed [ESEA]. School districts receiving benefits under the old program would get more under the new one. So unpopular was the Executive's recommendation to cut out the old program that *not a single Congressman could be found to introduce the Administration's bill,* although some privately admitted the "rationality" of the Administration's recommendation.[85] [Emphasis in original]

The Nixon Administration met with the same resistance, despite the new Battelle evidence about the perverse and unanticipated effect of the legislation. Congressmen have refused to consider any action that would reduce SAFA; such an action would not be popular back home. A USOE official wrote:

> On the basis of a comprehensive study conducted by the Battelle Memorial Institute the Impact Aid Reform Act was proposed in March 1970. This Act was not passed and no reform will be possible without an awareness of the political dynamism of the entire impact aid situation.[86]

There are a number of reasons why Congress has little taste for the sort of information ASPE thought was important. At a very practical level, most Congressmen have neither the time to wade through studies such as TEMPO or the 1968 survey nor the training to make sense of the technical language. A participant in Hill education debates has commented:

> We don't want that sort of information. The less involved the Senators get, the better off the program is. We'd rather be vague [in presenting education proposals] than get people bogged down in specifics they couldn't understand anyway.... Maybe in the House they can really spend time looking at "the issues." ... But, anyway, you could never do that in the Senate. Look at Pell; he is on 32 subcommittees, whereas a lot of Congressmen are only on 3. Pell can't spend time ... with impact studies. He just has to know where the money is going and that it is not being misused.[87]

In addition, many Congressmen do not share the conception of Title I that underlies an impact study. Many see Title I as general aid—a way to get money to the schools. Accordingly, achievement impact measures are not of great interest:

> Almost everyone I work with thinks of Title I as primarily political. To think that $1.5 billion dollars can make a difference is just ridiculous. Everybody knows that.
>
> There was never a coherent perception of what Title I was on the Hill. Perkins saw it as general aid; Robert Kennedy saw it as project oriented; Morse saw it as general aid, but not to the degree Perkins did. Perkins, after all, had begun to work on impact aid programs way back in the late 40's and early 50's. From the beginning, Title I has been seen as a political device for other things [lawmakers would like] to get done.[88]

Others involved in Congressional deliberations on educational policy concur that "most all of the senators see Title I as a political device."[89]

And like SAFA, Title I dollars have become institutionalized, and so the high-level policy decisions concerning federal aid to education presumed by an impact evaluation are not politically feasible in the instance of Title I. Impact evaluations furnish "yes" or "no" answers to the question "Is it working?" The policy implication of such information is either a "go" or "no go" decision about the legislative and fiscal future of the program, or about a decision regarding a new level of program funding. However, few believe that federal aid to the schools, such as Title I, is other than a permanent policy fixture.[90]

Genevieve Dane at USOE has said: "You couldn't just turn off the spigot on a $1.5 billion dollar program. Think of the number of jobs Title I supports at the local level."[91] Even within ASPE, it is widely acknowledged that no Congressman wants the program in his community phased out—or the project in his district shut down.[92]

Because Title I fulfills this hidden function, impact studies that lead to macronegative results constitute a threat for many Congressmen, in the same way they threaten program personnel at USOE.[93] Aaron Wildavsky argues that the politicians' "idea of desirability manifestly includes the support which programs generate for them.... Evaluations which are not congruent with these interests will be rejected and with it the men who do it."[94] The teachers, administrators, and others whose salaries are paid by Title I, or whose budgets are balanced by its funds, are, in practice, a more powerful constituency than those poor parents who are disillusioned by its unfulfilled promise.

Representative Carl Perkins from Kentucky, for example, has adopted just the attitude toward evaluators Wildavsky expects. Representative Perkins, a long-time champion of general aid to the schools, has often said that he "knows" Title I "works." "To me it is amazing that the [Title I] programs I have observed have been as successful as they have been."[95] In the midst of very encouraging testimony from a Kentucky schoolman concerning the positive effects of the Title I program, Perkins interjected:

> We have so much research money in Washington that is thrown away. Sometimes the Office of Education has hired friends to evaluate things, and you felt like kicking them in the pants, the way they run down these programs, where there is no true evaluation at all. . . . These so called research specialists receive grants for political reasons.[96]

Emerson Elliott puts the case of Congressional interest in evaluation a bit more soberly: "Congress is oriented toward where the money goes. They are more influenced by the conventional wisdom than by analytical studies."[97] Lawmakers want to be seen as thrifty, judicious, and wise.[98] Consequently, they prefer to have evidence about the success of their initiatives, not the failure, especially in the instance of an entrenched program such as Title I.[99] Organizational theorists see these information preferences as axiomatic: "If the political and administrative system has committed itself in advance to the correctness and efficacy of its reforms, it cannot tolerate learning of failure."[100]

Congressmen welcome reports on successful Title I programs, especially from their own states and districts. Contrary to the assumptions of technologists, most lawmakers have not expressed much interest in translating these reports into a more substantive federal education policy. Congressional interest in unusually successful compensatory programs stems primarily from a need for evidence about the wisdom of legislative action, not from a desire to legislate the model strategy, or to tighten up on Title I guidelines. A long-term participant in the Senate deliberations on education proposals said: "Congress likes to see success stories because they can point to them and tell the folks back home that they're spending their money wisely. Other than that, Congress really doesn't care [about evaluation]."[101]

In 1969, as ASPE was moving toward the identification of specific effective strategies (through initiation of Planned Variation, Right To Read, and Experimental Schools), debates in Congress continued to underline the principle of local control.[102] And President Nixon's "New Federalism" places even greater emphasis on local autonomy. Nixon initiatives, such as the proposal for education revenue sharing, imply that the federal role in education will become even less prescriptive than that contained in the broad categorical guidelines of Title I. The President describes his Education Revenue Sharing Program as a program "operated by the State—for the People ... a Federal Assistance Program without unnecessary Federal red tape."[103] This definition of a new federal role, in fact, suggests that federal imposition of the information about net benefit and relative costs that ASPE sought would be *contrary* to the interest of increasing the efficacy of local programs:

> I believe we must recognize that the Federal government cannot substitute
> its good intentions for the local understanding of local problems, for local
> energy in attacking these problems, and for local initiative in improving the
> quality of education in America.[104]

Thus, ASPE's expectation that a more concrete federal education policy only awaited information may not be an accurate reading of the inclinations or interests of lawmakers. The recent winds, although undoubtedly conditioned by historical developments, seemed to be blowing in just the opposite direction. A Senate Staff Assistant acknowledged that he shared the view of "technologists," but recognized that the current political climate was incompatible with such a federal policy. "Revenue Sharing," he concluded glumly, "is just the exact opposite."[105]

And while speculation about what could have happened is always risky, there is little evidence to suggest that substantive federal policy in the area of education could have evolved prior to Nixon and the new federalism, even if the national impact studies had been successful. Robert Kennedy's project orientation to Title I seems to have been the minority view. Even in the first year of Title I, before the disappointing evidence began to accumulate, Congress consistently supported the principle of local control, even in the face of USOE evidence on local misuse of Title I funds. If, as in the opinion of our informants, a majority of the more powerful figures in the Senate and the House saw Title I as general aid from the beginning, there is little reason to expect that a suggestion to legislate successful strategies of compensatory education would have received much support even in the early years.

Lawmakers on the whole do not seem to have much interest in the sort of information ASPE wanted. Were this not so, Congressional displeasure about the nature and timeliness of information available on Title I should have been evident by now. The 1968 survey report was the last "hard" data delivered to Congress on Title I. This report, covering the activities of Title I in FY 1967-68, was transmitted to Congress on April 24, 1970. The Glass report of 1968-1969 activities has not been released. In fact, the Congress did not even receive a report of USOE activities, as mandated by the 1967 amendments to ESEA, until the spring of 1972.[106] Had the deliberations and negotiations of Congress concerning the legislative and fiscal fate of Title I relied heavily on "evidence" of the program's overall effectiveness, this absence of data would have been intolerable. There has been no outrage, however; few have even asked about the Glass report or what's happened to data from FY

1969-70 and 1970-71. The Commissioner's apologies that an annual report of USOE activities "awaited further data" have been received with little more than a ripple of objection.

It is worth asking whether the fiscal policy units of the executive branch, on which the efforts of PPBS ultimately focus, tend to use information differently from the legislative branch. PPBS management principles were introduced to combat the "creeping incrementalism" that was seen to characterize program planning and fiscal management. OMB decisionmakers, however, do not seem to use information any more "rationally" in the instance of programs such as Title I than do their colleagues in Congress. In operation, PPBS has been little more than a band-aid measure; it has created a new matrix for planners and a new vocabulary, but it has not markedly altered the fundamental incentives and vested interests that shape the federal decisionmaking process. Writing about the introduction of PPBS, Elizabeth Drew observes: "As interesting as watching what happens when the government is confronted with program planning is observing what happens to program planning when confronted with government."[107]

The confrontation between PPBS and traditional styles of federal decisionmaking and behavior resulted in an outcome quite unanticipated by McNamara's "whiz kids" or the ASPE staff. When confronted with PPBS, the government did not significantly reform its style of decisionmaking; PPBS simply introduced a new set of rituals to adorn the traditional, incremental decisionmaking process. While PPBS may have forced some federal education planners to think in more analytical terms, on balance the planning and management of Title I seemed especially impervious to reform by these systematic decisionmaking strategies.

The institutionalization of a Title I, for example, placed the same constraints upon OMB policymakers as it did upon Congress. Thus, although a PPBS model assumes that the fundamental worth of a program will be reassessed in each budget cycle and that, on the basis of new evidence, a decision will be made about whether to expand, modify, or terminate the program, such "zero-base" thinking is rare at OMB and not feasible in the instance of Title I. For example, given that it is very unlikely that the level of federal investment in education represented by Title I could be substantially decreased (although it might be repackaged), decisions about allocation of resources among competing social strategies are unlikely to be made. That is, on the basis of an impact study of Title I, federal planners could not choose to invest Title I funds in another human-service strategy such as a Family Assistance Plan. Support for an alternative social strategy would represent an *addition* not a *substitution* to federal investment in social action programs.

The federal budget is not drawn anew each year. It is in large measure a recitation of previous commitments and represents the results of past negotiation and consensus building. Accordingly, most federal budget decisions are based on the established equilibrium—the previous year's budget. Budget decisions, then, are largely incremental and often more responsive to the nuances of the broader political and economic climate than to evidence. Charles Schultze pointed to the tension between the ideal of PPBS and the style of decisionmaking that has been typical of the federal government in his remark that "PBS impinges directly upon a complicated political process which is structured to achieve decisions by mutual adjustment among partisan advocates, each possessing different, or at least differently weighted, ends and values."[108]

On balance, the analytical model of the national surveys and the TEMPO study is congruent with the theoretical principles of PPBS, but the unstable nature of the information collected by these evaluation designs, combined with the constraints on Title I decisionmakers, leads to the use of information in an essentially political or advocacy fashion—a use that PPBS had hoped to replace or supplement. Information collected by Title I evaluations has not suggested clear policy alternatives, nor were substantively different policy alternatives available. Thus Title I evaluation has not been employed as a "rational" input to the decisionmaking process but instead has been used to impart an aura of rationality to what remains in education as fundamentally an incremental process of decisionmaking. A Staff Assistant to the Senate Subcommittee on Education remarked:

> There is absolutely no relationship between authorizations, appropriations, and evaluation. And OMB sure doesn't care about evaluation. It's just a political process. Evaluation is used when it fits.[109]

Genevieve Dane, a long-time USOE staff member, concurred:

> We live in a political world. Decisions [concerning the future on federal programs] are made in a political context. . . . It's all appropriations politics; it's not based on evidence.[110]

A former USOE administrator, Hendrick Gidenose, said:

> . . . it's pretty damn difficult for knowledge to affect policy in that kind of environment. . . . All of this [the lack of impact of information upon federal policy] is understandable, though, once you move away from a framework in which you believe knowledge should affect public policy. . . . the fallacy is between what is and what ought to be.[111]

Richard Carlson, former junior examiner at OMB and now Director of Planning, Office of the Deputy Commissioner for Renewal at USOE, also remarked:

> Evaluations get stuck on the shelf. Most of them aren't used unless they are evaluations of very large programs which are in someone's interest to pick up. It's all part of the adversary process.[112]

Thus both the way in which the national surveys were used and the general lack of substantive interest in the information produced by this approach to evaluation reveal yet another inconsistency in the assumptions that generated the national impact evaluations. In addition to an incongruence between the analytical paradigm and the Title I program, there is also a discrepancy between the expectations of federal evaluators and the role that information could play in the Title I policy system. Although the use made of these Title I evaluations reflects to some extent the instability and ambiguity of the information itself, it can also be seen as part of a more pervasive pattern of information use, at least in the instance of an institutionalized federal investment such as Title I. These federal evaluation efforts have been used predominately to defend policy, both because the evaluations failed to provide an incontrovertible basis for the formulation of policy and because the constraints of available policy alternatives precluded the fundamental reassessment of program worth assumed by an impact, cost-benefit study. An Urban Institute paper concludes:

> Traditionally, evaluation planning and design has been guided by an unrealistic interpretation or model of both operational and strategic decisionmaking. At the strategic level, the budget process and the paraphenalia of the PPBS have been seen as the vehicle through which evaluation would have

impact. This process is viewed as a budget planner making marginal trade-offs among programs. Unfortunately, there is much more myth than substance to this view of the federal decison process. Its acceptance has lead to a demand for OE to produce the impact/cost benefit type evaluation.[113]

Thus, while William Gorham and other reformers anticipated that new information could be used rationally—if only at the margins—there is little in the experience of these Title I evaluations to suggest information is (or can be) used that way. The notions that William Gorham brought to ASPE were based on particular assumptions concerning the availability of information, the ability of federal evaluators to collect and display this information, and the inclination or ability of participants within the Title I policy system to use it. A theme that recurs in the experience of the national surveys, however, is the slippage between these assumptions, which were generated by the science of systems analysis, and the realities of the Title I policy system.

Furthermore, the experience of the national surveys indicates that what is "learned" from programs such as Title I is often determined by factors having little to do with the program itself, and the consequences of evaluation are themselves difficult to evaluate. That is, the questions asked and the interpretation given the resulting evidence often reflect primarily the background and commitments of the enquirers and the consumers, as well as the suppliers of information. What is learned is often described by what needs to be known, or proved, or defended, not by what can be discovered.[114] Similarly, the role of information is often determined first of all by the constraints of the policy system, not the information itself, or even by the logic of the research. In this instance, the incongruities that existed among the analytical paradigm of the national surveys, the character of Title I as a social program, and the dominant policy system incentives generated evaluation that failed to meet the expectations of ASPE reformers or USOE program managers.

# Notes to Chapter 4

1. Bayla F. White to Alice Rivlin, Memo, "Title I Evaluation," December 8, 1967, p. 3.

2. E. J. Mosbaek and other TEMPO analysts suggested that "Aggregating data on the resources and participation in compensatory program for a whole school or aggregating student performance for a whole school is likely to mask the effects of compensatory education." (E. J. Mosbaek et al., "Analysis of Compensatory Education in Five School Districts: Summary," TEMPO, General Electric Company, Washington, D.C., n.d., pp. 32-33.)

3. The TEMPO analysts cautioned that ". . . it must be kept in mind that Title I funded programs were still relatively new at the time of 1966-1967 tests, and that it is not reasonable to expect conclusive evidence of enhancement in achievement so soon." (Ibid., p. 31.)

4. In the view of TEMPO analysts, the risk of Type I error was even more serious: "There can be a loss to society in failing to support a program that is actually successful but whose success cannot be clearly substantiated by available data." (Ibid.)

5. U.S. Department of Health, Education, and Welfare, "Recommended Human Investment Programs for FY 1968," n.d., pp. vii-3.

6. See, for example, Alice Rivlin's January 27, 1969, memo to the Secretary, "Thoughts on the Department's Role in Education," p. 3.

7. Bayla F. White, "The Design and Purpose of the 1968 Survey of Compensatory Education," paper presented at the meeting of the American Educational Research Association, Los Angeles, February 1969.

8. Bayla F. White to Robert Hartman, Memo, "Your 'Title I Evaluation' Memo of January 2," January 3, 1969, p. 2.

9. White to Rivlin, op. cit., p. 4.

10. Interview, Bayla F. White, February 7, 1972.

11. Interview, George Mayeske, June 16, 1972.

12. Ibid.

13. Interview, Bayla F. White, February 7, 1972.

14. See USOE/BESE memos to the CSSOs and SEAs concerning the conduct and analysis of the 1968 survey.

15. Interview, Joseph Froomkin, February 25, 1972. Dr. Froomkin did not believe that the resulting compromise survey design would result in either a useful policy document or in research relevant to program development. Froomkin felt that the national survey would make education "look bad" because no impact would be discovered and that the absence of process data precluded the usefulness of the survey as a program guide.

16. "Analysis of Data from the 1968 Survey on Compensatory Education," draft Request for Proposal, July 23, 1968.

17. The RFP states the survey purpose in this tone: "The legislation requires that the Title I program be evaluated at a national level on an annual basis and that an evaluation report be furnished by the Commissioner of Education to the Congress by January 31 of each calendar year." (Ibid., p. 3.)

18. Interviews I conducted with SEA personnel in the Spring of 1971 suggest that this view is not constrained to the federal level. Few SEA personnel seem to have any illusions about the quality of the state reports. In fact, an evaluator in a state widely touted as the "best" in program evaluation called the preparation of the annual report "an exercise in fantasy."

19. U.S. Office of Education, Bureau of Elementary and Secondary Education, ESEA Title I Program Information Letter No. 126, February 6, 1968.

20. Ibid.

21. Ibid.

22. Interview, Bayla F. White, February 7, 1972.

23. Ibid. Also, Interview, Susan Smith, June 1972.

24. Interview, Susan Smith, June 1972. Also, Bayla F. White, "The Role of Evaluation in Title I Program Management," paper presented at the National Academy of Public Administration Conference on Evaluation of Education Programs, Rockville, Maryland, May 26, 1972, p. 3.

25. Susan Smith reported the results of her study in an interview and made copies of her draft analysis available to me. It is questionable, however, even if all available data had been reported, whether or not the information would have been useful. Subsequent evaluations indicate that achievement data are seldom comparable from district to district, or even from program to program within districts. Different tests, different norming, and the like make comparisons difficult if not impossible.

26. Richard Jaeger, Chief, Evaluation Design, BESE, Memo, "Minutes of the September 23, 1968 Meeting on 1969 Title I Evaluation," p. 10.

27. Interviews: Susan Smith and Iris Lipkowitz, June 1972.

28. Participants in the writing of the 1968 report have said that the report went through five drafts. However, only three were compiled and disseminated for review.

29. U.S. Office of Education, *Education of the Disadvantaged: An Evaluative Report on Title I Elementary and Secondary Education Act of 1965, Fiscal Year 1968,* p. 1 (hereafter cited as *1968 Survey).*

30. Ibid., p. viii.

31. Ibid., pp. 6-10.

32. Indeed, questions of comparability and misuse received explicit Congressional attention only when they were publicly and bitterly raised by the report, *Title I of ESEA: Is It Helping Poor Children?* prepared by the Washington Research Project of the Southern Center for Studies in Public Policy and the NAACP Legal Defense and Educational Fund, Inc., Washington, D.C., 1970.

33. *1968 Survey,* p. 126.

34. This evaluation is called the "Glass Report" after the principal author, Gene Glass.

35. Interview, Susan Smith, June 1972. Also, Karl Hereford's Memo, "Recommendations for Organization and Format of the 1968 Elementary Survey," n.d.

36. Interview, Genevieve Dane, June 12, 1972. Furthermore, a staff assistant on the Hill has remarked that each administration tries to carve out its own style, and generally in quite explicit contrast to the character of preceding executive initiatives. (Interview, October 1972.)

37. Richard Jaeger to Jack Biren, Memo, "BESE Plan for Evaluation FY 1970 through 1974," May 5, 1969.

38. Request for Proposal, op. cit.

39. Gene V. Glass et al., *Data Analysis of the 1968-1969 Survey of Compensatory Education (Title I),* U.S. Office of Education, Bureau of Elementary and Secondary Education, August 1970, p. 193.

40. Interviews: Susan Smith and Iris Lipkowitz, June 1972.

41. Glass, op. cit.

42. In a July 1970 letter to David Cohen, Harvard Center for Educational Policy Research, Glass explained that he could not honor Dr. Cohen's request for a copy of the report as USOE had not yet authorized distribution.

43. Kathryn A. Hecht has written: "The fiscal 1968 report was technical and its implications difficult to understand. It was not written as guidance for SEA or LEA personnel or for dissemination purposes, and was not released in time to provide the useful material that it was expected to offer. The fiscal 1969 report suffered from the same problems, perhaps to a greater extent. It still has not been disseminated." ("Five Years of Title I Evaluation," revised version of a paper presented to the 1972 Annual Meeting of the American Educational Research Association, Chicago, Illinois, April 7, 1972, p. 10.)

44. Richard L. Fairley, "Accountability's New Tool," *American Education,* Vol. 8, No. 5, June 1972, pp. 33-35.

45. U.S. Department of Health, Education, and Welfare, Office of the Secretary, Memo to Education Staff from Robert Hartman, "Final Words on Title I, ESEA," January 16, 1969, p. 3.

46. U.S. Congress, Senate, Subcommittee on Education of the Committee on Labor and Public Welfare, 91st Cong., 1st sess., *Hearings on Elementary and Secondary Education Amendments* (Washington, D.C.: U.S. Government Printing Office, 1969), p. 228.

47. U.S. Congress, House, Committee on Education and Labor, *Hearings on the Extension of Elementary and Secondary Programs, Part IV* (Washington, D.C.: U.S. Government Printing Office, 1967).

48. Alice Rivlin believed that the failure of TEMPO and the 1968 survey to furnish input-output data, or to model effective strategies, was not inevitable. Dr. Rivlin thought that TEMPO or the 465 survey could have yielded the desired information had the Title I program been *designed* differently: "Headstart, Title I, model cities and other federal programs *could* have been designed to produce information on their effectiveness, but they were not." (Alice M. Rivlin, *Systematic Thinking for Social Action,* Washington, D.C.: The Brookings Institution, 1971, p. 86.)

49. Alice Rivlin asserted "that the federal government should take the leadership in organizing, funding and evaluating systematic experiments with various ways of delivering education, health, and other social services." (Ibid.)

50. Interview, Staff Assistant to House Subcommittee on Education, October 1972.

51. U.S. Congress, House, 91st Cong., 2d sess., "Message from the President of the United States on Educational Reform," March 3, 1970, Document No. 91-267.

52. Ibid.

53. Interview, Genevieve Dane, June 12, 1972.

54. Interview, Emerson Elliott, February 24, 1972.

55. A Senate Staff Assistant, knowledgeable in the area of educational policy, pointed to the need of every President to establish a "trademark" or administrative style: "Nixon's proposal for NIE was part of a legislative package [to take education out of the arena of politics]. NIE didn't look too political except for the word "national." Nixon's approach to education differed from LBJ's. Johnson designed the Great Society and wanted programs. Nixon's stamp, as a "rationalist," is the creation of "Institutions" and "Foundations." (Interview, October 1972.)

56. Interview, Genevieve Dane, June 12, 1972.

57. "Message from the President of the United States on Educational Reform," op. cit.

58. U.S. Congress, House, 92d Cong. 2d sess., "Message from the President of the United States Relative to Busing and Equality of Educational Opportunity, and Transmitting a Draft of Proposed Legislation To Impose a Moratorium on New and Additional Student Transportation," March 20, 1972, Document No. 92-195.

59. Michael Timpane made these comments in a panel discussion on "The Use and Abuse of Research Studies in Federal Educational Policy Making: Some Case Studies," American Educational Research Association 1973 Annual Meeting, New Orleans, February 25-March 1, 1973.

60. Ibid. Also, interviews: Genevieve Dane, June 12, 1972; Alan Ginsburg, February 1972; and Iris Lipkowitz, June 1972.

61. Interviews: Genevieve Dane and Larry LaMoure, June 12, 1972.

62. Michael J. Wargo, "Needs, Resources, Management, and Impact: A Comprehensive Evaluation of ESEA Title I Since 1965," American Institutes for Research in the Behavioral Sciences, Palo Alto, California, February 1972. Although this report was submitted by AIR as its final report, the study was rewritten at the request of Richard L. Fairley, head of DCE, and officially released in March 1972, under the title "ESEA Title I: A Reanalysis and Synthesis of Evaluation Data from Fiscal Year 1965 through 1970."

63. Interview, Joan Bissell, June 1972.

64. Interview, Wallace Cohen, June 14, 1972.

65. U.S. Department of Health, Education, and Welfare, "The Effectiveness of Compensatory Education: Summary and Review of the Evidence," n.d., p. 4.

66. Ibid., p. 5.

67. "Message from the President of the United States on Educational Reform," op. cit.

68. U.S. Department of Health, Education, and Welfare, "The Effectiveness of Compensatory Education: Summary and Review of the Evidence," n.d., p. 5.

69. Ibid., p. 6.

70. U.S. Department of Health, Education, and Welfare, Report to Congress for 1971-1972 on the Status of Department Programs.

71. U.S. Department of Health, Education, and Welfare, "The Effectiveness of Compensatory Education: Summary and Review of the Evidence," n.d., p. 9.

72. Ibid.

73. Ibid., p. 10.

74. Ibid.

75. Ibid., p. 11.

76. Personal communication.

77. Ibid.

78. Comments made in a panel discussion on "The Use and Abuse of Research Studies in Federal Educational Policy Making: Some Case Studies," American Educational Research Association 1973 Annual Meeting, New Orleans, February 25-March 1, 1973.

79. Interview, Staff Assistant to the Senate Subcommittee on Education, October 1972.

80. Interview, Alan Ginsburg, February 1972.

81. Interview, Larry LaMoure, June 12, 1972.

82. Interview, Richard Carlson, February 25, 1972.

83. Michael W. Kirst, "A Political Analysis of Title I ESEA Feedback," paper presented at the Annual Meeting of the National Council on Measurement in Education, New York City, February 5, 1971.

84. Commissioner Marland, writing to protest OMB action on the proposed USOE budget, referred to SAFA as a "sacred idol" of Congress.

85. William Gorham, "Sharpening the Knife That Cuts the Public Pie," paper presented at the International Political Science Association, Brussels, Belgium, September 1967, p. 6.

86. Acting Associate Commissioner for Elementary and Secondary Education to John W. Evans, Assistant Commissioner for OPPE, Memo, "Draft Program Memorandum for FY 1973-1977," September 1, 1971, p. 13.

87. Interview, Staff Assistant to Senate Subcommittee on Education, October 1972.

88. Ibid. This remark may represent the wisdom of hindsight and the reformulation of expectations.

89. Ibid.

90. Only one person said he thought that Title I could be substantially cut or terminated.

91. Interview, Genevieve Dane, op. cit.

92. Interviews: Michael Timpane, February 24, 1972; Joan Bissell, June 1972; Alan Ginsburg, February 1972.

93. Alan Ginsburg has said: "Program people and BESE see evaluation as a threat; even Congress does. What matters ultimately is money to the districts." (Interview, February 1972.)

94. Aaron Wildavsky, "Evaluation as an Organizational Problem," n.d., mimeo., p. 43.

95. U.S. Congress, House, Committee on Education and Labor, *Oversight Hear-*

*ing on Elementary and Secondary Education,* 92d Cong., 2d sess., hearings held in Lexington, Kentucky, January 13 and 14, 1972 (Washington, D.C.: U.S. Government Printing Office, 1972, p. 33).

96. Ibid., p. 40.

97. Interview, Emerson Elliott, February 24, 1972.

98. See Charles L. Clapp, *The Congressman: His Work as He Sees It* (Garden City, New York: Doubleday & Co., Inc., Anchor Books, 1964).

99. John Hughes, veteran USOE administrator, certainly understood this when, as the press picked up the TEMPO findings and made headlines of the failure of federal policy, he wrote to the CSSO: "It might be a good idea at this time for any of you who have news clippings or other reports concerning the effectiveness of Title I programs in your state to forward them to members of your Congressional delegation." (Program Information Letter No. 170.)

100. Donald T. Campbell, "Reforms as Experiments," in Francis Caro (ed.), *Readings in Evaluation Research* (New York: Russell Sage Foundation, 1971), pp. 233-261.

101. Interview, Staff Assistant to Senate Subcommittee on Education, October 1972.

102. For example, in 1969, the Senate Subcommittee Report suggested that ". . . local school districts may elect to use program funds for a variety of different special services. They have put Title I funds to work in providing such programs as remedial reading and other instructional projects, teaching teacher training, cultural enrichment, school health care, and nutritional services. The list is limited only to the ability of each local school system to create and explore special methods of helping deprived children to learn and to want to learn." It seems unlikely that this committee would have supported legislation that required local districts to select one of several prescribed options for delivering Title I services.

103. U.S. Department of Health, Education, and Welfare, and The Domestic Council, Executive Office of the President, *The Right To Learn: President Nixon's Proposal for Education Revenue Sharing* (Washington, D.C.: U.S. Government Printing Office, 1971), p. 5.

104. "Excerpts of the President's Message to Congress April 6, 1971," included with *Right To Learn* materials.

105. Interview, Staff Assistant to the Senate Subcommittee on Education, October 1972.

106. Michael Timpane noted USOE's delinquency in a memo to the ASPE staff: "This is the first time that OE has managed to fulfill a requirement of several years' standing. The general conclusion of the [Commissioner's] report is that we have learned very little from evaluation so far." (U.S. Department of Health, Education, and Welfare, Office of the Secretary, Memo from Director of Education Planning to Assistant Secretary for Planning and Evaluation, "Annual Report Evaluating the Results and Effectiveness of OE Programs and Projects," March 14, 1972.)

107. Elizabeth B. Drew, "HEW Grapples with PPBS," *The Public Interest,* Summer 1967, pp. 9-29.

108. Charles L. Schultze, *The Politics and Economics of Public Spending* (Washington, D.C.: The Brookings Institution, 1968), p. 16. Others have argued that PPBS is incompatible not only with the political process but also with the area of human activity to which it has been applied: "McNamarism is the marriage of abstract thought and quantitative method. It creates a remarkably restricted mentality. When applied to certain narrow problems of logistics or conditioning pigeons in a

laboratory, McNamarism can be excellent. But it fails utterly when social/political reality is to be understood. The argument can be made that rigid adherence to McNamarism, far from being the essence of rationality, is itself a virulent form of irrationalism." (Daniel Yankelovich, "The New Naturalism," *Saturday Review,* April 1972, pp. 31-37.)

109. Interview, Staff Assistant to Senate Subcommittee on Education, October 1972.

110. Interview, Genevieve Dane, June 12, 1972.

111. Comments made by Hendrick Gidenose in a panel discussion on "The Use and Abuse of Research Studies in Federal Educational Policymaking: Some Case Studies," American Educational Research Association 1973 Annual Meeting, New Orleans, February 25-March 1, 1973.

112. Interview, Richard Carlson, February 25, 1972.

113. John W. Scanlon, Joe N. Nay, and Joseph S. Wholey, *An Evaluation System To Support a Decentralized, Comprehensive Manpower Program* (Washington, D.C.: The Urban Institute, 1971), p. 3.

114. See, for example, the similar argument made by David N. Kershaw in "Issues in Income Maintenance Experimentation" in Peter H. Rossi and Walter Williams (eds.), *Evaluating Social Programs* (New York: Seminar Press, 1972), pp. 221-248.

# Chapter Five

# Case Studies of Exemplary Compensatory Programs

The national survey of compensatory education was only one solution advanced at the federal level in response to the outcome of the Kennedy scheme and the results of TEMPO. Concurrently with planning for the 1968 survey, Dr. Joseph Froomkin,[1] the newly appointed Assistant Commissioner for Program Planning and Evaluation (OPPE), was pursuing alternative research strategies to remedy the absence of Title I program data and evidence on the impact of compensatory programs. Dr. Froomkin, like ASPE and Senator Kennedy, had concluded that the three-tiered reporting scheme was a failure.[2] But Froomkin had a somewhat different perception of the character of Title I evaluation policy, and what should be done to solve the problems revealed by TEMPO.[3]

Joseph Froomkin had come to OPPE at a time when the major function of the office was writing budget justifications.[4] The 1967 ESEA amendments subsequently expanded USOE's evaluation requirements and thereby OPPE's responsibilities. OPPE's new duties involved providing data that Commissioner Howe could take to Congress as well as collecting evidence with which to defend USOE budget requests. Froomkin's information needs and evaluation policies were thus influenced by the advocacy requirements of USOE and the attendant responsibilities of his office. Like ASPE analysts, Froomkin wanted information on successful strategies, and on the impact of compensatory programs, but for different reasons. His most immediate concern was not with gathering information that could reform federal decisionmaking or local educational practices, but with conducting an evaluation that would enable OPPE to justify continuing federal investment in ESEA Title I, USOE's largest program.

Commissioner Harold Howe had to appear before Congress each February to explicate and defend USOE programs. Because of the time constraints imposed by Congressional calendars, Dr. Froomkin did not believe the 1968 survey evaluation model could meet OPPE's data requirements. The proposed survey and the subsequent analysis, in Froomkin's view, would take too long to be useful to him or to the Commissioner. Further, as we shall see, Froomkin did not believe the survey asked the right questions. These different views on evaluation precipitated a somewhat bizarre situation. Independently and simultaneously within USOE, two alternative evaluation plans were being developed in response to the failure of the Kennedy scheme, TEMPO, and USOE's expanded reporting requirement.

## "COLEMAN REVISITED": A NATIONAL IMPACT SURVEY

Dr. Froomkin made one false start and one true start at initiating evaluation congruent with his perceived responsibilities. The first alternative proposed to the national survey idea was the "Coleman Revisited" plan.[5] Joseph Froomkin reasoned that a more efficient way to collect evidence on the effectiveness of education and Title I as an intervention strategy would be to measure change in the achievement of disadvantaged children by comparing the 1964 EEOS achievement data with standardized achievement measures taken in the same schools and grades in 1967, or 2 years after the initiation of ESEA Title I. The proposed Coleman Revisited plan was essentially a replication of the Coleman survey, using the same sampling design and the same achievement instrument. Froomkin's major research interest lay in the trends that such a comparative analysis would reveal, particularly for inner-city children. Froomkin commented: "I wanted to know what was happening to poor kids in Cleveland, Chicago and New York City. I was curious to find out about migration and how the population sub-groups had shifted since the time the EEOS data was collected."[6] In a memo to the ASPE staff, Bayla White outlined the primary objectives of Froomkin's proposed Coleman Revisited plan:

> According to Joe, the new study seeks to answer three major questions:
>
> —what has happened to the gap in achievement between advantaged and disadvantaged kids since the fall of 1965?
>
> —has there been a change in attitudes and self-perceptions of children between 1965 and 1968?
>
> —what changes have occurred in achievement among specific sub-groups of the population: rural non-farm suburban, central cities, rural farm?
>
> He added that he believes that the new study will make education look good, rather than bad.[7]

Coleman Revisited was never done; the study was a casualty in the continuing struggle over federal evaluation efforts. While Foomkin viewed the politicking and compromising of ASPE evaluators somewhat disdainfully, his decision to ignore the purely political aspects of evaluation frustrated his own evaluation plans. Coleman Revisited, in that it could permit state, district, and school comparisons, ignored the critical principles of evaluation that had been forged with the passage of ESEA. Froomkin's plan contained all the bugaboos of assessment most firmly resisted by the CSSO. Bayla White has said:

> Froomkin didn't understand that if he wanted to do evaluation, he had to have the cooperation of the Chiefs and of the Council of Great City Schools. Froomkin was not very good at marketing his idea. The states got the impression that the feds were going to evaluate their performance and they didn't like it.[8]

Coleman Revisited was opposed at the federal level for both methodological and political reasons. ASPE watched the development of Froomkin's plan with concern. ASPE analysts didn't support Coleman Revisited because they believed that the study asked the wrong questions. For one, the study wouldn't gather descriptive information on local practices. Also, in a memo to Alice Rivlin, Joseph Wholey argued that Coleman Revisited "would have limited usefulness in getting at the cost effectiveness of different types of compensatory programs."[9] Further, ASPE was worried about the political fallout that would result from the study. It was feared that the furor that the Froomkin plan would cause among the Chiefs would abort ASPE's own evaluation plans.[10]

There was also opposition to Coleman Revisited within USOE. Dr. Karl Hereford, head of BESE evaluation, was mounting plans for Belmont, a massive data-collection scheme. (Belmont is discussed in the following chapter.) This new plan relied heavily on the cooperation of influential educational interest groups. BESE supported the long-range survey plan because it fitted into the Belmont scheme and was built on a consensus with CSSO. BESE worried that the one-shot Coleman Revisited would anger schoolmen and undermine plans for the Belmont effort. Michael Kirst commented that "BESE was convinced that local educators would not assent to a standardized test—this would be a threat to local control and cause more controversy than national assessment."[11]

Nonetheless, late in 1967 two evaluation plans were proposed as a solution to the failure of the Kennedy scheme and the disappointment of TEMPO. However, both of the plans could not be implemented; either the national survey or Coleman Revisited could be put in the schools in 1968, but not both. The question of which evaluation plan should be implemented was resolved primarily on political, not methodological, grounds. The position taken by CSSO was pivotal. The Chiefs learned of the Coleman Revisited plan just in advance of their annual meeting and were enraged.[12] They were so angry about Froomkin's proposal that ASPE observers at the February 1968 CSSO meeting thought the convention debate would result in the censure of Commissioner Howe for permitting the evolution of such a plan within USOE.[13] Howe, already in disfavor with the Chiefs because of his position in support of school desegregation, decided to drop the Coleman Revisited plan and go ahead with the plans for the 1968 survey. Froomkin remembers: "I was shot down by the Chief State School Officers and the Commissioner. The Chiefs didn't want the feds mucking around."[14]

Despite this defeat, Froomkin was "tenacious."[15] He presented his evaluation proposal once again at the June 1968 CSSO meeting, hoping to persuade them of his good intentions and the merit of the study. In preparation for the meeting, Froomkin sent a letter to the Chiefs, outlining his evaluation plan in great detail and attempting to dispel their fears. Joseph Froomkin's strength, however, did not lie in diplomacy; although he intended his letter to be an avuncular missive of reassurance, the letter implied instead a threat to the Chiefs:

> I am increasingly convinced that most evaluation activities are designed to document the failures of the American Education system. By contrast, I have tried to sponsor some evaluation activities which could document the problems of American education and present some evidence that American education is coping with those problems successfully.
>
> I will be candid: we would be getting a great deal of information [from Coleman Revisited]. Such information can cause you embarrassment if it is badly analyzed or used by people with narrow points of view. I intend to be here for another 12 months to see that this does not happen. *If you postpone your approval any longer you will be dealing with my successor. He may or may not be as sympathetic to your problems as I am.* [16] [Emphasis added]

According to ASPE personnel attending the June meeting, the Chiefs were "furious."[17] Anxious USOE officials took whatever ad lib action they could to appease the angry Chiefs:

> Graham Sullivan promised the conference that if it did not endorse the study, then OE *would not proceed with it.* On the way back to the office, Joe told me he was completely taken by surprise by Sullivan's promise.

It does appear that the survey will proceed. I don't know who in OE approves of it or how it will be coordinated with other efforts. Joe sounds as if he already has the $800,000 from Research money . . . therefore the plans for the study will not have to be reviewed by this office [ASPE has discretionary power over OPPE money].

Something has got to be done to get the Office of Education acting as one agency, instead of a series of competing fiefdoms.[18] [Emphasis in original]

It was fiefdom action that finally killed Coleman Revisited. As Joseph Froomkin continued to stand firm in his intent to do the study, Karl Hereford invited Henry Dyer of Educational Testing Service to arbitrate the now heated dispute between OPPE and BESE.[19] After reviewing the study, Dyer recommended that the proposal be dropped on the ground that its sampling procedure was inadequate and that any gains that might possibly be attributed to participation in the Title I program could be washed out by broader and uncontrolled socioeconomic status changes in the sample. Dyer's pronouncement, however, simply served to annoint with the holy oil of science a decision required by the political climate of the Title I policy system. Joseph Wholey and Bayla White wrote to the new head of OPPE, Dr. John W. Evans, at a later date:

That study failed to get off the ground because of resistance from the CSSO and because of a belief within OE that the political costs of such a study outweighed its potential usefulness. In other words, it was felt that the Office of Education might jeopardize its whole evaluation/data collection effort and the future cooperation of the states and local authorities for the sake of a one-shot effort to gather achievement data.[20]

The demise of Coleman Revisited highlights the purely political aspects of federal evaluation policy. Dr. Froomkin's choice to overlook these constraints upon possible evaluation design short-circuited OPPE's first attempt to gather useful data, and meant that Commissioner Howe had to resign himself to another year without "hard" data to take to Congress.

## "IT WORKS": CASE STUDIES OF EXEMPLARY PRACTICE

In its second approach to evaluation, OPPE explicitly embodied the lessons Froomkin had learned in the battle over Coleman Revisited. The 1968 rejection of his plan left Froomkin in the same position as in late 1967. The Commissioner still needed data he could use for his report to Congress; Froomkin still needed data he could use to justify USOE budget requests. To meet his own data needs as quickly as possible and with the least amount of fuss, Froomkin contracted with AIR to undertake a series of case studies of exemplary compensatory education projects. This plan was appealing in that it side-stepped the states, it did not involve the sophisticated and time-consuming data analysis required by the 1968 survey, and it promised to provide abundant process data on the activities of successful programs. Michael Kirst, who was at BESE when the AIR study plan was conceived, has commented:

Joe Froomkin wanted quick information that wouldn't have to rely on the states. "It Works" was information to placate people in Congress and OMB howling at the Commissioner for what works, program information and the like. Although there was some talk about LEAs [how they would use the study], the series was never for the LEAs. Froomkin never thought about dissemination. The study was done to satisfy political forces.[21]

The ASPE staff was no more enthusiastic about Joseph 'Froomkin's second proposal than it had been about Coleman Revisited.[22] Dr. Rivlin thought that the AIR study would probably encounter the same difficulties that had plagued the TEMPO effort—an absence of identifiable programs and reliable data. Too, ASPE was persuaded of the merits of the PCI suggested by James Mauch at DCE. The project-centered research model proposed for the AIR study would not, in ASPE's view, be as useful in identifying the multiple influences that might affect achievement and so would not be as helpful in specifying a "best" model of effective compensatory practices. Froomkin's motives in undertaking the AIR study, however, were different from ASPE's; he needed data not to reform the Title I program but to defend it.

The AIR study design carefully avoided many of the obstacles encountered by the TEMPO staff. Through an extensive literature search and follow-up site visits, AIR identified a number of potentially successful compensatory programs. Programs with inadequate data were weeded out in the literature screen; field visits eliminated programs that in practice did not conform to program evaluation reports. In this way, the AIR staff uncovered sufficient data to document "successful" compensatory strategies and to imply that schools were devising new and effective programs for disadvantaged youngsters as legislators had hoped with the passage of ESEA.

The AIR study resulted in a final report, *A Study of Selected Exemplary Programs for the Education of Disadvantaged Children,* [23] and in the "It Works" case study series, which described program populations, strategies, and achievements. A number of general conclusions were drawn from the AIR study and the "It Works" series:

Good program design and effective guidelines establishing criteria were crucial to effecting program evaluation.

Successful preschool programs all had certain common attributes: careful planning, including statement of objectives; teacher training in the methods of the program; small groups and a high degree of individualization; and instruction and materials closely relevant to the objectives.

Successful compensatory education at the elementary level largely depended upon: academic objectives clearly stated; active parental involvement, particularly as motivation; individual attention for pupils' learning problems and a high intensity of treatment.

"Successful" compensatory programs, in largest number, focused on the provision of remedial reading services for elementary school students.

## IMPACT ON THE TITLE I POLICY SYSTEM

If the outcome of an evaluation effort is measured by the degree to which it fulfills its intended objectives, the AIR study was an unqualified, resounding success. It furnished just the sort of positive, hopeful data that will justify budgets and that commissioners can take to Congress. In fact, the data from Froomkin's 1968 study are still being used for these purposes. The extensive use made of AIR data furnishes additional support for the earlier suggestion that the data ASPE considered to be important may not be the only type of information useful to the larger policy system. The enthusiastic reception to the AIR series within the executive and the legislative branches suggests that the policy system can and will use nonscientific, anecdotal evidence, and that the impact, cost-benefit evaluations pursued by ASPE are not obligatory.

"It Works" has been extremely popular with Congress. Samuel Halperin remembers Kennedy complaining (in response to TEMPO) that he "wasn't interested in methodological rhetoric like baseline and control"; that he and his constituents "wanted to see evaluations of working programs."[24] The AIR series provided Congress with thirty-one such examples from all parts of the country. The study offered evidence that compensatory programs could work, pointed to specific ways in which they have "worked," and so supported legislative investment in education.

Emerson Elliott has said that "Froomkin's studies were really helpful to OMB," in that they suggested better ways for spending money efficiently.[25] Further, Elliott remarked, "the studies which were done while Froomkin was around have had a lot to do with opinions [re: effective compensatory strategies] that have jelled. For example, we have not gone much beyond recognizing the importance of parent involvement and reading programs."[26] The AIR study, in sum, went farther to remedy the gaps in the knowledge base about effective educational strategies than did any of the impact, cost-benefit studies.[27] In view of the popularity and extensive citation of the AIR series, it is ironic that the AIR findings subsequently proved to be ephemeral. Follow-up studies conducted by AIR found that "successful" programs exhibited the regressive tendency that has been typical of innovative efforts for the past 15 years.[28] The AIR research staff has found that only a small portion of the original "It Works" projects were still "working" in following years.[29] Whatever it is that makes a program "work" appears to be in large part unstable or unspecified, or an artifact of measurement error.

The AIR study was successful in supplying the evidence that Commissioner Howe needed, but the impact of the study has been a disappointment in other ways. A major source of disappointment at the federal level has been the lack of interest by SEAs and LEAs in the study findings. Publication of the "It Works" series did not result in a marked upsurge of "Project Concerns" or "Project Early Starts" throughout the country, or even in a substantial number of inquiries.[30]

It does not seem that USOE made an extensive or concerted effort to distribute the information or publicize the series. Froomkin, responding to more immediate pressures, did not consider the question of dissemination at the outset. His most immediate concern was to gather information USOE could use in its reports to Congress and OMB. After the studies were completed, however, Dr. Froomkin did try to call attention to the AIR findings. He recalls that "I made speeches at the AERA meetings, the National School Association meetings and so on, but there was not a lot of interest."[31]

Froomkin's hope for the subsequent impact of the series was in many ways similar to ASPE's expectations that information would be self-winding. For example, in a memo on the Department's and the federal government's role in education, Alice Rivlin wrote:

> School systems are eager for information on how to do their job better. They
> do not know where to turn. If the Federal government were to take the

leadership in finding demonstrably better ways to teach children, I believe these methods would be put into practice by popular demand.[32]

Similarly, Dr. Froomkin believed that the mere identification of the exemplary projects would generate its own demand and interested consumer group. Froomkin now says: "Looking back, I made a mistake. I engaged in the highest form of halluci-nation: believing one's own [rhetoric]. I assumed that if 'truth' were known, it would be acted on and that working programs would be replicated."[33]

The necessary haste with which the study was conceived and executed, in combi-nation with Dr. Froomkin's assumption that "truth" would not have to be marketed, meant that no plans were made at the outset to disseminate the "It Works" studies. In fact, according to Gilbert Austin, the existence of the series was not even widely known within USOE or DHEW:

> [It has been] very difficult to find out what provision for the dissemination of the exemplary programs the original contract had made. To the best of my knowledge there were no plans made ahead of time to distribute these particular documents. The documents were first made available in the Office of Education in September 1968 and there was no knowledge of them on the part of many people until November 1968. . . . no allocations of money were made *nor* were there any *specific objectives* set up that the dissemination was to accomplish. One of the things that continues to amaze me is how many different things the Office of Education is doing that are similar and that so few people over there know about. The information flow within the Office of Education itself is very poor.[34] [Emphasis in original]

The general lack of interest displayed by LEAs in the AIR findings suggests that both Dr. Froomkin and the ASPE analysts made assumptions about the way deci-sions are made at the local level that are not entirely consistent with the realities of the local school policy system. Froomkin's belief that "truth" would be self-executing assumes a particular notion of how decisions are made and classroom policies are set at the local level. These expectations presume that the bringing about of reform or effective change will mainly be a matter of demonstrating the efficacy of a given innovation and that once the model is observed, it will be adopted by local practitioners.[35] An assumption about the self-executing nature of informa-tion underestimates or overlooks the multiplicity of influences that determine local school policy.

Local school policy is formed by many different considerations and constraints; only one of these multiple determinants (albeit an important one) is academic achievement or program effectiveness. An innovative or eager local project or school administrator cannot simply "require" the adoption of an educational strategy, even though it appears to be a promising alternative to current practice. Jeanne S. Chall, for example, has observed how little the conclusions of research have influenced the teaching of reading.[36] The explanation for the lack of impact of research evidence upon practice has to do with more than just the instability of knowledge. Local decisions of this type must be responsive to a number of sources of pressure from public, private, lay, and professional interest groups. And the values and priorities of each group are often not congruent.[37] For example, low-income parents may want a program that more explicitly emphasizes basic skills, while middle-income parents are interested in "the latest thing"; the school board may be reluctant to invest more money in the implementation of a new program; teachers may be unwilling to expend effort in implementing a program that requires retraining. Thus, within this organizational context, policy decisions typically are based on considerations beyond "evidence." Information is viewed and interpreted by each party in the light of its own vested interests and its own perceptions of consequence.

The existence of these countervailing powers within the local policy system generates what James S. Coleman calls a "conservative tendency" in school behavior:

> ... there is one general tendency of bureaucratic organizations [which] shapes the direction of [administrative] incentives. That is the equilibrating and self-maintaining character of bureaucratic organizations, what may be called the conservative tendency of such systems. For the primary interest of occupants of roles in a bureaucratic organization is toward self-maintenance and thus the manifestation of those interests in organizational behavior is ... not to disturb the functioning of the organization.[38]

The importance of equilibrium maintenance as a constraint means that the perceived response of important interest groups may eclipse the objective merits of a proposed course of action. Consequently, local action in behalf of formal school goals (such as academic achievement) is often contingent upon the congruence of the proposed action with maintenance of system status quo.

This conservative tendency has important consequences for ASPE's and Froomkin's expectations for the role of information. It suggests that school administrators will usually reject rapid or radical change that might upset the equilibrium of the organization, despite its purported educational value. Coleman contends:

> ... whenever [the administrator] considers an action ... which he believes might increase achievement, but which might upset the organizational equilibrium, he has a strong negative incentive against upsetting the equilibrium, and incentive to reject the action.[39]

Local implementation of "exemplary" models, then, may conflict with the more compelling administrative concern for maintaining stability of the school environment and the organizational status quo.[40]

Administrative interest in maintaining harmony in the school environment also puts a premium on predictable consequences for any proposed course of action. A school administrator would like to be confident that a new strategy will work at least as well as the one it replaces, if not predictably better. Unfortunately, no such high order of validity or reliability attends the outcomes of educational innovations or strategies. Research in education does not yield the same sort of certainty as does a laboratory experiment.[41] Thus, although an administrator may be intrigued by Jacksonville's "Learning To Learn" program or by Buffalo's "Plus Program," he cannot be sure that these models will also "work" for him in his school in the same way. Inherent in the adoption and implementation of any new strategy is the possibility of failure. Many school administrators, after weighing the possible gains of a new approach against the risks of failure and the subsequent organizational fallout, elect to stick with what they know, and outcomes they can more accurately anticipate.

Thus, a fallacy in the technologist's assumption about local actions and choices lies in the tacit equation of an individual actor's goals with the formal and explicit goals of schools as organizations.[42] Both Joseph Froomkin and Alice Rivlin, for example, equated the express goals or objectives of the school (academic achievement) with the goals and incentives guiding the action of individual participants in the local school policy system. This teleology of behavior suggests a market model of competition and a focus on "product." And, within such a market model, organizational survival is directly tied to ability of the organization to turn out a "better" product. Accordingly, this model posits that the administrative concern with information will be primarily determined by its potential to enhance a "product," not an assessment of its bureaucratic spin-off.[43] In reality, however, schools seldom operate in such a market-like setting.[44] In the absence of incentives that would turn primary administrative interest from maintenance of status quo to improvement of the educational product, it is unlikely that reform or revitalization of the educational system will come about in the manner ASPE originally presumed. On balance, the incentives operating in the educational policy system do not seem to run in that direction.

There is little congruence between the conditions under which an industrial manager operates and the milieu of the local school.[45] Even a superficial inspection of schools and the process of education indicates that the conditions attending the school function do not approximate those existing for private firms. Schools have little control over inputs—notably, money and students. No production function has been determined for the process of schooling; indeed, there is little agreement as to what the important variables of the equation should be.[46] There is only marginal agreement on preferred "output" or formal objectives for schools. And the state of the art of measurement is scarcely able at this time to provide clear and unequivocal evidence of success or failure.[47] It is not surprising, then, that local school districts generally have not rushed to implement "exemplary" strategies.

If this model of the incentives that influence local school policy suggests that "reform" is not likely to result from the mere identification of exemplary models, it also implies that the sort of reform Kennedy had in mind is in theory more consistent with the facts of life in the local school setting. Kennedy thought evaluation could provide parents with a new source of power. Kennedy hoped that parents could use this new power to make schoolmen pay attention to their particular priorities and preferences. He believed that political change was necessary to pedagogical change. Information, in Kennedy's view, could redefine the balance of power in the school policy setting. It is unlikely that a similar pressure to adopt more successful strategies emanating from federal agencies could pose the same threat as disruption in the immediate school environment. The federal government is too far removed from the local setting, and the local schools are too well protected by traditions of federalism and pluralism for federal directives to cause more than a ripple in the local policy system. Dissatisfied parents, Robert Kennedy expected, would be quite another matter.

But Kennedy underestimated the resistance of the system to this sort of public accounting. Local schools opposed this notion of accountability, and Kennedy's reform failed because the schools held predominant power. The schools could make sure that project evaluations would not be used to disrupt the school environment simply by not conducting them in the way Kennedy and other reformers expected. Many schools chose to head off possible dissatisfaction in the parent community and the school setting by publication of innocuous and idiosyncratic documents. Kennedy's expectations for the role of evaluation are consistent with the incentive structure influencing local school practice, but it may also be difficult to use evaluation in this way because of the predominant balance of power within the local educational system.

The impact of the AIR studies within the Title I policy system, then, suggests implications for both Kennedy's and ASPE's notions of reform. The AIR studies, unlike preceding Title I evaluation efforts, were above all self-serving: they were not motivated by expectations of reform but instead by the need to gather evidence that could advocate USOE policies and programs. ASPE initiated the impact, cost-benefit evaluation with the hope that the resulting information would make a difference in the quality of local practice and in the formulation of federal policy. The evaluation models pursued by ASPE have not had such an impact, but the AIR studies did make a substantive difference in the way people think about the components of compensatory education.

But the difference this information made is directly related to its support of the existing system, or status quo. Martin Rein observes that evaluation will seldom be used by those for whom it is intended if the evaluation challenges current practice:

> . . . research will be used by an organization to the extent that it does not bear on the central problems of the organization and to the extent that it avoids implications which deal with the organization's most central dynamics. (Of course, during internal power struggles, research may be picked up and used selectively.)[48]

The AIR series does not challenge the operational principles or central values of the policy system: The studies defend them. The "It Works" series is a public relations effort of the highest order. The programs selected for inclusion in the series could tell their communities and state educational agencies that they were among the "most effective" in the country. Educators at all levels were able to meet the challenge of Coleman by pointing to the AIR studies as evidence that schools can "work," as proof that local administrators are devising compensatory strategies for poor children, and that investment in education is justified as social policy. The AIR study made no comparisons, asked for no additional data, posed no embarrassing questions. The case studies were a boon, not only for USOE but for SEAs and LEAs across the country.

The success of the AIR series also is a counterpoint to the tension that exists between the federal (scientific) perception of evaluation and local preferences. Those evaluations initiated to enhance accountability or quantify program impact have generally been resisted by local programs, whereas descriptive evaluation of the type conducted by AIR has not encountered the same obstacles. Thus, the experience of Coleman Revisited and the AIR studies reinforces the suggestion raised by the experience of TEMPO and the national surveys—that the successful conduct and the consequent impact of an evaluation are often contingent on the extent to which the evaluation effort is congruent with dominant incentives in the local school policy system.

# Notes to Chapter 5

1. Joseph Froomkin came to USOE via IBM and the Department of the Army.
2. Interview, Joseph Froomkin, February 25, 1972.
3. See Michael W. Kirst, "Administrative Problems in Evaluation of Title I of the Elementary and Secondary Education Act," a paper included in an Urban Institute report on federal evaluation practices, December 1969, n.d., mimeo., p. 7.
4. Interview, Joseph Froomkin, February 25, 1972.
5. The study has also been called "Junior Coleman."
6. Interview, Joseph Froomkin, February 25, 1972.

7. Bayla F. White to Jack Biren, Memo, "Chief State School Officers Conference —Froomkin Presentation," June 24, 1968.

8. Interview, Bayla F. White, February 7, 1972. Similarly, another participant has remarked: "Joe Froomkin didn't understand bureaucracies or political systems." (Interview, Susan Smith, June 1972.)

9. Joseph S. Wholey to Alice Rivlin, Memo, "Title I Evaluation: 1967-1968 and Beyond," November 29, 1967, p. 2.

10. Interview, Bayla F. White, February 7, 1972.

11. Kirst, op. cit., p. 8.

12. A number of participants allege that Hereford's BESE staff "sabotaged" the Coleman Revisited study. It is claimed that Hereford dispatched a number of BESE "informants" to some of the more influential Chiefs to "warn" them of the forthcoming Froomkin proposal, and urge their opposition. (Interviews, February and June 1972.)

13. Interview, Bayla F. White, February 7, 1972.

14. Interview, Joseph Froomkin, February 25, 1972.

15. Interview, Bayla F. White, February 7, 1972.

16. Joseph Froomkin, Letter to CSSO, June 20, 1968.

17. Interview, Bayla F. White, February 7, 1972.

18. White to Biren, op. cit.

19. Some participants have said that Henry Dyer was brought in with specific instructions from Karl Hereford to "find a methodological reason for rejecting the Froomkin study plan." (Interviews, February and June 1972.)

20. Joseph S. Wholey and Bayla F. White, Letter to John W. Evans, Assistant Commissioner, Office of Program Planning and Evaluation, November 18, 1970.

21. Interview, Michael W. Kirst, July 31, 1972.

22. Interview, Joseph Froomkin, February 25, 1972.

23. D. G. Hawkridge, A. B. Chalupsky, and A. O. H. Roberts, *A Study of Selected Exemplary Programs for the Education of Disadvantaged Children, Parts I and II,* American Institutes for Research in the Behavioral Sciences, Palo Alto, California, September 1968.

24. Interview, Samuel Halperin, February 22, 1972.

25. Interview, Emerson Elliott, February 24, 1972.

26. Ibid.

27. Even ASPE has used the AIR findings. Many observers contend that the present "Right To Read" program was based on the AIR conclusion that investment in reading programs seems to have a greater probability of "success" in terms of achievement gain than expenditure on other compensatory services.

28. See, for example, Charles E. Silberman, *Crisis in the Classroom* (New York: Vintage Books, Inc., 1970), for a discussion of the instability of "success."

29. Personal communication, Michael J. Wargo. See also Michael J. Wargo et al., "Further Examination of Exemplary Programs for Educating Disadvantaged Children," American Institutes for Research in the Behavioral Sciences, Palo Alto, California, July 1971.

30. But, as ASPE analyst Alan Ginsburg has noted, there has really never been an investigation of the degree to which information was disseminated to the local school districts: "[USOE has provided the states] with literature on supposedly replicable programs. There has been no real follow-through. It is not known whether states have passed this information on to the local districts and if they have, whether these programs have really been replicated." (Alan Ginsburg et al., "Title I of ESEA—Problems and Prospects," DHEW paper, ca. 1970, p. 7.)

31. Interview, Joseph Froomkin, February 25, 1972.

32. Alice Rivlin to the Secretary, Memo, "Thoughts on the Department's Role in Education (Follow-up on Conversation of January 16)," January 27, 1969, p. 3.

33. Interview, Joseph Froomkin, February 25, 1972.

34. Gilbert R. Austin to Willard I. Zangwill, Memo, "Some Further Information on the Dissemination of the AIR 'It Works' Series," June 1, 1970. Indeed, so strained were the communications between the OPPE staff and the Title I staff that DCE was concurrently preparing a similar document, "Profiles in Quality Education," which detailed information about successful programs nominated by the SEAs. The DCE effort was initiated quite in ignorance of Froomkin's study at OPPE.

35. See, for example, R. Chin and K. Benne, "General Strategies for Effecting Changes in Human Systems," in W. G. Bennis, K. Benne, and R. Chin (eds.), *The Planning of Change*, 2d ed. (Toronto: Holt, Rinehart and Winston of Canada, Ltd., 1969); and Graham Allison, *Essence of Decision Making* (Boston: Little Brown & Co., Inc., 1971). Chin and Benne argue that these assumptions are part of an "empirical-rational" model of decisionmaking, and Allison includes them in his description of "Model I" or "The Rational Actor Model."

36. Jeanne S. Chall, *Learning To Read: The Great Debate* (New York: McGraw-Hill Book Company, 1967).

37. See, for example, the analysis of Frederick M. Wirt and Michael W. Kirst, *The Political Web of American Schools* (Boston: Little Brown & Co., Inc., 1972).

38. James S. Coleman, "Incentives in Education, Existing and Proposed," n.d., mimeo., p. 13.

39. Ibid.

40. This may be a partial explanation of the observed gap between innovation in name and innovation in reality. Formal adoption of an "innovation" appeases federal monitors and grants managers, while substantive adherence to familiar patterns of practice placates some parents, teachers, and line administrators.

41. See, for example, Benjamin S. Bloom, "Twenty-five Years of Educational Research," *American Educational Research Journal*, Vol. 3, 1966, pp. 211-221; and Richard A. Dershimer and Laurence Iannaccone, "Social and Political Influences on Educational Research," in R. M. W. Travers (ed.), *Second Handbook of Research on Teaching* (Chicago: Rand McNally & Company, 1973).

42. Daniel Katz and Robert L. Kahn, *The Social Psychology of Organizations* (New York: John Wiley & Sons, Inc., 1966).

43. See Robert E. Klitgaard, "Models of Educational Innovation and Implications for Research," P-4977 (Santa Monica, Calif., The Rand Corporation, March 1973).

44. The Voucher Demonstration and the Performance Contracting experiments are attempts to simulate the market settings of private firms for education.

45. Henry Levin argues that none of the conditions that underlie expectations for efficiency in the private sector exist in the educational policy arena: "Technical efficiency for an industry presumes that there exist: (1) managerial knowledge of the technical production process; (2) substantial managerial discretion over input mix; (3) a basic competitive environment with all of its attendant assumptions (freedom of entry, many firms, perfect information); (4) managerial knowledge of prices for both inputs and outputs; (5) an objective function that is consistent with maximizing output such as profit maximization; and (6) clear signals of success or failure (profits, losses, sales, costs, rate of return, share of market)." (Henry M. Levin, "Concepts of Economic Efficiency and Educational Production," paper presented at the Confer-

ence on Education as an Industry, sponsored by the National Bureau of Economic Research, New York, June 4-5, 1971.)

46. See, for example, Herbert Gintis, "Non-cognitive Outcomes of Schooling: Priorities for Research in the Economics of Education," n.d.; Zvi Griliches and William M. Mason, "Education, Income, and Ability," January 1972; Levin, op. cit.

47. See Robert E. Klitgaard and George Hall, *A Statistical Search for Unusually Effective Schools* (Santa Monica, Calif.: The Rand Corporation, 1973), monograph; Lee J. Cronbach and L. Furby, "How Should We Measure 'Change'—Or Should We?" *Psychological Bulletin,* Vol. 74, No. 1, 1970, pp. 68-80.

48. Martin Rein, *Social Policy: Issues of Choice and Change* (New York: Random House, Inc., 1970), p. 469.

# Chapter Six

# Belmont: Joint (Federal/State) Coordinated Evaluation Effort

• The expressly political nature of federal evaluation policy has been a recurring theme in the experience of evaluation prompted by Title I reporting requirements. These evaluation efforts were all shaped in important ways by the cross pressures over evaluation and the balance of power in the Title I policy arena. They were also disappointing to reformers. Federal efforts to evaluate compensatory education, generally, and Title I, specifically, came to little in terms of the expectations motivating them.

These evaluation efforts failed chiefly because reliable data on program accomplishments, specifically academic achievement, were not available. The tensions built into the Title I policy system—between federal evaluators and state and local administrators, and between lay and professional-interest groups—encouraged a defensive and promotional response to evaluation. The compromises that shaped the Kennedy and ASPE evaluation models were unable to dissolve these tensions.

The politicization of federal evaluation efforts reached its zenith with the planning and implementation of the Joint (Federal/State) Coordinated Evaluation Effort, or Belmont as this massive consolidated information reporting system is popularly known.

## THE BELMONT SYSTEM

In August 1968, a group of state and federal officials met at Belmont House, near Elkridge, Maryland, to discuss the creation of a joint federal-state task force on evaluation. The outgrowth of the meeting was Belmont, a new reporting, management, and evaluation system.

The Belmont project set itself five major objectives:[1]

1. To consolidate, into one comprehensive reporting system, Congressionally mandated statistical and evaluation reports in elementary and secondary education in federal, state, and local jurisdiction.

2. To reduce the amount of duplication and overlap in data collection.

3. To furnish useful data to Congress, USOE, SEA, and LEA by designing a system that would provide information for making decisions and an example on which

SEAs and LEAs could draw as they worked to improve their own information systems.

4. To act as a data base for federal and state evaluators, administrators, and planners.

5. To institutionalize federal data collection.

The data system subsequently established was calculated to meet federal, state, or local mandated annual reports in the following programs.[2]

| Congressional Mandated Report | USOE | SEA | LEA |
|---|---|---|---|
| ESEA I (general) | x | x | x |
| ESEA I (migrant) | x | x | — |
| ESEA I (neglected) | x | x | — |
| ESEA I (delinquent) | x | x | — |
| ESEA II | x | x | x |
| ESEA III | x | x | x |
| ESEA IV (402) | x | x | — |
| ESEA V (503) | x | x | — |
| ESEA V (505) | x | x | x |
| ESEA VII | x | — | x |
| ESEA VIII | x | — | x |
| NDEA III | x | x | x |
| NDEA V-A | x | x | — |
| Vocational Education | x | x | — |
| Follow Through | x | — | x |
| EDPA (Part B) | x | x | — |

Belmont Instruments and Guides included:[3]

A. Consolidated Program Information Report (CPIR)
B. Elementary School Survey (ESS) (informally referred to in the past as the Pupil Centered Instrument or PCI)
C. Secondary School Survey (SSS)
D. Preparing Evaluation Reports: A Guide for Authors
E. Common Status Measures (CSM)
F. Master Data Analysis Plan (MDAP)
G. SEA-Management Assessment System (MAS)
H. Anchor Test and New Cognitive Measures
I. User's Guides
J. Management Information System Project (MIS)

Belmont was a last ditch, all-out effort to revivify federal evaluation and to institutionalize a reporting system. The Belmont plan attempted to combine, under one administrative umbrella, the program reporting scheme that Kennedy had initiated and the impact survey model that had been developed in response to the disappointment of TEMPO. These previous evaluation efforts had been built on compromise; Belmont was based on explicit and careful manipulation of the dominant incentives and interests within the Title I policy system.

The principal architect of the Belmont system was Karl Hereford, head of BESE evaluation. Hereford came to BESE in February 1968 from the North Dakota State

Department of Education and was unhappy to find what he regarded as a passive USOE approach to program administration. Based on his experience in North Dakota,[4] Karl Hereford thought that consolidation of program administration was a strategy that could pave the way for a stronger USOE role. He believed that Title I and other categorical elementary and secondary education programs could be made to "work" if they were made to work *through* the existing SEA incentive structure. Since continuance and expansion of federal support are powerful incentives, Hereford reasoned that discretionary program dollars could be used as a lever or a "carrot" to force SEA compliance with categorical objectives for federal programs such as Title I. "He saw the discretionary programs as backstopping [the whole of] state grant programs."[5]

Thus, soon after he arrived at USOE, Hereford moved to gain control for BESE of elementary and secondary education programs:

> He wanted to consolidate programs in BESE so he could run it. Hereford thought he could manipulate Estes [Bureau Chief]. Only through the consolidation could he gain enough power to implement Bureau objectives.[6]

This straightforward plan of programmatic consolidation ran into trouble in that it touched the sensitive issue of organizational status. Dr. Nolan Estes, BESE chief, stood to gain staff positions and new money from Hereford's plan, and so supported it.[7] Conversely, administrators who would lose staff and resources if their programs were swept up in a consolidation move quickly objected. They argued that consolidation would result in less effective administration because important expertise, personal contacts, and oversight would be lost.[8]

Hereford's plan to achieve administrative consolidation was abandoned in the face of these objections from within USOE. The Belmont plan for a consolidated reporting scheme was subsequently developed by Hereford as a way to let "information" run interference for his plan of programmatic control. Michael Kirst commented:

> Hereford came at all this through what was a purely rational concept. An information system was part of a total planning strategy and could therefore be used as a wedge to get into the whole planning package.[9]

Karl Hereford's notion of enhancing BESE's leverage over elementary and secondary education programs was essentially a three-step process that involved, first, control of program information systems; second, increased federal involvement in program planning; and, consequently, third, more control for USOE and BESE over state and local implementation of federal programs.[10]

The motivation that led to BESE's Belmont plan, then, was different from those generating previous Title I evaluation efforts. Although the Belmont system contained the evaluation models suggested by other reformers, Karl Hereford and his staff did not see *information* per se as a vehicle of reform in the way that Robert Kennedy and ASPE analysts did. Instead, BESE's Belmont staff saw the construction and implementation of a consolidated *information system* as the first step in administrative and programmatic reform. Hereford wanted to upgrade local education practices not through information, but by means of a more aggressive USOE role.

Implementation of the Belmont plan required the appropriation of substantial new funds for BESE evaluation, as well as the cooperation of other federal and state participants in the Title I policy system.

BESE's efforts to gather support for the Belmont idea were explicitly political in their appeal to dominant constraints and incentives. The banner of knowledge and efficiency was raised to argue to ASPE that Belmont could succeed where the national surveys and the three-tiered reporting scheme had failed. According to Richard Jaeger, BESE evaluator, Belmont "is an attempt to make rational a complex set of decision processes." And Dr. Hereford wrote:

> In producing a more efficient system, the single data base for several programs would reduce the collection of redundant data, and allow comparable cross-program information to be collected and total impact to be studied, more in line with the purposes of the ESEA legislation.[11]

In a memo to ASPE analyst Jack Biren, Jaeger expressed BESE's confidence that Belmont could contribute to the "renewal" of American education at all levels:

> ... the plan is unique in several respects.... the plan presumes the use of evaluation as a tool for program managers. Evaluation thus becomes a positive implement for the renewal of American education at all levels of government.... within present personnel constraints of the Office, through proper program management, we can do a credible, even superior, job of elementary and secondary education evaluation.[12]

The BESE evaluation plan presented to ASPE outlined the role of information in the educational policy arena and spoke specifically to ASPE's point of view and data needs, as well as to the concerns expressed by the Secretary's Office:

> Management is a vital link in the renewal of American education. Evaluation is a necessary tool for effective education management. For our policies to be effective, management actions at governmental levels must be sound, and the research base connecting project implementation and educational results must be utilized correctly. Evaluation allows the testing and remediation of both requirements for program effectiveness.... evaluation must support policy formation, program development and program management by providing answers to critical policy questions for federal decision makers and state managers and school district program directors.[13]

Both the Secretary's Office and ASPE supported the Belmont idea because the new system promised to provide the information necessary to PPBS, and to gather it more efficiently.

In presenting the Belmont plan to Congress—with whom the funding decision ultimately rested—BESE again invoked the canons of efficiency and rational planning. The Title I statutory evaluation requirements were parlayed into a request for funds to support a data system as massive as Belmont:

> At the present level of fund commitment, we will be attempting to secure data vital for legislative planning, program impact evaluation and administrative decisionmaking through an expenditure of two one-hundredths of one percent of our total educational budget. In short, we will be spending scant thousands to plan the expenditure of billions. In the private sector, such a practice would be viewed as lunatic.[14]

Congress responded to this "irrationality" by substantially increasing support for USOE evaluation, thereby furnishing BESE with new resources for Belmont.

BESE's marketing of Belmont within USOE played on different incentives. Belmont was presented to DCE as a way to quiet the "violent objections" the states were beginning to raise about the extent of federal reporting requirements, as well as about federal requests for achievement data. In a memo informing Joseph Froomkin of OPPE about plans for Belmont, Dr. Estes wrote that the plan was

> designed to strengthen administrative and policy decisions with respect to the programs administered by BESE. . . . The plan is so constructed as to satisfy the complex requirements for valid data as well as to meet constructively the sensitive conditions under which evaluation information is collected.[15]

And Hereford did not tiptoe around the states, but went directly to CSSO and sought the Chiefs' support for his plan. Whereas ASPE and Mauch had reached a testy consensus with CSSO as they built a national survey design, and while Froomkin challenged the Chiefs, lost, and subsequently bypassed them altogether, Hereford created a role for them. He brought them into the center of the evaluation policy arena, as nominal full partners in the federal evaluation effort. Hereford wrote:

> This OE plan to develop and install a joint federal state information system —accompanied by federal program evaluation and federal technical assistance for state and local evaluation efforts—takes a long step forward recognizing the genuine need of the states for evaluation of *their* (not *our*) objectives. . . . Belmont is important as a demonstration that federal and state administrators can discover and satisfy common data needs for their similar but not identical purposes.[16] [Emphasis in original]

Hereford argued to the Chiefs that cooperation with Belmont would allow them to have a voice in the determination of federal evaluation policy—something they had wanted since the passage of ESEA.

In addition to entree into the arena of federal evaluation policy, reduction in the amount of paper work required by federal programs was another important incentive offered for state cooperation with the Belmont plan. Federal red tape had long been a gripe among schoolmen. As a practitioner from Vermont said: "If it is true that public schools are not doing as good a job as they might be, one of the major reasons is that they are slowly suffocating in a sea of Federal and State paper work."[17] In presenting his ideas to CSSO, Hereford implied, further, that successful implementation of the Belmont scheme would mean not only a consolidation of reporting, but also the end of new federal requests for local and state data.

Regardless of their view of Belmont itself, most participants in and observers of the initiation of Belmont agree that Hereford was politically and tactically masterful in involving the states. Michael Kirst commented that "Hereford worked through the states because he knew that no one at OE could challenge the states. Karl Hereford understood where the power was and so he went to the power."[18] And another participant observer in the implementation of Belmont has said that "Hereford sold a bill of goods to fewer than a half-dozen of the strongest Chiefs. They then talked their colleagues into it. The genius of Hereford was that he knew that as long as Belmont was entangled with the states, OE couldn't pull out."[19]

Response to BESE's Belmont idea within USOE was not enthusiastic. Joseph Froomkin at OPPE did not support the Belmont scheme, but chose not to make an issue of it. Froomkin's objections to Belmont were substantive and methodological. In Froomkin's view, the program impact and survey data that Belmont proposed to gather were not data that would contribute either to knowledge or change.[20] Michael Kirst recalled that "Froomkin washed his hands of Belmont. It wasn't his kind of thing, but he said he wasn't going to fight it. Froomkin and Piccariello [Froomkin's deputy] made a conscious and explicit decision to stay out of it."[21]

Others within the Office of Education, however, could not choose to ignore Belmont. Just as Dr. Hereford's original suggestion of program consolidation threatened to take positions and funds away from other policy units, so did Belmont threaten individual and unit status:

> Title I program people [in DCE] really balked when Hereford announced his massive data system. Belmont was a threat to those people whose job it was to collect data about programs. Karl Hereford's system would take their jobs away.[22]

Larry LaMoure, who worked closely with Hereford in the development of Belmont, said, "Hereford built an empire. He took staff away from Title I [DCE] and that made the people in Title I very bitter."[23]

Despite this opposition from within USOE, Belmont was begun in late 1968 with ambitious promises to gather the data both breeds of reformers had anticipated:

> With increasing amounts of federal, state and local monies being invested in education and with an increasing concern over the effectiveness of educational institutions, and practices, educational administrators, teachers, and parents need to know what the financial investment in education is achieving. The Belmont system has been developed to meet this need by providing hard data on a variety of educational delivery systems and programs as well as the public involved.[24]

Belmont, in practice, has fulfilled neither these information objectives nor the longer-range administrative goals Hereford had in mind. Belmont, in almost every respect, has been a very expensive flop. The cost of Belmont in dollar terms is difficult to estimate; its true costs were hidden at the outset and there is no accurate way to assess the investment of time and resources at the state and local level. However, it has been estimated that the net cost of Belmont from 1968 through 1972 is "at least 40 million dollars."[25]

## BELMONT'S UNMET PROMISE

The expressed objective of Belmont—to provide policy relevant data to the states and the federal government—was unmet. In a memo to the Title I Task Force, Susan Smith, then of BESE's Planning and Evaluation Unit, noted these deficits in Belmont activities:

> Relatively little emphasis has been placed by the Belmont staff in the following areas:
>
> —preparation of concise reports with data for use within OE in program decisionmaking
>
> —preparation of feedback to states and local districts on national survey data
>
> —preparation of Congressional reports
>
> —obtaining the assistance of more highly trained analytical types who know educational evaluation
>
> —specific assistance to the DCE staff

Belmont should place less emphasis on the administrative management process of coordination within the elaborate set of Belmont Committees and more emphasis on the quality of projects undertaken.[26]

As of spring, 1972, there was no substantive analysis and interpretation of Belmont data, and no statistical report to Congress based on Belmont data (the 1968 survey report was the last report sent to Congress). Although the data from the 1970 survey were analyzed, they were not interpreted and no report was written. In the spring of 1972, the 1970 survey data existed as approximately 1200 coded tables, meaningless to anyone except those in possession of the elusive code book. At that time, no analysis had been done of the 1971 data. And there was no feedback or "products" to the states. A 1970 ASPE memo concerning Belmont observed that "many states are beginning to ask the question—when are we going to get some benefits from all the data the Belmont project is collecting?"[27]

Nor was there use or feedback of the Belmont data at the federal level. A former Belmont staff member reports that she was assigned the task of reviewing 2 years of Senate and House testimony to find some evidence that the data supplied by the CPIR instrument (Consolidated Program Information Report) had been used by USOE officials and lawmakers. The objective of this research was to find incidence of use "so letters could be written to the states to tell them how their efforts had been used and that it [their participation] had all been worthwhile."[28] However, no such evidence of use of the Belmont data could be found in USOE testimony before the committees of Congress.[29]

Belmont also failed in another respect. Despite the trade-offs made to the states, and the nominal control offered the SEAs over the use and design of evaluation, and despite the court paid the critical educational interest groups, Belmont was no more successful than preceding evaluation efforts in collecting nationally representative achievement data. Proportionately, Belmont has returned no more achievement data than did previous federal evaluation efforts.[30]

Susan Smith did an exploratory study to estimate the impact of Belmont on the quality and quantity of information on Title I received by USOE. She found that there were *no differences* in either the quality, type, or the amount of data returned by the local programs and the SEAs as a result of Belmont.[31] And, as ASPE analyst Gilbert Austin notes, the states have not changed the manner of their response to federal evaluation requirements as a result of Belmont:

> In the specific guidelines which went to the various state educational agencies for the preparation of their 1968-1969 annual reports, there was a request that the state should provide the Federal Office with *hard data* on the results of Title I activities. It was specifically noted that this was not to be opinion, and it was not to be based on subjective judgments. It was to be based on hard data. Most of the state reports show little, if any, evidence of having complied with this specific direction. Most of the reports suggest that whatever they are saying about Title I and its achievements is based much more on their subjective judgments than on test evidence. There seems to be little evidence that the State Departments of Education have provided much leadership in complying with the federal requirement for the collection of hard data, either at state or local levels. Until this is done, there is little hope of much progress.[32] [Emphasis in original]

The Belmont system failed to collect reliable and representative data on student achievement and so the descriptive data and the background variables were useless to ASPE analysts interested in correlational studies.

If an important question posed by the Belmont experience is whether cajoling, compromise, positive incentives, and the leadership of someone as politically skilled as Karl Hereford can breathe life into federal evaluation efforts, and federal attempts to establish an information system, the answer must be no. With the implementation of Belmont, everything about evaluation changed in form, but in terms of outcome, very little was different.

The failure of Belmont to live up to its promises left USOE unable to meet its own reporting and data requirements. The Belmont system had assumed responsibility for "all Congressionally mandated statistical and evaluation reports in elementary and secondary education in federal, state and local jurisdictions."[33] Participation in the Belmont system met not only the mandated reporting requirements for ESEA Title I, but for fifteen other USOE programs as well. Thus Belmont's failure left USOE bereft of information not just on ESEA Title I, whose statutory reporting requirements had paved the way for a consolidated reporting scheme, but also on the activities and achievements of fifteen other programs in the area of elementary and secondary education.

The USOE Commissioner, S. P. Marland, Jr., was consequently unable to fulfill the annual reporting requirements outlined by the 1967 ESEA until the spring of 1972. The report that the Commissioner submitted to Congress[34] suggests that little had been learned in 7 years of compensatory education evaluation.[35] Commissioner Marland's report is remarkable chiefly in its similarity to the ambiguous and promotional USOE documents that began to appear with the first annual Title I report. The caveats raised concerning the quality and nature of the data echo the preface Commissioner Howe wrote to the first annual Title I report 5 years before. In a draft document prepared for inclusion in the Commissioner's report, OPPE evaluators wrote the following assessment of "The Status of Educational Evaluation":

> This report falls far short of providing ... the kind of rigorous, objective, quantitative evaluation data which both the executive and legislative branches should have if good funding and management decisions are to be made about these programs. ... We must simply note that systematic efforts at evaluating education programs have only a brief history ... not least because of lack of funds to carry out such studies.[36]

Indeed, although Commissioner Marland acknowledged Title I was "the most wide-ranging, ambitious, and heavily funded of OE administered programs targeted directly on the disadvantaged," after 6 years and several billion dollars of Title I funding, the Commissioner was unable to make a substantive, comprehensive, or definitive report on the accomplishments of Title I. He was only able to report that:

> The widest sample of achievement data yet examined on students assisted by Title I ... showed that children at all these grade levels were progressing at a rate approaching the norm for nondisadvantaged students. However, even the realization of a normal rate of achievement leaves the Title I-assisted student behind his peers since students must show pronounced learning deficits to be eligible for Title I help.

> National surveys conducted in 1968, 1969, and 1970 indicate that Title I has been relatively successful in targeting money on school districts serving the disadvantaged population and in focusing upon many of the critical needs of that population. However, many improvements need to be made in the delivery system.[37]

The utility and the credibility of the Commissioner's 1972 report were diminished by the failure of Belmont to fulfill its promise to do a "superior job of elementary and secondary education evaluation." The platitudes and qualified conclusions contained in the Commissioner's annual report suggest instead that the approximately $52 million[38] estimated to have been spent on education evaluation since the passage of Title I have done little to provide a social report on federal investments in education or to increase the knowledge base that could give substantive guidance to educational policymaking.

The failure of Belmont has also had an impact on USOE's other major reporting responsibility, the submission of the annual budget. Recent USOE budget submissions have drawn sharp criticism from the executive level and from the Secretary's Office. As Belmont assumed full responsibility for elementary and secondary evaluation in late 1968, and as the "It Works" series wore thin as a source of budget justifications, USOE had little program data to draw upon. Charles Miller, OMB, complained about the quality of USOE budget submissions in a memo to John Ottina, USOE Deputy Commissioner for Planning, Evaluation, and Management:

> [In the past] it was my view that OE did the best and timeliest work of any of the operating agencies on budget submittals. . . . It seemed to me that the reason for this was not simply that the OE budget shop did a better technical job. Their relationship with OE programs was such that they could request and receive timely and well prepared products. I am sorry to say I no longer feel this is as true. There has been a significant decline. . . . Several of the OE budget justifications that I saw were really very poor and practically nothing was timely. Yet the same cast of characters exist in the Budget Division with I believe the same ability to produce and the same motivation. The difference, it seems to me, is that the budget no longer occupies a very high priority in the policy levels of OE.[39]

In view of the failure of Belmont to result in any useable data, Miller most likely misspecified the cause of the decline in the quality of USOE budget submissions. The USOE budget justifications were "poor" and were not "timely" because the data on which they were based were also poor and out of date. Not surprisingly, the point at which Miller notes the decline in USOE preparations was the point at which Belmont took over the major portion of USOE evaluation. Further, Joseph Froomkin had left OPPE, and so the sorts of "trend" studies and case studies that he did and that OMB found useful were no longer being done. As Belmont got underway, and twenty-seven states joined the system, many of the nonparticipating states stopped sending in annual reports altogether.[40] The data that were returned were not being analyzed. Timely and useful data on elementary and secondary education programs just did not exist, so rather than reflecting a change in USOE priority for budget submissions, thinness of the USOE budget more likely represents USOE's attempt to make a silk purse from a sow's ear.

The reasons for the failure of the Belmont system are not elusive or obscure. In fact, the major components underlying the failure of Belmont parallel those that crippled the Kennedy reporting scheme. Neither the three-tiered reporting scheme nor the Belmont system was implemented with substantive attention to the type of information the system should generate or how the information would be used within the policy system. Just as the 1965 evaluation guidelines were seen as a temporary measure that would establish the precedent of evaluation as gently as possible, so too were the bulk of BESE efforts aimed at finding financial and political support for the expensive new information system—simply getting the Belmont plan off the ground. Hereford and his staff perceived the most difficult problem of Belmont to lie simply in its implementation. Thus, BESE's Belmont staff (like DCE evaluators in 1965) left many of the substantive details to be worked out once the information system was financed and underway.

Although the communications and publications issued by the Belmont staff implied that considerable planning had gone into Belmont,[41] development of the Belmont structure and data-collection instruments proceeded largely on an ad hoc basis.[42] Little, if any, of the planning one would expect of a "tool for sound program management" actually took place. Certainly, much of the planning for the Belmont system, like the formulation of the ESEA evaluation guidelines, was done under severe time constraints. The substantial sum Congress appropriated for Belmont in March of 1969 had to be spent by the close of the fiscal year in June.

However, even when free of these time pressures, the planning and development of Belmont displayed scant attention to the quality and function of the information Belmont was to gather. Just as the DCE staff was interested in 1965 in the evaluation guidelines as *guidelines,* and their reception in the Title I policy system, so did the BESE Belmont staff focus on the Belmont information system as a *system,* not on the quality and function of the data to be collected. The planning for Belmont did not display the orderly, focused, or thoughtful planning that would suggest overriding concern for policy-relevant information. One participant in the Belmont planning stages recalls that the planning "was like a gin mill. I saw Karl Hereford drum up ideas for contracts off the top of his head and then ask another member of the meeting to write up the RFP."[43] Nor were the Belmont instruments developed with careful attention to usefulness or policy relevance. According to a staff member, "The data questionnaires were never designed with use in mind. Nobody ever thought about what a final report should look like and then go back and think through the analysis plan."[44]

Other participants have commented that the awarding of Belmont contracts reflected in large part the desire of the Belmont staff to establish a minimum financial precedent for the new system, rather than the quality of product:

> I asked that the PDI [Project Descriptor Instrument] contract not be funded because the only two bidders were clearly incompetent for the job. But Don Rose and Larry LaMoure said that one of the bidders had to get the contract. That was a quarter of a million dollar contract![45]

BESE's overriding concern with establishing a system can be inferred from the fact that the program management and policy planning appropriate to Belmont's stated objectives did not take place until 2 and 3 years after the system was initiated, and then only at the prodding of the ASPE staff.[46] In 1970, Michael Kirst, now on the faculty of Stanford's Graduate School of Education, was hired to construct a management system for the Belmont project.[47] In 1971, Dr. Kirst was commissioned to formulate policy questions appropriate for the Belmont information system.[48]

Nor did there exist the symbiotic relationship between evaluators and program personnel that would suggest that the rhetoric about "informed decisionmaking" was more than verisimilitude. The federal policy units most interested in the outcome of Belmont—DCE and ASPE—were rarely consulted. For the most part, Belmont planning was done by BESE alone. Almost everyone else at the federal level was kept in the dark on Belmont:

> After all the lovely talk about coordination and consolidation to improve the effectiveness of scarce resources [by Nolan Estes], Hereford proceeded to describe a program which apparently has been funded within the past few weeks to train state evaluation personnel. Dave Pollen hit the ceiling since

Bureau of Research knows nothing about the project and we both suspect that Froomkin is in the dark about it. ... [The] Hereford creation, conceived and executed without consulting other parts of OE ... doesn't bode well for cooperative planning.[49]

A former Belmont staff member commented:

Larry LaMoure and Karl Hereford never did prepare anything that would let anyone know where they were. They tried to keep relations with outsiders as muddy as possible. They never put any summative statements on paper. One could never find out how much things cost or where they were [in the development of the Belmont plan].[50]

The program people themselves, both at federal and state levels, were consulted only in the interest of "good form." Title I staff in DCE, for example, recall that the Belmont staff only rarely asked about their information needs, priorities, or preferences. Such solicitations were mainly pro forma, and the substance of the suggestions was ignored. For example, a former BESE staff member said that "all DCE wanted was process information, so we [BESE] just forgot about it when we put Belmont together."[51]

An additional incongruence between rhetoric and reality is seen in the role of the states. Although Belmont is formally known as the "Joint (Federal/State) Coordinated Evaluation Effort," the involvement of the state program people was no more substantive or significant than that of federal program personnel.[52] The illusion of a federal/state "partnership" was important to protect Belmont from attack from within USOE. However, the "partnership" had scant basis in reality; the states were allowed to contribute little to the design and implementation of Belmont. A former Belmont staff member has said:

The whole Belmont thing was gerrymandered and engineered. The object in meeting with the states was not discussion but to jam Belmont down their throats. Belmont was a forum for Herefordism and later for LaMourism.[53]

Another staff member concurs:

The state meetings with the feds weren't work sessions, they were political strategy sessions. Hereford used them to make the states believe that he was following their wishes, but in fact he didn't pay any attention to what the states wanted. The states had little or no part in the actual planning of Belmont.[54]

The only substantive influence of the states is seen in the few compromises Karl Hereford made to secure agreement from the Chiefs concerning the collection of achievement data. Hereford agreed to develop and include the CPIR, a fiscal document to replace the narratives required by the Title I regulations, in return for standardized achievement data:

This was the one trade Hereford made in order to get them to give nationally representative achievement data. Apparently the states wanted state fiscal data.[55]

As part of the "trade," BESE agreed to constraints upon USOE analysis of achievement data:

USOE agreed that individual [LEA or SEA] forms would not be examined:

that OE would put it all in a computer and then look only at aggregate data.[56]

Any additional "joint planning" that was done, however, was simply undertaken to keep the state/federal coalition alive. On balance, the chief contribution the states made to the Belmont system was their political influence.

The implementation of Belmont evidenced the same absence of substantive federal interest that had characterized the drafting and administration of the original evaluation guidelines. And, somewhat paradoxically, just as the passive role of USOE and the SEAs left the Kennedy evaluation scheme in the hands of those who opposed it from the outset—the local schoolmen—so did the machinations and negotiations necessary to the launching of Belmont leave predominant power in the hands of the other group that had long opposed federal evaluations, CSSO. A former USOE analyst remarked:

> While the state people feel they lost, in that they didn't achieve the degree of influence over federal evaluation policy they had been promised, I think that the SEA people really coopted federal responsibility for the evaluation of Title I. *Congress mandated a national evaluation requirement for Title I, and then OE and Hereford let into the policy group the very people who objected to evaluation.* But this may have been politically very astute on Hereford's part.[57] [Emphasis added]

Karl Hereford had a notion about program consolidation that he believed could upgrade the effectiveness of USOE leadership and local programs. The establishment of an information system was the first step in this plan; the information itself was of secondary importance. Thus the force of Hereford's energies and the energy of his staff focused on the establishment of the system, and the substantive evaluation policy was shaped—in the absence of a strong federal plan or policy—by the fears and concerns of schoolmen. Seven years of experience with ESEA had given schoolmen ample demonstration of the fickleness of federal initiatives, and the inability of federal officials either to stick to their objectives or to enforce them. Although the BESE Belmont staff offered—for the first time in federal evaluation history—explicitly positive reasons for the SEAs and LEAs to go along with the evaluation effort, it may be that many program personnel had scant faith in the longevity of this new federal program and the promises that accompanied it. Genevieve Dane of DCE has remarked:

> People at the SEA didn't believe it [the promise of Belmont]; program people at the LEA and federal level didn't believe it either. But nobody could fight Hereford at the time. Hereford rammed it through. Commitments were made to the states: "If you do this, we'll never ask you for any other data." But times and interests change. The states know this. You can't hold to such promises. You may have to go after massive data for some other issues.[58]

Program people at the local, state, and federal levels often view "the latest" federal objective as transitory. An attitude of "this too shall pass" is commonly encountered among program people charged with implementing the most recent bureaucratic initiative. Whether or not the SEAs believed Karl Hereford, they likely had little confidence in the long-range commitments he made for the federal government. Hereford, too, would pass. Perception of government initiatives and commitments as inherently unstable, together with a basic defensiveness about achievement measures, most probably will continue to frustrate federal attempts to secure objective, reliable program-outcome measures.

There is further parallel between the experience of the Kennedy scheme and the Belmont plan. Just as the most voluble, immediate, and critical response to the failure of the Kennedy three-tiered reporting scheme came primarily from ASPE, so too did the failure of Belmont bring a swift and trenchant response from ASPE analysts. But whereas the ASPE response to the disappointment of the Kennedy reporting scheme essentially urged the program people to try harder, their response to the failure of Belmont was to sweep evaluation effectively from the purview of USOE programs. BESE had made extravagant promises concerning the potential of Belmont in an effort to generate support for the mandated reporting system, and to pave the way for further consolidation. But, at the same time, the pressure upon ASPE for useful, reliable information had been consistent and firm since the debut of PPBS in 1965. Thus, the failure of Belmont was not simply a disappointment to ASPE. In light of the Secretary's (and the President's) continuing stress on evaluation and program information, the nonfulfillment of Belmont's promises posed a challenge to ASPE's position and credibility within the policy system.

The demise of Belmont and evaluation within BESE was in the air and seemed inevitable even before Dr. Hereford left BESE in the summer of 1970 to become Dean of Education at the Virginia Polytechnic Institute. But in his wake, Karl Hereford left considerable bitterness at both the state and federal level over Belmont and its outcomes:

> By the time Hereford left, there was an enormous amount of dissatisfaction. Golden boy's promises hadn't come through. There was no feedback, no participation by the states and the amount of data collection had not been reduced.[59]

Or, as another participant put it, "Just before Hereford left, all of the balls he had in the air were about to crash down."[60] With Dr. Hereford's departure, the Belmont system lost its major source of political strength. Larry LaMoure, Hereford's successor, was not able to keep together the coalition that had been formed to support Belmont. But it is unlikely that even the political skills of Hereford could have mollified ASPE analysts by that time.

## BELMONT'S FAILURE AND FALLOUT

ASPE's disenchantment with Belmont ensued with the results of the first year of Belmont's operation and was based on absence of nationally representative achievement data. Dr. James Abert, Deputy Assistant Secretary for Evaluation and Monitoring, conducted a study of evaluation at DHEW that focused chiefly on USOE evaluation activities. Abert's investigation resulted in an extensive and detailed memo to Secretary Richardson, which presented an analysis of USOE evaluation activities since the implementation of the Belmont system. The report argued that BESE personnel had neither the time, interest, nor incentives to undertake the type of evaluation that could be useful to federal policymakers. In Abert's view, program people perceived evaluation as a threat and had no reason to work hard at it. Abert wrote to the Secretary: "Left to their own devices, program managers did not initiate effective evaluations. They did not use their resources for evaluation."[61] Michael Timpane, former Director of Educational Planning for ASPE, concurred with Abert's conclusions:

> Program operators are ambiguous [about evaluation] for much the same reasons as Congress. One, they do want to improve their programs. But

second, . . . they're worried about their own egos and sub-government surviv-al. The temptation is very strong for program operators to do non-threaten-ing evaluation.[62]

In his memo to the Secretary, Abert recommended radical changes in the ad-ministration and philosophy of USOE evaluation. Abert contended that USOE evaluation would be crippled as long-as it was tied to the program units; he recom-mended removing responsibility for the evaluation of Title I and other categorical programs from BESE and centralizing USOE evaluation activities within OPPE. This recommendation had important implications for BESE, since the transferral of all USOE evaluation to OPPE would mean the loss of Belmont evaluation funds and staff positions.

Further, James Abert was a proponent of impact evaluation.[63] Accordingly, he sought someone to head OPPE who would conduct USOE evaluation in this style. Thus Dr. John W. Evans, who was responsible for OEO's Westinghouse-Ohio impact study of the Head Start program, was brought to USOE with the charge to centralize evaluation within OPPE and to begin undertaking impact evaluations.

Evans saw BESE's administration of Belmont as conflicting with his own plans for strengthening OPPE. John F. Hughes, former Director of DCE and now Assistant Superintendent for Schools, diplomatically stated: "Belmont ran afoul of the statisti-cal program OPPE wanted."[64] The issue of Belmont was not, however, simply one of conflicting statistical approaches to evaluation. The issue of Belmont was the power and status that the Belmont system represented. Evans didn't want a compet-ing evaluation shop within USOE; he and others also wanted the resources of Belmont.[65] Larry LaMoure interpreted the demise of Belmont and BESE's loss of evaluation responsibilities to OPPE primarily in terms of predominant powers with-in the federal policy system:

> ASPE, Ginsburg, Abert and all really let Belmont and BESE have it; OPPE [Evans] converged on BESE at the same time. So BESE and Belmont lost everything. Belmont was caught in a big power struggle as to who is going to run OE.[66]

Thus, after Karl Hereford left BESE, Belmont became a bureaucratic and politi-cal donnybrook, which involved substantial funds and staff positions. One staff member, whose own position was traded off numerous times, commented:

> After Hereford left, everybody got into the fight over Belmont. They weren't fighting over substantive issues of evaluation. They were fighting for the money, power and positions attached to Belmont.[67]

Michael Kirst agrees that the primary interest in Belmont centered on the increase in power that would come to whomever "won the prize":

> I urged Hereford to run to Guilford [as BESE control of Belmont was threat-ened by Evans], because she had the only shop in town [National Center for Educational Statistics] with a serious interest in information. But Davies wanted Belmont, and he had the Commissioner's ear. Davies wanted the money and positions only. He wasn't interested in information.[68]

It is fitting perhaps that what began as an expressly political effort to establish a new information system should come to such an expressly political end. But even though the rise and fall of Belmont had little to do with issues of information or methodology, the failure of Belmont has had important implications for Title I evaluation within USOE and for the different expectations of reform that generated the Title I mandate to evaluate. The effective demise of Belmont marked the end of federal efforts to resuscitate the Title I information system that had been created in response to Robert Kennedy's demands, and that ASPE analysts had hoped would provide input to PPBS. As a result of the collapse of the Belmont system, Title I evaluation, as it was conceived originally by Robert Kennedy and William Gorham, is no longer being done at USOE.

The evaluation resources of USOE are now centered in OPPE under the direction of John Evans, and the remnants of the Belmont system are administered by NCES. The removal of evaluation from BESE has removed evaluation from the locus of program management and development and cut off the access of program people to information about the activities of the Title I program. OPPE does not collect program data, and NCES, according to program personnel, is always too late with too little to be useful to BESE or DCE.[69]

After the initiation of the Belmont system, many of the states stopped sending in annual reports altogether. Genevieve Dane of DCE reports that since only thirty-five states send in reports, and since program staff are allowed only nine telephone calls a year to SEAs, program people have no accurate information concerning even basic program statistics. Although Mrs. Dane is responsible for writing the USOE budget justifications for DCE programs, she says that she was unable to locate data even on the number of children participating in the Title I program last year. "When you are not working with the program data," says Mrs. Dane, "and when you have no access to them, you have no sense of what is going on in the program."[70] Thus program personnel have neither the information to fulfill the oversight role Kennedy defined nor the data to frame USOE budget justifications or program policy in a manner congruent with PPBS management principles. Several different actors in the Belmont effort have said that the "net effect of the failure of Belmont has been to destroy relevant program evaluation within the Office of Education and BESE."[71] Certainly John Evans, who is responsible for the overall focus of USOE evaluation activities, has taken quite another approach to evaluation. The impact studies that Evans' OPPE staff are currently pursuing may have some import for high-level, go/no-go decisions, but they have scant relevance for program development.[72] With the transfer of BESE evaluation resources to OPPE, and the removal of Belmont to NCES, federal evaluation of and for the Title I program essentially came to an end.

The end of Belmont also marked the end, for all practical purposes, of the struggle over Title I evaluation that began in 1965 with the demands of Robert Kennedy and the passage of ESEA. The local education agencies control the outcome of the three-tiered evaluation system, and the SEAs dominate the remnants of Belmont. The failure of the Belmont system suggests that the assumptions made by Robert Kennedy and William Gorham concerning the availability of relevant and objective program information and the role of evaluation were inconsistent with the reality of the policy system. Reformers underestimated the importance of the balance of power and the dominant incentives within the Title I policy system for the conduct of evaluation. Federal officials could neither impose a federal reporting requirement on state or local education agencies nor force program people to furnish data. Belmont was an all-out effort to secure the cooperation of SEA and LEA personnel in the development and implementation of a viable information system. But no amount of cajoling, urging, or court on the part of USOE was sufficient to entice schoolmen to see evaluation as much more than a burden.

The experience of Belmont, viewed together with the outcomes of the Kennedy reporting scheme, TEMPO, and the national survey efforts, suggests that notions of reform and evaluation, which are complementary in theory, may conflict with each other in practice—especially when both the interest in reform and the incentive to evaluate originate at the federal level.

## Notes to Chapter 6

1. Adapted from a memo from Gilbert R. Austin to Willard I. Zangwill, "Belmont Project," August 10, 1970.

2. Ibid. Some of these instruments are designed to meet the Congressionally mandated reporting requirements for ESEA Titles I, II, III (NDEA Title V-A included), V, VII, VIII; NDEA Title III; Vocational Education Amendments of 1968 (elementary and secondary portions); EOA, Follow Through; EPDA (Part B); and CRA Title IV.

3. U.S. Office of Education, *Joint Federal/State Task Force on Evaluation: An Overview (Belmont System)*, February 1971, p. 19. See pp. 20 ff. of this work for a complete description of these items.

4. For full expression of Hereford's plan and philosophy, see *Educational Development for North Dakota: 1967-1975* and its companion volume, *An Overview*, published by the University of North Dakota, 1967.

5. Interview, Michael W. Kirst, July 31, 1972.

6. Ibid.

7. Ibid.

8. Ibid.

9. Ibid.

10. Richard Jaeger, a member of the Belmont staff, commented to David Cohen, Harvard Graduate School of Education, that he did not think Michael Kirst's interpretation of Karl Hereford's motives was correct. Jaeger told Cohen that Hereford was simply interested in a better data-collection scheme, and did not see a consolidated information scheme as the "first step to programmatic control." Kirst, responding to these comments, disagreed with Jaeger and said: "We've [he and Jaeger] talked about this often and have basically agreed about what was going on in Hereford's mind."

11. U.S. Office of Education, Bureau of Elementary and Secondary Education, "Current and Future Evaluation Activities: A Report and a Proposal," n.d., mimeo.

12. Richard Jaeger, Chief, Evaluation Design, BESE, to Jack Biren, Special Assistant, Program Analyses, ASPE, Memo, "BESE Plan for Evaluation FY 1970 through 1974," May 5, 1969.

13. U.S. Office of Education, Bureau of Elementary and Secondary Education, "A Forward Plan for the Evaluation of Elementary and Secondary Education, 1970 through 1974," May 4, 1969.

14. U.S. Office of Education, Bureau of Elementary and Secondary Education, "1968 Evaluation Report," n.d., mimeo.

15. Nolan Estes, Associate Commissioner BESE, to Joseph Froomkin, Assistant Commissioner OPPE, Memo, "FY 1969-1970 Evaluation Plan," May 28, 1968.

16. U.S. Office of Education, Bureau of Elementary and Secondary Education, "Current and Future Evaluation Activities: A Report and a Proposal," n.d., mimeo.

17. U.S. Congress, Senate, Subcommittee on Education of the Committee on Labor and Public Welfare, 91st Cong., 1st sess., *Hearings on Elementary and Second-*

*ary Education Amendments* (Washington, D.C.: U.S. Government Printing Office, 1969), p. 209.

18. Interview, Michael W. Kirst, July 31, 1972.

19. Interview, June 1972.

20. Joseph Froomkin's approach to the administration and philosophy of evaluation is outlined in an Office of Education unpublished position paper, "Major Policy Issues and Implementation Problems in the Office of Education," 1969.

21. Interview, Michael W. Kirst, July 31, 1972.

22. Interview, Former Belmont Staff Member, June 1972. The Belmont system, for example, completely undercut James Mauch who as head of DCE/PPE was responsible for Title I SEA and USOE reports. Mauch had hoped that the development of the PCI and the DCE administration of the 1968 survey would enhance DCE status. And although Mauch was a principal architect of the survey and the PCI instrument, 2 months after the inception of the survey, administration and staffing for it was shifted to Hereford at BESE, under the aegis of Belmont. Kirst has said: "Hereford recognized the PCI immediately as a good thing and so swept it into the Belmont system." In consequence, Mauch left DCE for Pittsburgh and the Cathedral of Learning.

23. Interview, Larry LaMoure, February 23, 1972.

24. U.S. Office of Education, *Joint Federal/State Task Force on Evaluation: An Overview (Belmont System)*, February 1971.

25. Interview, General Accounting Office Examiners, June 1972.

26. Susan Smith, Memo to the Title I Task Force, n.d.

27. Gilbert R. Austin to Willard I. Zangwill, Memo, "A Summary of Recent Reports on Title I," May 6, 1970.

28. Interview, Former Belmont Staff Member, June 1972.

29. Ibid.

30. According to some participants, Karl Hereford believed that the political manuevering that preceded Belmont would result in achievement data. "Karl Hereford thought if you just approached the Chiefs in the right way, you could get achievement data." (Interviews, Former Belmont Staff Members, June 1972.)

31. Susan Smith, unpublished paper prepared for the Title I Task Force.

32. Gilbert R. Austin to Willard I. Zangwill, Memo, "A Summary of Recent Reports on Title I," May 6, 1970.

33. Michael W. Kirst, "Proposed Management System for the Belmont Program," U.S. Office of Education (OEC-0-70-2920), June 12, 1970, p. 2.

34. *Annual Report of the U.S. Commissioner of Education, Fiscal Year 1971* (Washington, D.C.: U.S. Government Printing Office, 1972).

35. In a memo to the ASPE staff, Michael Timpane noted that "This is the first time that OE has managed to fulfill a requirement of several years' standing. The general conclusion of the report is that we have learned very little from evaluation so far." (Director of Education Planning to Assistant Secretary for Planning and Evaluation, Memo, "Annual Report Evaluating the Results and Effectiveness of OE Programs and Projects," March 14, 1972.)

36. U.S. Department of Health, Education, and Welfare, Office of Program Planning and Evaluation, "Annual Evaluation Report to Congress on Office of Education Programs, FY 1971," January 19, 1972, mimeo.

37. *Annual Report of the U.S. Commissioner of Education, Fiscal Year 1971* (Washington, D.C.: U.S. Government Printing Office, 1972), pp. 23-24.

38. This estimate of $52 million was made by two General Accounting Office

examiners, one of whom had been a member of the BESE evaluation staff. The exact amount expended on evaluation cannot be documented.

39. Charles Miller, Deputy Assistant Secretary, Budget, to Dr. John R. Ottina, Deputy Commissioner for Planning, Evaluation, and Management, Office of Education, Memo, "Organization of Budget Activities in the OE Commissioner's Office," April 11, 1972.

40. Interview, Genevieve Dane, June 12, 1972.

41. See, for example, Jaeger to Biren, op. cit. See also U.S. Office of Education, *Joint Federal/State Task Force on Evaluation: An Overview (Belmont System)*, February 1971.

42. As his testimony before the Select Subcommittee indicates, even Secretary Robert Finch was led to believe that substantive planning underlay the BESE proposal for Belmont: "We are ... recommending that the Office of Education be authorized, upon application from the states, to permit the states to consolidate all federal funds authorized for administration of education programs. The educational agencies in these states would account for the funds in a single report [which would be fed into the Belmont system].

"Here again we think we are achieving flexibility and economy.... We think that the states could receive greater immediate benefit, since this program has already had considerable planning within the Office of Education." (U.S. Congress, Senate, Subcommittee on Education of the Committee on Labor and Public Welfare, 91st Cong., 1st sess., *Hearings on Elementary and Secondary Education Amendments*, Washington, D.C.: U.S. Government Printing Office, 1969, p. 181.)

43. Interview, Former Belmont Staff Member, June 1972.

44. Ibid.

45. Ibid.

46. Interview, Michael W. Kirst, July 31, 1972.

47. The results were described in Michael W. Kirst, "Proposed Management System for the Belmont Program," U.S. Office of Education (OEC-0-70-2920), June 12, 1970.

48. Interview, Michael W. Kirst, July 31, 1972.

49. Bayla F. White to Jack Biren, Memo, "Conference of Chief State School Officers, June 20th and 21st," June 21, 1968.

50. Interview, Former Belmont Staff Member, June 1972. Research for this study confirms this statement. For example, Karl Hereford apparently "hid" the true costs of the Belmont system among the other budget line items. No one at USOE in 1972, even those responsible for the USOE budget, knew how much Belmont really cost.

51. Interview, Former Belmont Staff Member, June 1972.

52. Interview, Former BESE Administrator, February 1972. Interview, Former Belmont Staff Member, June 1972.

53. Interview, Former Belmont Staff Member, June 1972.

54. Ibid.

55. Interview, Susan Smith, June 1972.

56. Ibid.

57. Ibid.

58. Interview, Genevieve Dane, June 12, 1972

59. Interview, Former Belmont Staff Member, June 1972.

60. Ibid.

61. James Abert, "Evaluation at HEW: 1969-1971," April 8, 1971, mimeo.

62. Interview, Michael Timpane, February 24, 1972.

63. Former ASPE evaluator Joan Bissell commented, "Jim Abert saw evaluation as a narrative action/reaction." (Interview, February 24, 1972.)

64. Interview, John F. Hughes, February 8, 1972.

65. Interviews, Michael W. Kirst, July 31, 1972, and former Belmont Administrator, February 1972. Another interpretation of John Evans' stake in Belmont has been offered by a former BESE staff member: "John Evans knows that Belmont stinks but that he can't cut off Belmont completely. He's afraid he'd lose his job. The Chiefs would complain to the Commissioner and he'd lose his job. He also thinks that Perkins would have his job if he pulled the plug on Belmont." (Interview, June 1972.)

66. Interview, Former Belmont Administrator, February 1972.

67. Interview, Former Belmont Staff Member, June 1972.

68. Interview, Michael W. Kirst, July 31, 1972.

69. Interviews, BESE and DCE Program Personnel, February 1972 and June 1972.

70. Interview, Genevieve Dane, June 12, 1972.

71. This specific comment was made by Susan Smith (Interview, June 1972).

72. For example, the Director of DCE, Richard Fairley, has said: "The impact evaluations are useless to us because the data are not representative of the Title I program and it takes too long to do the sophisticated kind of analysis Evans wants to do. We need general information about the program, but we don't get it." (Interview, February 24, 1972.)

# Chapter Seven

# Conclusions

The evaluations undertaken in response to the Title I reporting requirement have been a mixture of reform, counterreform, demand, and compromise. The disappointing outcome and impact of these activities served to confirm Senator Robert Kennedy's worst fears about the slippage between federal intent and local practice, and to suggest that even less rationality exists at the margins of the Title I policy system than William Gorham expected. The experience of evaluation undertaken in response to the Title I requirement indicates that the multiple units within the Title I policy system are even more impervious to information and to the intent of federal policies than reformers had expected. The history of this evaluation effort also suggests that assessment of the impact of a broad-aim social action program such as Title I is a very difficult task that may be impossible to accomplish by means of an analytical paradigm that assumes a single program objective and comparability of program inputs, or that relies on local data-collection activities.

The USOE does not "run" Title I. The design and content of the more than 30,000 Title I projects across the country are determined by LEAs. Consequently, the use of Title I dollars reflects multiple and diverse goals, which are not easily transformed into measurable overarching objectives. The federal approach to Title I evaluation tended to reduce a very complex, broad-aim and largely unspecified process to deceptively simple, unidimensional terms, even though neither the objectives nor the independent variables are established.

The problems resulting from lack of consensus on program goals and treatments are compounded by the fact that the federal government has little effective control over the data collected and reported by LEAs. Thus the evaluation data returned by local projects tend to reflect local not federal interest in evaluation. Title I evaluation strategies ignored this and underestimated LEA resistance to or disinterest in evaluation. Thus these evaluations resulted in information that was not useful either as a management tool or as a means of informing parents about the activities and accomplishments of their local Title I project, as reformers had hoped.

But the information gathered through the Title I reporting schemes has been used and has had an impact on the Title I policy system. Ironically, the outcome of the Title I evaluation efforts has been in some ways just the opposite of the expectations expressed by reformers. The three-tiered reporting scheme that Robert Kennedy hoped would make school administrators accountable and augment the power of low-income parents has resulted in promotional and anecdotal program reports, compiled primarily in the interest of the local programs, not in compliance with the intent of the evaluation mandate. And the impact, cost-benefit model developed by ASPE and perpetuated by OPPE has not been able to reduce "creeping incremental-ism." Instead, these evaluations have been used selectively to lend a raiment of rationality to this essentially political mode of decisionmaking.

The net result of the Title I evaluation is also somewhat paradoxical in that these efforts to reform the governance and practice of education may have done more harm than good. For example, ASPE hoped its efforts would give stature to evaluation as a "tool for decisionmaking." But the highly political way in which Title I evaluation has been conducted and used has corroded the credibility of evaluation as an instrument of policy in the eyes of many program personnel. A former BESE evaluator remarked that "Evaluation at USOE is prostituted to such an extent now that it can't possibly have an impact [on policy or practice] because everyone knows it is just fun and games."[1] Certainly, Representative Edith Green found little evidence in her inquiry into federal evaluation practice to suggest that evaluation is taken seriously:

> It is my judgment that we are spending hundreds of millions of dollars on evaluation research that is absolutely worthless. Nobody looks at it. Nobody studies it. . . . Right now we are concentrating on the Office of Education where there are just under 1,400 live contracts. We've been looking at con-tracts for $130,000, $500,000 and $900,000 and we've found that it is really complete chaos at OE. They don't know to whom the contracts have been given, or for how much, or for what purpose, or what's been done with them after the final reports come in.[2]

Further, the federal evaluation efforts that were initiated to strengthen the education system have functioned instead to undermine it, and to demoralize educa-tion personnel at all levels. As a result of TEMPO and its progeny, many social planners and policymakers have abandoned investment in education as a social strategy, and the evaluations have been used as a basis for attacks on the school as a social institution. These evaluations have given education a black eye, but they have provided no guidance to program managers or education administrators about how to do better.

Ironically, another major impact of the outcome of Title I evaluation has been the spawning of more evaluations. No one has stood back and reassessed the value of the process of evaluation itself or the assumptions underlying the evaluation models, or wondered if the cost of acquisition was in this instance worth paying. If the evaluations being done at present are a yardstick of what has been learned from 7 years and over $50 million of Title I evaluation, the conclusion must be that we have learned very little.[3] As a former BESE administrator, who has been involved with Title I evaluation since 1966, has observed: "At this point in time [spring 1972], USOE would be hard pressed to show where evaluation findings impacted legislative or management proposals."[4]

But information gathering has become a necessary activity (qua activity) in the policy system, and faith in the science of systems analysis remains undiminished at the higher echelons of the federal government. The Title I evaluations have general-ly set to rest the uncritical optimism of the mid-sixties concerning the effects of school and the role of education as an antipoverty strategy. But the scientific move-ment in education (which has been dominant for more than a century) continues on unperturbed by the experience of Title I.

The history of Title I evaluation also suggests a number of implications about the conduct and use of evaluation in a multilevel government structure. These lessons raise both methodological and functional questions about the wisdom of a continuing pursuit of scientific rationality, especially in the instance of broad-aim social action programs, such as Title I, which represent an institutionalized federal investment. The Title I experience has shown how resistant the educational policy > system is to assessment of achievements and accomplishments, and also that a number of obstacles to this confirmatory style of reporting are inherent in the system itself. The structure and control of the nation's education system hampers all reporting, and it may preclude the accountability and impact reports reformers wanted. The obstacles to the successful implementation of evaluation policy are symptomatic of the barriers to the implementation of all categorical federal policy. In a federal system of government, and especially in education, the balance of power resides at the bottom, with special interest groups. Accordingly, the implementation of federal initiatives relies in large measure on the incentives and preferences of local authorities; there is little effective muscle at the top. Thus a federal evaluation policy that conflicts in fundamental ways with local priorities is unlikely to succeed. Specifically, data on the relative effectiveness of teaching strategies or allocation of resources will be difficult to gather not only because of the unsystematic and decentralized data-collection practices existing at the local level, but also because local programs have little interest in these data and are disinclined to collect them or furnish them. Federal evaluators, then, are faced with a specifically political dilemma generated by their inability to insist upon accurate information on school effects and program impact.[5] And the existence of powerful social sanctions against a strong federal data requirement means that these barriers to the implementation of federal evaluation policy will remain.

Furthermore, in the instance of Title I, the disinclination of the operating units to furnish impact information was matched by a general lack of appetite for data that assessed overall program or project effectiveness. Contrary to the expectations of reformers, neither federal decisionmakers nor local school personnel showed much interest or ability to use these evaluations to formulate Title I policy or practice. The experience of Title I evaluation implies that anyone who looks to evaluation to take the politics out of decisionmaking is bound to be disappointed. Evaluation is just one input into a complex process that, inherently and predominately, is not rational. But Title I evaluations failed to supply information that could add even marginal rationality to the decisionmaking process. We have argued that this failure was in part a result of the instability of the information itself. But the disappointing impact of Title I evaluation also reflects a lack of systematic attention to the structure of the decision process—or the decision space actually available to Title I decisionmakers. The information needs of a policymaker are determined by the decisions that he can make. In part, the evaluations undertaken by the federal government represented the data requirements of an "ideal" management model—PPBS—not the actual policy choices available to program managers.

The reformer's approach to evaluation embodied legitimate expectations for a social report and for reform by means of better information. But the incongruities between these expectations, the consequent analytical paradigm, policy system constraints on information collection and use, as well as the character of the Title I program itself, led to evaluations that were valuable neither as reports, nor as ways to manage Title I better, nor as ways to learn about Title I.

Evaluation embraces two separate dimensions. It is both a logic of inquiry and a part of a complex system of social and political relations. A recurring theme in this study is the extent to which these two components interact and shape each other. An important lesson of the Title I experience is that the logic of inquiry should be perceived as relative, not absolute, and that a realistic and useful evaluation policy should acknowledge the constraints of the policy system and the behavior of bureaucracies. Evaluation efforts based on expectations for reform by means of a social report, or better information on program accomplishments, certainly find justification in theory. But in practice they may turn out to be little more than empty ritual.

## Notes to Chapter 7

1. Interview, Former Belmont Staff Member, June 14, 1972.

2. Edith Green, "The Business of Education," in Frank J. Sciara and Richard K. Jantz (eds.), *Accountability in American Education* (Boston: Allyn & Bacon, Inc., 1972), pp. 53-54. Similarly, a General Accounting Office investigation of USOE evaluation practices concluded that USOE evaluation funds are wasted because of the inattention of USOE administrators. See, for example, John Matthews, "GAO Probe Sees Waste in Research: Educational Evaluation Is Wasteful, GAO Says," *The Evening Star,* Washington, D.C., August 18, 1971, Sec. A-6.

3. This is not to say that people have not learned anything at all from the experience of Title I. In some quarters, principally the academy, the outcome of these evaluations has raised issues unthought of in 1965, and pushed the logic of research back to more basic questions.

4. Wallace Cohen, "The Structure and Organization of the United States Office of Education Evaluation Function," n.d. (prepared in the spring of 1972).

5. See Robert A. Levine, *Public Planning: Failure and Redirection* (New York: Basic Books, Inc., 1972), for a discussion of this point and its implication for OEO evaluation efforts and the expectations of social planners.

# Bibliography

Abert, James G. "Evaluation at HEW: 1969-1971." Mimeographed, April 8, 1971.

Acland, Henry D. *Social Determinants of Educational Achievement.* Ph.D. thesis, Oxford University, February 1973.

Allen, James E., Jr. "Strengthening the Office of Education for Service to the States." Address before the Annual Meeting of the Council of Chief State School Officers, Phoenix, Arizona, November 17, 1969.

Allison, Graham T. *The Essence of Decision Making.* Boston: Little, Brown & Co., Inc., 1971.

*The Analysis and Evaluation of Public Expenditures: The PPB System.* Compendium of papers submitted to the Subcommittee on Economy in Government of the Joint Economic Committee, Congress of the United States, 91st Cong., 1st sess. Washington, D.C.: U.S. Government Printing Office, 1969, 3 vols.

Archibald, Kathleen. "Three Views of the Expert's Role in Policymaking: Systems Analysis, Incrementalism, and the Clinical Approach." *Policy Sciences,* Vol. 1, No. 1, Spring 1970, pp. 73-86.

Argyris, Chris. *Personality and Organization.* New York: Harper & Row, Publishers, 1957.

Bailey, Stephen K., and Edith K. Mosher. *ESEA: The Office of Education Administers a Law.* Syracuse: Syracuse University Press, 1968.

Barkin, David, and Walter Hettich. *The Elementary and Secondary Education Act: A Distributional Analysis.* St. Louis, Mo.: Washington University, April 1968.

Barro, Stephen M. *An Approach to Developing Accountability Measures for the Public Schools.* Santa Monica, Calif.: The Rand Corporation, 1970. Monograph.

Bauer, Raymond A. *Social Indicators.* Cambridge: The M.I.T. Press, 1966.

Bauer, Raymond A., and Kenneth J. Gergen (eds.). *The Study of Policy Formation.* New York: The Free Press, 1968.

Bellack, Arno A. "The National Assessment of Educational Progress: Issues and Problems," in Arthur Kroll (ed.), *Issues in American Education.* New York: Oxford University Press, 1970.

Bendiner, Robert. *Obstacle Course on Capitol Hill.* New York: McGraw-Hill Book Company, 1965.

Bickner, Robert F. "I Don't Know PPB at All." *Policy Sciences,* Vol. 2, 1971, pp. 301-304.

Blau, Peter M. *Bureaucracy in Modern Society.* New York: Random House, Inc., 1956.

Blau, Peter M. *The Dynamics of Bureaucracy.* Rev. ed. Chicago: University of Chicago Press, 1955.

Bloom, Benjamin S. *Taxonomy of Educational Objectives Handbook. I: Cognitive Domain.* New York: David McKay Company, Inc., 1971.

Bloom, Benjamin S. "Twenty-five Years of Educational Research." *American Educational Research Journal,* Vol. 3, 1966, pp. 211-221.

Bloom, Benjamin S., Allison Davis, and Robert Hess. *Compensatory Education for Cultural Deprivation.* New York: Holt, Rinehart & Winston, Inc., 1967.

Braybrooke, David, and Charles E. Lindblom. *A Strategy of Decision: Policy Evaluation as a Social Process.* New York: The Free Press, 1970.

Bruner, Jerome S. *The Process of Education.* New York: Vintage Books, Inc., 1960.

Buchanan, Garth N., Bayla White, and Joseph S. Wholey. *Political Considerations in the Design of Program Evaluation.* Paper presented at the American Sociological Association, Denver Hilton Hotel, September 1, 1971.

Callahan, Raymond E. *Education and the Cult of Efficiency.* Chicago: University of Chicago Press, 1962.

Campbell, Donald T. "Factors Relevant to the Validity of Experiments in Social Settings." *Psychological Bulletin,* Vol. 54, No. 1, 1957.

Campbell, Donald T. "Methods for the Experimenting Society." Preliminary draft of a paper presented at the American Psychological Association, Washington, D.C., September 1971.

Campbell, Donald T. "Reforms as Experiments," in Francis Caro (ed.), *Readings in Evaluation Research.* New York: Russell Sage Foundation, 1971, pp. 233-261.

Campbell, Donald T., and Julian C. Stanley. *Experimental and Quasi-Experimental Designs for Research.* Skokie, Ill.: Rand McNally & Company, 1963.

Campbell, Roald F., et al. *The Organization and Control of American Schools.* 2d ed. Columbus, Ohio: Charles E. Merrill Books, Inc., 1970.

Campbell, Roald F., and Gerald R. Sroufe. "Toward a Rationale for Federal-State-Local Relations in Education." *Phi Delta Kappan,* Vol. 47, No. 1, September 1965, pp. 2-7.

Capron, William M. "The Impact of Analysis on Bargaining in Government," in James W. Davis, Jr. (ed.), *Politics, Programs and Budgets.* Englewood Cliffs: Prentice-Hall, Inc., 1969.

Carnoy, Martin. *Schooling in a Corporate Society.* New York: David McKay Company, Inc., 1972.

Caro, Francis G. "Issues in the Evaluation of Social Programs." *Review of Educational Research,* Vol. 40, No. 2, April 1971, pp. 87-114.

Caro, Francis G. (ed.). *Readings in Evaluation Research.* New York: Russell Sage Foundation, 1971.

Chall, Jeanne S. *Learning To Read: The Great Debate.* New York: McGraw-Hill Book Company, 1967.

Chin, R., and K. Benne. "General Strategies for Effecting Changes in Human Systems," in W. G. Bennis, K. Benne, and R. Chin (eds.), *The Planning of Change.* 2d ed. Toronto: Holt, Rinehart and Winston of Canada, Ltd., 1969.

Clapp, Charles L. *The Congressman: His Work as He Sees It.* Garden City, New York: Doubleday & Co., Inc., Anchor Books, 1964.

Clifford, Geraldine J. "A History of the Impact of Research on Teaching," in Robert

M. W. Travers (ed.), *Second Handbook of Research on Teaching.* Skokie, Ill.: Rand McNally & Company, 1973.

Cohen, David K. "Politics and Research: Evaluation of Social Action Programs in Education." *Review of Educational Research,* Vol. 40, No. 2, April 1970, pp. 213-238.

Cohen, David K. "The Schools and Social Reform: The Case of Compensatory Education." Cambridge: Harvard Graduate School of Education, Center for Educational Policy Research, August 30, 1970.

Cohen, David K. "Social Accounting in Education: Reflections on Supply and Demand." *Proceedings of the 1970 Invitational Conference on Testing Problems— The Promise and Perils of Educational Information Systems,* 1971.

Cohen, David K., et al. "The Effects of Revenue Sharing and Block Grants on Education." Cambridge: Harvard Graduate School of Education, September 1970.

Cohen, Elizabeth G. *A New Approach to Applied Research: Race and Education.* Columbus, Ohio: Charles E. Merrill Books, Inc., 1970.

Cohen, Michael D., James G. March, and Johan P. Olsen. "A Garbage Can Model of Organizational Choice." *Administrative Science Quarterly,* Vol. 17, No. 1, March 1972, pp. 1-25.

Cohen, Wallace. "Structure and Organization of United States Office of Education Evaluation Function." N.d. (prepared in the spring of 1972).

Coleman, James S. "Incentives in Education: Existing and Proposed." Mimeographed, n.d.

Coleman, James S., et al. *Equality of Educational Opportunity.* Washington, D.C.: U.S. Government Printing Office, 1966.

Conant, James B. *Shaping Educational Policy.* New York: McGraw-Hill Book Company, 1964.

Cremin, Lawrence A. *The Transformation of the School.* New York: Vintage Books, Random House, Inc., 1961.

Cronbach, Lee J., and L. Furby. "How Should We Measure 'Change'—Or Should We?" *Psychological Bulletin,* Vol. 74, No. 1, 1970, pp. 68-80.

Cronbach, Lee J., and Patrick Suppes. *Research for Tomorrow's Schools.* London: Collier-Macmillan Ltd., 1969.

Cronin, Thomas E., and Norman C. Thomas. "Educational Policy Advisers and the Great Society." *Public Policy,* Fall 1970, pp. 659-686.

Crozier, Michael. *The Bureaucratic Phenomenon.* Chicago: University of Chicago Press, 1964.

Cyert, Richard M., and James G. March. *A Behavioral Theory of the Firm.* Englewood Cliffs: Prentice-Hall, Inc., 1963.

Dahl, Robert A. *Who Governs?* New Haven: Yale University Press, 1968.

Dahl, Robert A., and Charles E. Lindblom. *Politics, Economics, and Welfare.* New York: Harper & Row, Publishers, 1953.

Dentler, Robert A. "Urban Eyewash: A Review of 'Title I/Year II.'" *The Urban Review,* Vol. 3, No. 4, February 1969, pp. 32-33.

Dershimer, Richard A., and Laurence Iannaccone. "Social and Political Influences on Educational Research," in R. M. W. Travers (ed.), *Second Handbook of Research on Teaching.* Skokie, Ill.: Rand McNally & Company, 1973.

Derthick, Martha. *The Influence of Federal Grants: Public Assistance in Massachusetts.* Cambridge: Harvard University Press, 1970.

Dorfman, Robert (ed.). *Measuring Benefits of Government Investments.* Washington, D.C.: The Brookings Institution, 1965.

Downs, Anthony. *Inside Bureaucracy.* Boston: Little, Brown & Co., Inc., 1967.

Drew, Elizabeth B. "Education's Billion Dollar Baby." *The Atlantic Monthly,* Vol. 218, July 1966, pp. 37-43.

Drew, Elizabeth B. "HEW Grapples with PPBS." *The Public Interest,* Summer 1967, pp. 9-29.

Dror, Yehezkel. "PPBS and the Public Policy-Making System: Some Reflections on the Papers by Bertram M. Gross and Allen Schick." *Public Administration Review,* Vol. 29, No. 2, March-April 1969, pp. 152-160.

Dror, Yehezkel. *Public Policymaking Reexamined.* San Francisco: Chandler Publishing Company, 1968.

Duncan, Otis Dudley. *Social Forecasting—The State of the Art.* Paper presented at the Technological Forecasting Conference, University of Texas, April 22-26, 1969.

Dye, Thomas R. *Politics, Economics and Public Policy Outcomes in the American States.* Skokie, Ill.: Rand McNally & Company, 1966.

Easton, David. *A Framework for Political Analysis.* Englewood Cliffs: Prentice-Hall, Inc., 1965.

"Economics and Public Policy." *The Public Interest,* Summer 1968, pp. 67-129.

Eidenberg, Eugene, and Roy D. Morey. *An Act of Congress.* New York: W. W. Norton & Company, Inc., 1969.

Etzioni, Amitai. *Modern Organizations.* Englewood Cliffs: Prentice-Hall, Inc., 1964.

Etzioni, Amitai. "Policy Research." *The American Sociologist,* Vol. 6, 1971, pp. 8-12.

Etzioni, Amitai. "Shortcuts to Social Change?" *Public Interest,* No. 12, Summer 1968, pp. 40-51.

Etzioni, Amitai, and Edward W. Lehman. "Some Dangers in Valid Social Measurement." *The Annals of the American Academy of Political and Social Science,* Vol. 373, September 1967, pp. 1-15.

Evans, John. "Evaluating Social Action Programs." Mimeographed, June 12, 1969.

Fairley, Richard L. "Accountability's New Tool." *American Education,* Vol. 8, No. 5, June 1972, pp. 33-35.

Fenno, Richard F., Jr. *The Power of the Purse: Appropriations Politics in Congress.* Boston: Little, Brown & Co., Inc., 1966.

Freeman, Howard E., and Clarence C. Sherwood. *Social Research and Social Policy.* Englewood Cliffs: Prentice-Hall, Inc., 1970.

Fullan, Michael. "Overview of the Innovative Process and the User." *Interchange,* Vol. 3, Nos. 2-3, 1972, pp. 1-46.

Gage, N. L. (ed.). *Handbook of Research on Teaching.* Skokie, Ill.: Rand McNally & Company, 1963.

Gardner, John W., Chairman. *Report of the President's Task Force on Education.* Washington, D.C., 1964. Mimeographed.

Ginsburg, Alan, et al. "Title I of ESEA—Problems and Prospects." U.S. Department of Health, Education, and Welfare paper, ca. 1970.

Gintis, Herbert. "Non-cognitive Outcomes of Schooling: Priorities for Research in the Economics of Education." N.d.

Gittell, Marilyn, and Alan G. Hevesi. *The Politics of Urban Education.* New York: Praeger Publishers, Inc., 1969.

Glass, Gene V. "The Growth of Evaluation Methodology." Laboratory of Educational Research, University of Colorado. Mimeographed, n.d.

Glazer, Nathan. "The Limits of Social Policy." Paper presented at City College of New York, September 1970.

Glennan, Thomas K. *Evaluating Federal Manpower Programs: Notes and Observations.* Santa Monica, Calif.: The Rand Corporation, September 1969. Monograph.

Goodlad, John I., and M. Frances Klein and Associates. *Behind the Classroom Door.* Worthington, Ohio: Charles A. Jones Publishing Co., 1970.

Gordon, Edmund W., and Doxey A. Wilkerson. *Compensatory Education for the Disadvantaged.* New York: College Entrance Examination Board, 1966.

Gorham, William. "Notes of a Practitioner." *The Public Interest,* Summer 1967, pp. 4-8.

Gorham, William. "The Political and Administrative Context of Federal Decision Making." Lecture No. 1. International Summer School, Milan, Italy, June 1967.

Gorham, William. "Sharpening the Knife That Cuts the Public Pie." Paper presented at International Political Science Association, Brussels, Belgium, September 1967.

Green, Edith. "The Business of Education," in Frank J. Sciara and Richard K. Jantz (eds.), *Accountability in American Education.* Boston: Allyn & Bacon, Inc., 1972, pp. 52-61.

Green, Mark J., James M. Fallows, and David R. Zwick. *Who Runs Congress?* New York: Bantam Books, Inc., 1972.

Greer, Colin. *The Great School Legend.* New York: Basic Books Inc., 1972.

Griliches, Zvi, and William M. Mason. "Education, Income, and Ability." January 1972.

Guba, Egon G. "The Failure of Educational Evaluation," in Carol H. Weiss (ed.), *Evaluating Action Programs: Readings in Social Action and Education.* Boston: Allyn & Bacon, Inc., 1972, pp. 250-266.

Guba, Egon G., and Daniel Stufflebeam. "Evaluation: The Process of Aiding and Abetting Insightful Action." Mimeographed, n.d.

Guthrie, James R. "What the Coleman Reanalysis Didn't Tell Us." *Saturday Review,* Vol. 55, No. 30, July 22, 1972, p. 45.

Halperin, Samuel. "ESEA: Five Years Later." *Congressional Record,* House, September 9, 1970, pp. 8492-8494.

Hand, Harold C. "National Assessment Viewed as the Camel's Nose." *Phi Delta Kappan,* Vol. 47, No. 1, September 1965, pp. 8-13.

Hannah, John A., et al. *Racial Isolation in the Public Schools.* Report of the U.S. Commission on Civil Rights, Vol. 1, 1967.

Hanushek, Eric A. *Longitudinal Surveys of Educational Effects.* Washington, D.C.: Council of Economic Advisers, 1972.

Harrington, Fred, et al. "Compensatory Education: What We Must Do." Paper presented at the National Invitational Seminar on Compensatory Education, University of Wisconsin, April 1969.

Hartman, Robert. "Evaluation of Multi-Purpose Grant-in-Aid Programs." Mimeographed, n.d.

Harvard Center for Law and Education. "A Litigation Packet for Title I of the Elementary and Secondary Education Act."

HARYOU (Harlem Youth Opportunities Unlimited). *Youth in the Ghetto: A Study of the Consequences of Powerlessness and a Blueprint for Change.* New York, 1964.

Hawkridge, D. G., Peggie Campeau, and Penelope Trickett. *A Guide for Authors of Evaluation Reports of Educational Programs.* American Institutes for Research in the Behavioral Sciences, Palo Alto, California, 1969.

Hawkridge, D. G., A. B. Chalupsky, and A. O. H. Roberts. *A Study of Selected Exemplary Programs for the Education of Disadvantaged Children, Parts I and II.* American Institutes for Research in the Behavioral Sciences, Palo Alto, California, September 1968.

Hecht, Kathryn A. "Five Years of Title I Federal Evaluation." Revised version of a paper presented to the 1972 Annual Meeting of the American Educational Research Association, Chicago, Illinois, April 7, 1972.

Heller, Barbara R., and Richard S. Barrett. *Expand and Improve ... A Critical Review of the First Three Years of ESEA Title I in New York City.* New York: Center for Urban Education, July 1970.

Hellmuth, Jerome (ed.). *Disadvantaged Child.* Vol. 3. *Compensatory Education: A National Debate.* New York: Brunner-Mazel, Inc., 1970.

Henry, Jules. *Culture Against Man.* New York: Random House, Inc., 1965.

Horowitz, Irving Louis. "The Academy and the Polity: Interaction Between Social Scientists and Federal Administrators." *Journal of Applied Behavioral Science,* Vol. 5, No. 3, 1969, pp. 309-335.

Horowitz, Irving Louis (ed.). *The Use and Abuse of Social Science.* New Brunswick, N.J.: Transaction Books, 1971.

Houston, Tom R., and Julian C. Stanley. "The Behavioral Sciences Impact Effectiveness Model." Paper presented at Evaluation of Social Action Programs Conference, May 2-3, 1969.

Hyman, Herbert, and Charles Wright. "Evaluating Social Action Programs," in Francis Caro (ed.), *Readings in Evaluation Research.* New York: Russell Sage Foundation, 1971, pp. 185-220.

Iannaccone, Laurence, and Frank Luta. *Politics, Power and Policy: The Governing of Local School Districts.* Columbus, Ohio: Charles E. Merrill Books, Inc., 1970.

*Innovations in Planning, Programming, and Budgeting in State and Local Governments.* Compendium of papers submitted to the Subcommittee on Economy in Government of the Joint Economic Committee, Congress of the United States, 91st Cong., 1st sess. Washington, D.C.: U.S. Government Printing Office, 1969.

Jencks, Christopher, et al. *Inequality: An Assessment of the Effect of Family and Schooling in America.* New York: Basic Books, Inc., 1972.

Johnson, Harry G. "The Economic Approach to Social Questions." *Public Interest,* No. 12, Summer 1968, pp. 68-79.

Jones, James A. "Education in Depressed Areas: A Research-Sociologist's Point of View," in HARYOU, *Youth in the Ghetto: A Study of the Consequences of Powerlessness and a Blueprint for Change.* New York, 1964.

Jordan, Daniel C., and Kathryn A. Hecht (Spiess). *Compensatory Education in Massachusetts: An Evaluation with Recommendations.* Amherst: The University of Massachusetts Press, 1970.

Katz, Daniel, and Robert L. Kahn. *The Social Psychology of Organizations.* New York: John Wiley & Sons, Inc., 1966.

Katz, Michael B. *Class, Bureaucracy, and School.* New York: Praeger Publishers, Inc., 1971.

Katz, Michael B. *The Irony of Early School Reform.* Cambridge: Harvard University Press, 1968.

Katz, Michael B. "From Voluntarism to Bureaucracy in American Education." *Sociology of Education,* Vol. 44, No. 3, Summer 1971, pp. 297-332.

Katzman, Martin T., and Ronald S. Rosen. "The Science and Politics of National Educational Assessment." *The Record,* Vol. 71, No. 4, May 1970, pp. 571-586.

Kaysen, Carl. "Model-makers and Decision-makers: Economists and the Policy Process." *Public Interest,* No. 12, Summer 1968, pp. 80-95.

Kearney, Charles Phillip. "The 1964 Presidential Task Force on Education and the Elementary and Secondary Education Act of 1965." Ph.D. diss., University of Chicago, 1967.

Keppel, Francis. *The Necessary Revolution in American Education.* New York: Harper & Row, Publishers, 1966.

Kershaw, David N. "Issues in Income Maintenance Experimentation," in Peter H. Rossi and Walter Williams (eds.), *Evaluating Social Programs.* New York: Seminar Press, 1972, pp. 221-248.

Kimbrough, Ralph B. *Political Power and Educational Decision-Making.* Skokie, Ill.: Rand McNally & Company, 1964.

Kirst, Michael W. "Administrative Problems in Evaluation of Title I of the Elementary and Secondary Education Act." Paper included in an Urban Institute report on federal evaluation practices, December 1969. Mimeographed.

Kirst, Michael W. "Delivery System for Federal Aid to Disadvantaged Children: Problems and Prospects," in U.S. Congress, Senate, *Hearings before the Select Committee on Equal Educational Opportunity of the U.S. Senate.* 92d Cong., 1st sess., pt. 17. Washington, D.C.: U.S. Government Printing Office, October 7, 1971.

Kirst, Michael W. "Federalism and Urban Education: A Washington Perspective." Mimeographed, n.d.

Kirst, Michael W. "The Growth and Limits of Federal Influence in Education." Occasional Paper 72-9. School of Education, Stanford University, September 1972.

Kirst, Michael W. "A Political Analysis of Title I ESEA Feedback." Paper presented at the Annual Meeting of the National Council on Measurement in Education, New York City, February 5, 1971.

Kirst, Michael W. "Proposed Management System for the Belmont Program." U.S. Office of Education (OEC-0-70-2920), June 12, 1970.

Kirst, Michael W. "What Types of Compensatory Education Programs Are Effective." Paper presented for the National Conference on Equal Educational Opportunity in America's Cities, sponsored by the U.S. Commission on Civil Rights, Washington, D.C., November 16-18, 1967.

Klitgaard, Robert E. "Models of Educational Innovation and Implications for Research." Santa Monica, Calif.: The Rand Corporation, March 1973. Paper P-4977.

Klitgaard, Robert E., and George Hall. *A Statistical Search for Unusually Effective Schools.* Santa Monica, Calif.: The Rand Corporation, 1973. Monograph.

Knezevich, Stephen J. *Program Budgeting (PPBS).* Berkeley: McCutchan Publishing Corp., 1973.

Koerner, James D. *Who Controls American Education?* Boston: Beacon Press, 1969.

Kuhn, Thomas S. *The Structure of Scientific Revolutions.* 2d ed. *International Encyclopedia of Science,* Vol. 2, No. 2. Chicago: University of Chicago Press, 1970.

Land, William G. "The Shakeout in USOE." *Phi Delta Kappan,* Vol. 47, No. 1, September 1965, pp. 31-33.

Lane, Robert E. "The Decline of Politics and Ideology in a Knowledgeable Society." *American Sociological Review,* Vol. 31, No. 5, 1966, pp. 649-662.

Levin, Henry M. "Concepts of Economic Efficiency and Educational Production."

Paper presented at the Conference on Education as an Industry, sponsored by the National Bureau of Economic Research, New York, June 4-5, 1971.

Levine, Daniel U., and Robert J. Havighurst (eds.). *Farewell to Schools???*Worthington, Ohio: Charles A. Jones Publishing Co., 1971.

Levine, Murray. "A Social Systems Analysis of Research Methods: Some Preliminary Thoughts." Psycho-Educational Clinic, Yale University. Mimeographed.

Levine, Robert A. *The Poor Ye Need Not Have with You: Lessons from the War on Poverty*. Cambridge: The M.I.T. Press, 1970.

Levine, Robert A. *Public Planning: Failure and Redirection*. New York: Basic Books, Inc., 1972.

Lindblom, Charles E. *The Intelligence of Democracy*. New York: The Free Press, 1965.

Lindblom, Charles E. *The Policy-Making Process*. Englewood Cliffs: Prentice-Hall, Inc., 1968.

Lindblom, Charles E. "The Science of 'Muddling Through.'" *Public Administration Review*, Vol. 19, Spring 1959, pp. 79-88.

Lindvall, C. M., and Richard C. Cox. *Evaluation as a Tool in Curriculum Development: The IPI Evaluation Program*. Skokie, Ill.: Rand McNally & Company, 1970.

Lipson, Joseph. "An Overview of Educational Problems." Commissioner's Planning Unit for NIE, August 30, 1971. Mimeographed.

Lyons, Gene M. *The Uneasy Partnership: Social Science and the Federal Government in the 20th Century*. New York: Russell Sage Foundation, 1969.

Mann, Dean E. *The Assistant Secretaries*. Washington, D.C.: The Brookings Institution, 1965.

March, James G., and Herbert A. Simon. *Organizations*. New York: John Wiley & Sons, Inc., 1958.

Marcus, Sheldon, and Harry N. Rivlin. *Conflicts in Urban Education*. New York: Basic Books, Inc., 1970.

Marris, Peter, and Martin Rein. *Dilemmas of Social Reform*. New York: Atherton Press, 1969.

Matthews, John. "GAO Probe Sees Waste in Research: Educational Evaluation Is Wasteful, GAO Says." *The Evening Star*, Washington, D.C., August 18, 1971, Sec. A-6.

McClure, Phyllis. Statement before the Congressional Black Caucus Hearings on Government Lawlessness, June 29, 1972.

Meltsner, Arnold J. "Political Feasibility and Policy Analysis." *Public Administration Review*, Vol. 32, No. 6, November-December 1972, pp. 859-867.

Meranto, Philip. *The Politics of Federal Aid to Education in 1965: A Study in Political Innovation*. Syracuse: Syracuse University Press, 1967.

Merton, Robert K., et al. (eds.). *Reader in Bureaucracy*. New York: The Free Press, 1952.

Mosbaek, E. J., et al. "Analysis of Compensatory Education in Five School Districts: Summary." TEMPO, The General Electric Company, n.d.

Mosteller, Frederick, and Daniel P. Moynihan. *On Equality of Educational Opportunity*. New York: Random House, Inc., 1972.

Moynihan, Daniel P. *Maximum Feasible Misunderstanding*. New York: The Free Press, 1970.

Munger, Frank, and Richard Fenno. *National Politics and Federal Aid to Education*. Syracuse: Syracuse University Press, 1962.

Murphy, Jerome T. *Grease the Squeaky Wheel: A Report on the Implementation of Title V of the Elementary and Secondary Education Act of 1965, Grants To Strengthen State Departments of Education.* Cambridge: Harvard Graduate School of Education, Center for Educational Policy Research, February 1973.

Murphy, Jerome T. "Title I of ESEA: The Politics of Implementing Federal Education Reform." *Harvard Educational Review,* Vol. 41, No. 1, February 1971, pp. 35-63.

Musgrave, Richard A. (ed.). *Essays in Fiscal Federalism.* Washington, D.C.: The Brookings Institution, 1965.

"National Educational Assessment: Pro and Con." National Education Association, Washington, D.C., 1966.

Neustadt, Richard E. *Presidential Power.* New York: John Wiley & Sons, Inc., 1960.

*The New York Times.* "Gardner Departs with No Fanfare." March 2, 1968, p. 1.

*The 1971 Annual Report to the President and the Congress.* Washington, D.C.: National Advisory Council on the Education of Disadvantaged Children, 1971.

Niskanen, William A. "Why New Methods of Budgetary Choices? Administrative Aspects." International Institute of Public Finance, Germany, 1971.

Novick, David (ed.). *Program Budgeting: Program Analysis and the Federal Budget.* 2d ed. Cambridge: Harvard University Press, 1967.

Olson, Mancur, Jr. "Economics, Sociology and The Best of All Possible Worlds." *Public Interest,* No. 12, Summer 1968, pp. 96-118.

Passow, Harry A. (ed.). *Developing Programs for the Educationally Disadvantaged.* New York: Teachers College Press, Teachers College, Columbia University, 1963.

Passow, Harry A. *Education in Depressed Areas.* New York: Teachers College Press, Teachers College, Columbia University, 1963.

Pauly, Edward W. *The Struggle over Title I.* A.B. thesis, The Woodrow Wilson School of Public and International Affairs, Princeton University, April 16, 1971.

Phi Delta Kappa. *Education and the Structure of Knowledge.* Fifth Annual Phi Delta Kappa Symposium on Educational Research. Skokie, Ill.: Rand McNally & Company, 1964.

Phi Delta Kappa National Study Council on Evaluation. *Educational Evaluation and Decision Making.* Itasca, Ill.: F. E. Peacock Publishers, Inc., 1971.

Piccariello, Harry. "Evaluation of Title I." N.d.

Porter, David O., et al. "The Mobilization of Federal Aid by Local Schools: A Political and Economic Analysis." Report submitted to the Syracuse University Research Corporation.

Quade, E. S. "Systems Analysis Techniques for Planning-Programming-Budgeting." Santa Monica, Calif.: The Rand Corporation, March 1966. Paper P-3322.

Rainwater, Lee, and William L. Yancey. *The Moynihan Report and the Politics of Controversy.* Cambridge: The M.I.T. Press, 1967.

Ransom, Harry Howe. *The Intelligence Establishment.* Cambridge: Harvard University Press, 1970.

Rein, Martin. *Social Policy: Issues of Choice and Change.* New York: Random House, Inc., 1970.

Ribich, Thomas I. *Education and Poverty.* Washington, D.C.: The Brookings Institution, 1968.

Rivlin, Alice M. "PPBS in HEW: Some Lessons from Experience." Paper presented to the Joint Economic Committee, March 1969.

Rivlin, Alice M. *Systematic Thinking for Social Action.* Washington, D.C.: The Brookings Institution, 1971.

Rivlin, Alice M., and Joseph Wholey. "Education of Disadvantaged Children." *Socio-Economic Planning Sciences,* Vol. 2, 1969, pp. 373-380.

Roberson, E. Wayne (ed.). *Educational Accountability through Evaluation.* Englewood Cliffs: Educational Technology Publications, 1971.

Robinson, Mary E., and Arlyne Pozner. "Compensatory Education in the War on Poverty." Office of Economic Opportunity, Research and Plans Division, May 1966.

Rossi, Peter H. "Boobytraps and Pitfalls in the Evaluation of Social Action Programs," in Carol H. Weiss (ed.), *Evaluation Action Programs: Readings in Social Action and Education.* Boston: Allyn & Bacon, Inc., 1972.

Rossi, Peter H. "Testing for Success and Failure in Social Action," in Rossi and Williams (eds.), *Evaluating Social Programs.* New York: Seminar Press, 1972, pp. 11-49.

Rossi, Peter H., and Walter Williams (eds.). *Evaluating Social Programs.* New York: Seminar Press, 1972.

Rothenberg, Jerome. "Cost-Benefit Analysis: A Methodological Exposition." Working Paper No. 46. Massachusetts Institute of Technology, October 1969.

Sarason, Seymour B. *The Culture of the School and the Problem of Change.* Boston: Allyn & Bacon, Inc., 1971.

Scanlon, John W., Joe N. Nay, and Joseph S. Wholey. *An Evaluation System To Support a Decentralized, Comprehensive Manpower Program.* Washington, D.C.: The Urban Institute, June 1971.

Schick, Allen. "From Analysis to Evaluation." *The Annals of the American Academy of Political and Social Science,* March 1971, pp. 57-71.

Schick, Allen. "The Road to PPB: The Stages of Budget Reform." *Public Administration Review,* Vol. 26, No. 4, December 1966, pp. 243-258.

Schultze, Charles L. *The Politics and Economics of Public Spending.* Washington, D.C.: The Brookings Institution, 1968.

Sciara, Frank J., and Richard K. Jantz. *Accountability in American Education.* Boston: Allyn & Bacon, Inc., 1972.

Scientific Educational Systems, Inc. *Joint Federal/State Task Force on Evaluation— Comprehensive Evaluation System: Current Status and Development Requirements.* 1970.

Scriven, Michael. "The Methodology of Evaluation." *Perspectives of Curriculum Evaluation,* AERA Monograph Series on Curriculum Evaluation. Skokie, Ill.: Rand McNally & Company, 1967.

Seidman, Harold. *Politics, Position, & Power.* New York: Oxford University Press, 1970.

Sheldon, Eleanor B., and Wilbert E. Moore. *Indicators of Social Change.* New York: Russell Sage Foundation, 1968.

Silberman, Charles E. *Crisis in the Classroom.* New York: Vintage Books, Inc., 1970.

Simon, Herbert A. *Administrative Behavior.* 2d ed. New York: The Free Press, 1965.

Simon, Herbert A. "On the Concept of Organizational Goal." *Administrative Science Quarterly,* Vol. 9, June 1964, pp. 1-22.

Stephens, J. M. *The Process of Schooling.* New York: Holt Rinehart & Winston, Inc., 1967.

Stone, Richard. "Input-Output and Demographic Accounting: A Tool for Educational Planning." *Minerva,* Vol. 4, No. 3, Spring 1966, pp. 365-380.

Stone, Richard. "A Model of the Educational System." *Minerva,* Vol. 3, No. 2, Winter 1965, pp. 172-186.

Suchman, Edward A. *Evaluative Research.* New York: Russell Sage Foundation, 1967.

Sundquist, James L. *On Fighting Poverty.* New York: Basic Books, 1969.

Sundquist, James L. *Making Federalism Work.* Washington, D.C.: The Brookings Institution, 1969.

Sundquist, James L. *Politics and Policy: The Eisenhower, Kennedy, and Johnson Years.* Washington, D.C.: The Brookings Institution, 1968.

Teaching and Learning Research Corp. *Utilizing Available Information from Compensatory Education Surveys.* New York, June 1971.

Technomics, Inc. *A Study of Cost/Effectiveness in Title I Schools.* February 1968.

Thomas, Norman C. "Bureaucratic-Congressional Interaction and the Politics of Education." *Journal of Comparative Administration,* Vol. 2, 1970, pp. 52-80.

Tiedt, Sidney. *The Role of the Federal Government in Education.* New York: Oxford University Press, 1966.

Timpane, P. Michael. "Educational Experimentation in National Social Policy." *Harvard Educational Review,* Vol. 40, No. 4, November 1970, pp. 547-566.

Timpane, P. Michael. "Hard Lessons in the Assessment of Social Action Programs: The Case of ESEA Title I." Mimeographed, n.d.

Travers, Robert M. W. (ed.). *Second Handbook of Research on Teaching.* Skokie, Ill.: Rand McNally & Company, 1973.

Tukey, John W. "The Future of Data Analysis." *Annals of Mathematical Statistics,* Vol. 33, 1962, pp. 1-67.

Tyler, Ralph W. "Assessing the Progress of Education." *Phi Delta Kappan,* Vol. 47, No. 1, September 1965, pp. 13-16.

Tyler, Ralph W., Robert M. Gagne, and Michael Scriven. *Perspectives of Curriculum Evaluation.* Skokie, Ill.: Rand McNally & Company, 1967.

U.S. Bureau of the Budget. Executive Office of the President. "'Supplement to Bulletin No. 66-3'; Subject: Planning-Programming-Budgeting," February 21, 1966.

U.S. Commission on Civil Rights. *Racial Isolation in the Public Schools.* Washington, D.C.: U.S. Government Printing Office, 1967.

U.S. Congress. House. *Hearings before the Subcommittee on Education of the Committee on Labor and Public Welfare.* 89th Cong., 1st sess., 1965.

U.S. Congress. House. Committee on Education and Labor. *Hearings on the Extension of Elementary and Secondary Programs, Part IV.* Washington, D.C.: U.S. Government Printing Office, 1967.

U.S. Congress. House. *The Use of Social Research in Domestic Programs.* Staff Study for the Research and Technical Programs Subcommittee, Committee on Government Operations. 90th Cong., 1st sess., 1967.

U.S. Congress. House. Joint Economic Committee. *The Analysis and Evaluation of Public Expenditures: The PPB System.* 91st Cong., 1969.

U.S. Congress. House. "Message from the President of the United States on Educational Reform," March 3, 1970. 91st Cong., 2d sess. Document No. 91-267.

U.S. Congress. House. "Message from the President of the United States Relative to Revenue Sharing," February 4, 1971. 92d Cong., 1st sess. Document No. 92-44.

U.S. Congress. House. Committee on Education and Labor. *Oversight Hearing on Elementary and Secondary Education.* 92d Cong., 2d sess. Hearings held in Lexington, Kentucky, January 13 and 14, 1972. Washington, D.C.: U.S. Government Printing Office, 1972.

U.S. Congress. House. "Message from the President of the United States Relative to Busing and Equality of Educational Opportunity, and Transmitting a Draft of Proposed Legislation To Impose a Moratorium on New and Additional Student Transportation," March 20, 1972. 92d Cong., 2d sess. Document No. 92-195.

U.S. Congress. Senate. Subcommittee on Education of the Committee on Labor and Public Welfare. *Hearings on Elementary and Secondary Education Amendments.* 91st Cong., 1st sess. Washington, D.C.: U.S. Government Printing Office, 1969.

U.S. Congress. Senate. *Education Amendments of 1972.* 92d Cong. Report 92-604, February 7, 1972.

U.S. Congress. Senate. *Conference Report: Education Amendments of 1972.* 92d Cong. Report No. 92-798, May 22, 1972.

U.S. DHEW. Office of the Assistant Secretary for Program Coordination. *Human Investment Programs: Elementary and Secondary Education,* September 1966.

U.S. DHEW. "Program Memorandum on Education Programs of DHEW: Fiscal Years 1969-1973," November 1967.

U.S. DHEW. Joseph S. Wholey. "Title I Evaluation: 1967-1968 and Beyond," November 1967.

U.S. DHEW. "Recommended Human Investment Programs for FY 1968," n.d.

U.S. DHEW. Office of the Secretary. Joseph S. Wholey. "TEMPO Contract," January 15, 1968.

U.S. DHEW. John Brandl. "FY 1969 Evaluation Plan," November 1968.

U.S. DHEW. "Program Memorandum on Education Programs of the Department of Health, Education, and Welfare: Fiscal Years 1970-1974," December 1, 1968.

U.S. DHEW. Alice Rivlin. "Thoughts on the Department's Role in Education," January 27, 1969.

U.S. DHEW. Office of the Secretary. "1970 Evaluation Digest," 1970.

U.S. DHEW and The Domestic Council, Executive Office of the President. *The Right To Learn: President Nixon's Proposal for Education Revenue Sharing.* Washington, D.C.: U.S. Government Printing Office, 1971.

U.S. DHEW. Office of the Secretary. "Education Program Memorandum," September 1971.

U.S. DHEW. Office of the Secretary. "Research and Evaluation Guidance," December 30, 1971.

U.S. DHEW. Office of Secretary, Director of Education Planning. "Annual Report Evaluating the Results and Effectiveness of OE Programs and Projects," March 1972.

U.S. DHEW. *The Effectiveness of Compensatory Education: Summary and Review of the Evidence,* April 1972.

U.S. DHEW. *Operational Planning System Handbook,* May 1972.

U.S. DHEW. Office of the Assistant Secretary for Legislation. "Highlights of the Education Amendments of 1972," June 1972.

U.S. DHEW. "Justifications of Budget Estimates Fiscal Year 1973."

U.S. Office of Education. "Comprehensive Educational Planning and Evaluation in the States," n.d.

U.S. Office of Education. Bureau of Elementary and Secondary Education. ESEA Title I Program Information Letter No. 126, n.d.

U.S. Office of Education. Division of Compensatory Education. The Council of Great City Schools. *Title I in the Great City Schools: An Analysis of Evaluation .Practices and Exemplary Projects,* n.d.

U.S. Office of Education. "Position Paper Concerning the Office's Future Role and Relationships with Large City School Districts and State Education Agencies," August 1965.

U.S. Office of Education. *A Chance for a Change: New School Programs for the Disadvantaged*, 1966.

U.S. Office of Education. *Summer Education for Children of Poverty*, 1966.

U.S. Office of Education. *Title I/Year II: The Second Annual Report of Title I of the Elementary and Secondary Education Act of 1965, School Year 1966-1967.*

U.S. Office of Education. *The States Report: The First Year of Title I, Elementary and Secondary Education Act of 1965.* Washington, D.C.: U.S. Government Printing Office, 1967.

U.S. Office of Education. Bureau of Elementary and Secondary Education. "Title I Evaluation Model in FY 1968," September 1967.

U.S. Office of Education. *Education of the Disadvantaged: An Evaluative Report on Title I Elementary and Secondary Education Act of 1965, Fiscal Year 1968.*

U.S. Office of Education. "Major Policy Issues and Implementation Problems in the Office of Education," 1968.

U.S. Office of Education. *Profiles in Quality Education*, 1968.

U.S. Office of Education. "Conference of Chief State School Officers, June 20th and 21st," June 1968.

U.S. Office of Education. Harold Howe, II. "Improving the Quality of Local Title I Compensatory Education Programs." ESEA Title I Program Guide No. 48, November 1968.

U.S. Office of Education. Bureau of Elementary and Secondary Education. "A Plan for Program Evaluation: FY 1969." Mimeographed, n.d.

U.S. Office of Education. *Programs for the Disadvantaged*, January 1969.

U.S. Office of Education. *Bureau of Elementary and Secondary Education Programs*, March 1969.

U.S. Office of Education. Bureau of Elementary and Secondary Education. "Participants in 1967-68 Elementary Compensatory Education Programs in Title I Schools in the United States," March 1969.

U.S. Office of Education. Bureau of Elementary and Secondary Education. "Some Results of Compensatory Reading Programs for Second, Fourth, and Sixth Grade Pupils in Elementary Schools Receiving Funds under Title I, ESEA 1967-1968," March 1969.

U.S. Office of Education. Bureau of Elementary and Secondary Education. "A Forward Plan for the Evaluation of Elementary and Secondary Education, 1970 through 1974," May 4, 1969.

U.S. Office of Education. *History of Title I ESEA*, June 1969.

U.S. Office of Education. Wilson O. Riles and John F. Hughes. *Report of the Task Force on Urban Education*, October 1969.

U.S. Office of Education. *Preparing Evaluation Reports: A Guide for Authors*, 1970.

U.S. Office of Education. *Statistical Report Fiscal Year 1968: A Report on the Third Year of Title I Elementary and Secondary Education Act of 1965*, 1970.

U.S. Office of Education. *History of Title I ESEA*, February 1970.

U.S. Office of Education. James E. Allen. "Memorandum to Chief State School Officers." ESEA Title I Program Guide No. 57, February 1970.

U.S. Office of Education. *Summary of Title I*, July 1970.

U.S. Office of Education. Division of Compensatory Education. "Information Needs," 1971.

U.S. Office of Education. "Summary of FY 1970 Evaluation Contracts as of February 11, 1971," 1971.

U.S. Office of Education. *Joint Federal/State Task Force on Evaluation: An Overview (Belmont System),* February 1971.

U.S. Office of Education. "1971 Evaluation Plan," March 1971.

U.S. Office of Education. "Need for Improving the Administration of Study and Evaluation Contracts," August 1971.

U. S. Office of Education. "Appeal on Fiscal Year 1973 Office of Management and Budget Allowance for the Office of Education," December 1971.

U.S. Office of Education. *Annual Report of the U.S. Commissioner of Education, Fiscal Year 1971.* Washington, D.C.: U.S. Government Printing Office, 1972.

U.S. Office of Education. "Basis for the FY 72 Evaluation Plan," n.d.

U.S. Office of Education. "Comments on Draft Evaluation Report on Title I by AIR," 1972.

U.S. Office of Education. Michael Wargo et al. *Needs, Resources, Management, and Impact: A Comprehensive Evaluation of ESEA Title I Since 1965,* 1972.

U.S. Office of Education. *Every Child Has a Future,* February 1972.

U.S. Office of Education. Bureau of Elementary and Secondary Education. Associate Commissioner for Elementary and Secondary Education. "1972 OE Evaluation Plan," May 6, 1972.

Wargo, Michael J., et al. *Further Examination of Exemplary Programs for Educating Disadvantaged Children.* American Institutes for Research in the Behavioral Sciences, Palo Alto, California, July 1971.

Washington Research Project of the Southern Center for Studies in Public Policy and the NAACP Legal Defense and Educational Fund, Inc. *Title I of ESEA: Is It Helping Poor Children?* Washington, D.C., 1970.

Weber, Max. "The Essentials of Bureaucratic Organization: An Ideal-Type Construction," in Robert K. Merton et al. (eds.), *Reader in Bureaucracy.* New York: The Free Press, 1952.

Weiss, Carol H. (ed.). *Evaluating Action Programs: Readings in Social Action and Education.* Boston: Allyn & Bacon, Inc., 1972.

Weiss, Robert S., and Martin Rein. "The Evaluation of Broad-Aim Programs: A Cautionary Case and a Moral." *The Annals of the American Academy of Political and Social Science,* Vol. 385, September 1969.

Weiss, Robert S., and Martin Rein. "The Evaluation of Broad-Aim Programs: Experimental Design, Its Difficulties, and an Alternative." *Administrative Science Quarterly,* Vol. 15, No. 1, 1970, pp. 97-109.

White, Bayla F. "The Design and Purpose of the 1968 Survey of Compensatory Education." Paper presented at the Meeting of the American Educational Research Association, Los Angeles, February 1969.

White, Bayla F. "The Role of Evaluation in Title I Program Management." Paper presented at the National Academy of Public Administration Conference on Evaluation of Education Programs, Rockville, Maryland, May 26, 1972.

Wholey, Joseph S. "Notes on the Belmont Joint Federal/State Task Force on Evaluation Meeting." Paper presented at Cherry Hill, New Jersey, June 1970. Washington, D.C.: The Urban Institute, June 30, 1970.

Wholey, Joseph S., et al. *Federal Evaluation Policy: Analyzing the Effects of Public Programs.* Washington, D.C.: The Urban Institute, June 1970.

Wholey, Joseph S., et al. *Title I Evaluation and Technical Assistance: Assessments and Prospects.* Washington, D.C.: The Urban Institute, October 1970.

Wickline, Lee E. "Educational Accountability," in E. Wayne Roberson (ed.), *Educational Accountability through Evaluation.* Englewood Cliffs: Educational Technology Publications, 1971.

Wildavsky, Aaron. "Does Planning Work?" *The Public Interest,* No. 24, Summer 1971, pp. 95-104.

Wildavsky, Aaron. "Evaluation as an Organizational Problem." Mimeographed, n.d.

Wildavsky, Aaron. "The Political Economy of Efficiency." *The Public Interest,* No. 8, Summer 1967.

Wildavsky, Aaron. *The Politics of the Budgetary Process.* Boston: Little, Brown & Co., Inc., 1964.

Wildavsky, Aaron. "Rescuing Policy Analysis from PPBS." *The Analysis and Evaluation of Public Expenditures.* Compendium of papers submitted to the Subcommittee on Economy in Government of the Joint Economic Committee, Congress of the United States, 91st Cong., 1st sess. Washington, D.C.: U.S. Government Printing Office, 1969.

Wilensky, Harold L. *Organizational Intelligence.* New York: Basic Books, Inc., 1967.

Wilhelms, Fred T. *Evaluations as Feedback and Guide.* Washington, D.C.: Association for Supervision and Curriculum Development, NEA, 1967.

Williams, Walter. *Social Policy Research and Analysis.* New York: American Elsevier Publishing Co., Inc., 1971.

Wilson, O. Meredith. *Title I Report.* Washington, D.C.: National Advisory Council on the Education of Disadvantaged Children, 1967.

Wirt, Frederick M., and Michael W. Kirst. *The Political Web of American Schools.* Boston: Little, Brown & Co., Inc., 1972.

Wood, Robert C. "When Government Works." *The Public Interest,* Vol. 40, Winter 1970.

Yankelovich, Daniel. "The New Naturalism." *Saturday Review,* April 1972, pp. 31-37.

Zimiles, Herbert. "Has Evaluation Failed Compensatory Education?" in Jerome Hellmuth (ed.), *Disadvantaged Child,* Vol. 3. New York: Brunner-Mazel, Inc., 1970.

Zurcher, Louis A., Jr., and Charles M. Bonjean. *Planned Social Intervention.* Scranton: Chandler Publishing Co., 1970.

# Index

# About the Author

**Dr. McLaughlin** received her B.A. degree in Philosophy from Connecticut College for Women, her Ed.M. degree in Education and Social Policy from Harvard Graduate School of Education, and her Ed.D. degree in Education and Social Policy from Harvard in 1973.

Her research interests are centered on compensatory education theory and practice, planned change in complex organizations, and evaluation of social action programs. She is the author or co-author of several publications in these areas.

Dr. McLaughlin became a consultant to The Rand Corporation in 1971, and joined the staff in July 1973. At Rand she had worked on problems of evaluating large-scale social action programs and, most recently, on the educational change agent study sponsored by the U.S. Office of Education.

# Rand Educational Policy Studies

*John Pincus, General Editor*

**PUBLISHED**

Averch, Harvey A., Stephen J. Carroll, Theodore S. Donaldson, Herbert J. Kiesling, and John Pincus. *How Effective Is Schooling? A Critical Review of Research.* Englewood Cliffs, New Jersey: Educational Technology Publications, 1974.

Pincus, John (Ed.) *School Finance in Transition: The Courts and Educational Reform.* Cambridge, Mass.: Ballinger Publishing Company, 1974.

Carpenter–Huffman, P., G.R. Hall, G.C. Sumner. *Change in Education: Insights from Performance Contracting.* Cambridge, Mass.: Ballinger Publishing Company, 1974.

McLaughlin, Milbrey Wallin, *Evaluation and Reform: The Elementary and Secondary Education Act of 1965, Title I.* Cambridge, Mass.: Ballinger Publishing Company, 1975.

**OTHER RAND BOOKS IN EDUCATION**

Bruno, James E., (Ed.) *Emerging Issues in Education: Policy Implications for the Schools.* Lexington, Mass.: D.C. Heath and Company, 1972.

Coleman, James S. and Nancy L. Karweit. *Information Systems and Performance Measures in Schools.* Englewood Cliffs, New Jersey: Educational Technology Publications, 1972.

Haggart, Sue A. (Ed.) *Program Budgeting for School District Planning.* Englewood Cliffs, New Jersey: Educational Technology Publications, 1972.

Levien, Roger E. *The Emerging Technology: Instructional Uses of The Computer in Higher Education.* New York: McGraw-Hill Book Company, 1972.